A Customized version of *An Exploration of World Religions*
by Robert Y. Owusu and Richard Bennett
Designed Specifically for Robert Y. Owusu
at
Kennesaw State University and Morehouse College

Introduction to Religion

Robert Y. Owusu

Kendall Hunt
publishing company

www.kendallhunt.com
Send all inquiries to:
4050 Westmark Drive
Dubuque, IA 52004-1840

Copyright © 2016 by Kendall Hunt Publishing Company

ISBN 978-1-4652-9835-5

Printed in the United States of America

Contents

Introduction

PREVALENCE OF RELIGIOUS EXPERIENCE

As old as the age of human beings on earth, *religion is pervasive in all cultures*. Religion, also considered an art of worship, possibly predates human existence and has been practiced in the heavenly or divine realm where spirit beings have worshipped and nature has "declared the glory of God." Religion is found in every human community—among those who dwelt in the hamlets and those in the metropolis. Religious beliefs and practices are expressed in peoples' songs, dirges, occupations, conversations, relationships, behaviors, their dos and don'ts (about right and wrong), paintings, artifacts, buildings, monuments, and in other forms of cultural expressions. Across nations and cultures, visible signs of the pervasiveness of religion are demonstrated by the varieties of temples, shrines, emblems, images, inscriptions, music compositions, and clothing.

In the United States, for example, wherever you go, you see temples, church buildings, people in religiocultural costumes and apparel, religious marks, and symbols. In my home country of Ghana in West Africa, almost every automobile or shop has a kind of religious inscription on it—some of which are hilarious. I read something on a newly bought vehicle which said, "Behold, the Goodness of God," and on the other side of the road was a broken vehicle with the inscription "Is it too hard for God?" The writing on the second automobile was not done at the time of the breakdown, but, at that moment, it spoke to the situation in which the owner found himself. At another instance, a young man called S. K. was rushing out from one taxi to another to reach his church destination. When stopped for a short inquiry, he asserted, "As for us we breathe, eat, drink and smell religion. Don't delay me, please. Let me go." Generally, people are religious as shown in the global religious landscape in figure 1.1.

Religion is a social phenomenon. Religion influences peoples' behaviors and actions in society and it is because of this that there is such a prevalence and importance of religion in human cultures. Religion has inspired violence as well as peace movements and humanitarian actions. In many societies it is impossible for people to separate religion from the rest of their everyday life. Their religion is everything, and everything is religious. Through the eyes of their religions they understand themselves, the world, their purpose here, and the way they should live. Their religion informs and transforms them and their

©Joseph Sohm/Shutterstock.com

1

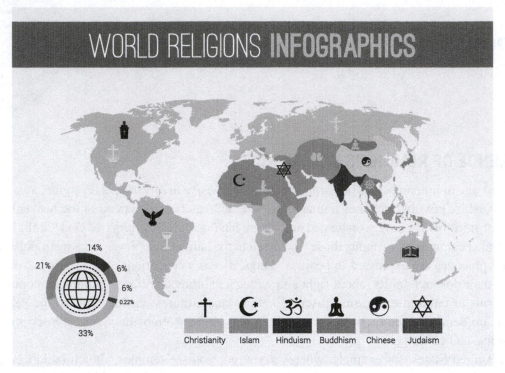

Figure 1.1 Global Religious Landscape

surroundings. At birthday parties, marriage ceremonies, death and funeral rites, festivities, sports, and political activities, people come across religious rituals, religious songs and dance over and over again. Such is the social power of religion.

Religious understanding and practice is diverse. In spite of many common things that peoples across cultures share, they are, at the same time, different from others. People do not speak the same language, wear the same clothes, eat the same food, observe similar rituals, understand the world, or live and die in the same way. Mary Pat Fisher is right when she says, "Religion is such a complex and elusive topic" that some scholars want us to discard studying it (Fisher 2011). The reason is that no matter how open you think your definition is, you still leave something out, and to include everything also tends toward disingenuity. But, in reality, the complexity and diversity of religion points to the breadth and depth of religious experience, which makes the study of religion difficult and necessary. Mahatma Gandhi, who, it is believed, read all the sacred scriptures of the world's major religions, once said about religious diversity that for all his life he had not met any two people who believe the same thing about their religion all the time even if both of them share one common faith. He said, "The golden rule of conduct . . . is mutual toleration, seeing that we will never all think alike and we shall always see Truth in fragment and from different angles of vision. Even amongst the most conscientious persons, there will be room enough for honest differences of opinion." (WorldofQuotes.com 2013). Bishop Burnet also affirmed that people differ in their understanding of religion and religious matters. "But men of sense are really but of one religion." When asked, "What religion?" he answered, "Men of sense never tell it" (WorldofQuotes.com 2013).

WHAT IS RELIGION?

There is no discipline that has attracted so much criticisms and affections as religion. There are many who quarrel about it but never practiced it, and as many others who had provided confident definitions of it but never "knew" it. There are those who think of it as an illusion, a kind of human fantasy for people seeking to run away from pragmatic questions. Others still consider it as something belonging to the private realm that has no business in the public square. Yet, there are also those who speak of religion as if it has no problem at all. Varying definitions or explanations have been given to answer the question, "What is religion?" from diverse viewpoints and disciplines. Sometimes it appears religion cannot be portrayed in its own terms without resorting to reductionism—a dependence on other fields of study for legitimacy. Of course, certain actions of some practitioners have provided the feed for such perception. Let us explore some definitions of religion:

Albert Einstein (scientist): "My religion consists of a humble admiration of the illimitable superior spirit who reveals himself in the slight details we are able to perceive with our frail and feeble mind." To seek to understand and admire is virtuous. In his advice to a young man, *Einstein* talked about the necessity of being a little curious about the mysteries of life. He called such questioning "a holy curiosity." He said, "The important thing is not to stop questioning. Curiosity has its own reason for existence. One cannot help but be in awe when he contemplates the mysteries of eternity, of life, of the marvelous structure of reality. It is enough if one tries merely to comprehend a little of this mystery every day. Never lose a holy curiosity" ("Old Man's Advice to Youth: Never Lose A Holy Curiosity," *Life Magazine, May 2, 1955, 64)*.

Actor, Activist and Religious critic Bertrand Russell (1872-1970) stated "Religion is something left over from the infancy of our intelligence, it will fade away as we adopt reason and science as our guidelines."

English philosopher and religious leader James Martineau (1805–1900) stated "Religion is the belief in an ever-living God; that is, in a Divine Mind and Will ruling the universe and holding relations with mankind."

English philosopher Herbert Spencer (1820–1903) stated "Religion is the recognition that all things are manifestations of a Power that transcends our knowledge."

English idealist philosopher F. H. Bradley (1846–1924) believed "Religion is rather the attempt to express the complete reality of goodness through every aspect of our being."

English poet, social and literary critic Matthew Arnold (1822–1888) stated "Religion is ethics heightened, enkindled, lit up by feeling."

British metaphysician J. M. E. McTaggart (1866–1925) stated "It seems to me that it [religion] may best be described as an emotion resting on a conviction of a harmony between ourselves and the universe at large."

Scottish philosopher Edward Caird (1835–1907) stated "A man's religion is the expression of his ultimate attitude to the universe, the summed-up meaning and purport of his whole consciousness of things."

Protestant theologian Paul Tillich (1886–1965) stated that Faith is "the state of beings ultimate concern."

Sociologist Emile Durkheim (1858–1917) "a unified system of beliefs and practices relative to sacred things, that is to say set apart and forbidden, beliefs and practices which unite into one single moral community, called a church, all those who adhere to them."

Cultural anthropologist Clifford Geertz (1926–2006) discussed how religion is "a system of symbols which acts to establish powerful, pervasive and long-lasting moods and motivations in men by formulating conceptions of a general order of existence and clothing these conceptions with such an aura of factuality that the moods and motivations seem uniquely realistic."

Religious scholar and theologian Bolaji 'Idowu (1913–1993) talked about how "Religion is the means by which God as a spirit and man's essential self communicate; therefore sees religion as the result of humanity's spontaneous awareness of a living Power."

Religious philosopher Y. Turaki stated that religion consists of a "theory of being and a theory of meaning."

Theologian and philosopher Jaco Beyers "Religion is an effort by humans to search for meaning, to understand reality and place themselves in a relationship with reality." Religion is therefore an epistemological activity."

* * *

Religion deals with the whole of human life, including death. A religious quest is a search for meaning and end of human existence, of the meaning and end of nature and the universe. Religion seeks to answer the questions:

1. Where do we come from? (origin of humanity and creation)
2. Why are we here? (purpose of life or existence)
3. Where are we going? (the hereafter)
4. What is the nature of reality? (about a Supreme Being, God or the Transcendent)
5. How do I encounter or know the existence of this reality? (experiencing or encountering the Transcendent)

Religious practice is as old as the origin of human beings and, as a Hindu puts it, preceded human existence. The Akan people of Ghana say, *Obi nkyerɛ abɔfra Nyame*, translated "no one teaches the child about God," which means knowledge of God is inherent and universal, a kind of prescience.

Religious communities are also described as "communities of people who share practices and beliefs (often in God or gods), who gather in special places for worship or meditation, and who live in special ways in the world" (Bowker 2006, 6).

©Pavel Vakhrushev/Shutterstock.com

The word "religion" comes from the Latin, *religio*; the verb, *religare* means "to bind closely together." It binds people to their god or gods (*Etymology Dictionary Online*). Religion draws and binds people together in common beliefs and practices, provides a common goal of life, and acts as a shield of protection. Religion, therefore, is a means of protecting a whole community by binding them together to stop extinction; that is, religion serves as an antidote to or a weapon against natural selection by creating a bond of people and making them fit to survive. For survival and continuity of the community, these beliefs and practices are passed on from generation to generation. An organization becomes necessary, hence the formation of religious organization(s) to promote the identity and continuity of that community.

Religion also helps the community to explore the things around them such as the sea, rivers and lakes, land or earth, animals, plants, the sky, planets, and others.

Religion and culture: The word "culture" is derived from the Latin word *cultus,* which is used to mean "worship of the gods or of a supreme being." Thus belief in worship of a higher being forms the foundation of culture. Culture and religion are thus tied together.

Religion is not all of human endeavor to grasp the divine or understand reality. It is also an act of the divine to reach out to human beings. In religion, human beings and the divine meet each other. Thus, religion is seen as humans' response to the divine or God's act of creation and providence.

Religion emphasizes freedom: Religion provides the basis and motif of freedom and thus enhances democracy. John Wycliffe, the fourteenth-century English Bible translator and reformer said, "This Bible is for the government of the people, by the people and for the people" (WorldofQuotes.com 2013). For Ralph Waldo Emerson, author, thinker, and lyricist, "Religion is to do right. It is to love, it is to serve, it is to think, it is to be humble" (WorldofQuotes.com 2013). Are these qualities not the very ones that uphold freedom and establish democracy?

Religion provides prophetic voices to guide nations on issues of eternal consequences such as social justice, peace, and human dignity. Cardinal Murphy O'Connor says, ever since the Romans, the state has been wary of Christianity, because Christianity defends the law of God, which places limits on the state's power. Faith points to a power and authority that the state cannot control (*Catholic Herald*, December 16, 2008).

Having explored a variety of definitions of religion, it will be helpful to have a working definition for this study. We understand religion as *the divine-human encounter and the consequent relationship involving the divine and the transformed individual or community leading to an assertion of beliefs and a following of certain moral order and ritual practices.*

WHY DO WE HAVE RELIGIONS?

Part of the answer to this question has been answered in our exploration of what religion is. There are various reasons why people follow religions. Scholars of religion, however, have grouped the responses into three categories: the materialist perspective, the functionalist perspective, and the substantive or faith perspective. The materialists regard reality as that which can be verified by scientific means according to the nineteenth-century school of positivism or scientific materialism. For the materialists, religious claims are too subjective and unverifiable and therefore cannot be real or true. They go ahead to make propositions about the nature of religion and why religions exist. Ludwig Feuerbach criticized religion as an illusion, the imagination and invention of humans; for Karl Marx, "Man makes religion, religion doesn't make man. Religion is the self-consciousness and

©Everett Historical/Shutterstock.com

Courtesy of the Library of Congress

self-esteem of man who has either not yet found himself or has already lost himself again." He goes on to state that "Religion is the sigh of the oppressed creature, the heart of a heartless world, just as it is the spirit of a spiritless condition. It is the opium of the people" (Marx, Critique of Hegel's Philosophy of Right, 261–313).

Sigmund Freud thought religion is "childhood neurosis" good for people who cannot stand for themselves as adults and that when they grow up they will abandon it (Fisher, 2011, 5). For the materialists, religions exist as a coping mechanism created out of and for humans' fantasies and to control people.

The functionalist view represented by Emile Durkheim and John Bowker argues that religion is useful and good for people and society. It strengthens and supports community and social structures and helps people find meaning for their existence. They point to the social role of religion. Governments and monarchs in world history understood the social phenomenon of religion and have used religion to foster their political and social agendas. The nomadic Aryans of central Asia who invaded Indus valley culture used religion to establish their kind of social order in the new territory. Emperor Constantine used Christianity to stratify his reign and society. The faith or essentialist view (also called substantive view) asserts that religion points to the existence of Ultimate Reality and an encounter with this transcendent reality. This

Michael Nicholson/Getty Images

Imagno/Hulton Archives/Getty Images

is known not by the senses but through experience. The knowledge of this beyond the limit of reason is called "experiential knowledge." Faith is the means by which one engages reality. It is the substance of religion. To discount or disregard it is to take away the mystery and the fascinating elements and reducing religion to other disciplines. Among the chief proponents are Pierre Teilhard de Chardin, George William Russel, and Rudolf Otto. For the functionalists and essentialists, religions serve a useful purpose, advocate for peace, and provide meaning for the world and human life.

Radical religious conflicts, wars, and killings in the name of religion in the twentieth century and the first decade of the twenty-first century have made some describe religion as anti-liberalism and an antisocial institution that still lives in the dark ages. Of course, this criticism is not new as the interpretation and practice of religious beliefs and messages have had serious violent outcomes in the course of world history.

BASIC CONSTITUENTS OF RELIGION

Many world religion books make reference to Ninian Smart's seven dimensions of religion:

> The mythic (sacred narrative)
> The doctrinal (philosophical or creeds) The ethical (legal, praxis)
> The ritual (practical)
> The experiential (emotional)
> The social (community or relational)
> The material (symbols, images, artistic expressions)

We can also add sacred persons, those designated as "interpretive and ritual specialists," as a key dimension of religion (Esposito, Fasching, and Lewis 2012, 16).

When a person encounters the divine or when the divine engages the attention of a person, a bond is often established. The expression of reverence takes the form of *worship* in which the worshipper pays homage to the divine. To relive the experience, *symbols* are created or developed. Symbols are images borrowed from the material world that appeal to the emotions and imaginations rather than to the rational mind of the worshippers. The event or the encounter must be told and preserved. Religious myths, which are stories based on the symbols and the divine–human encounters, are told to express the divine reality or basic truths of life and its meaning. According to the Judeo-Christian traditions, the creative world is a symbol of God's presence that tells of the glory of God. Creation is also God's message to humanity:

> *The heavens declare the glory of God;*
> *the skies proclaim the work of his hands.*
> *Day after day they pour forth speech;*
> *night after night they reveal knowledge.*
> *They have no speech, they use no words;*
> *no sound is heard from them.*
> *Yet their voice goes out into all the earth,*
> *their words to the ends of the world.*

(Psalms 19:1–4, NIV)

*For what can be known about God is plain
to them,
because God has shown it to them. For his
invisible
attributes, namely, his eternal power and
divine nature,
have been clearly perceived, ever since the
creation of
the world, in the things that have been made.*

(Romans 1:19–20)

Myths are therefore, sacred stories regarded as demonstrations of inner meaning of the universe and human life (see *The Hymn of Creation* insert). The believing community, either by their own initiative or divine instructions and commands, develop rituals that are practical actions that the community and individuals perform. A religious ritual is defined as "an agreed-on and formalized pattern of ceremonial movements and verbal expressions carried out in a sacred context" (Livingston 2008, 98). Then, doctrines or dogma, which are the systematic teachings or statements proclaimed as absolutely true and accepted as such, are formulated to guide the adherents and offer some rational explanations to the narrative. Ethics and morality set the legal and relational boundary of dos and don'ts for the people. Thus ethics and morality serve as the way of life of the entire group or the individual within the believing community.

* * *

To summarize, myths point to ultimate truths about identity and relationships, and provide guidelines for the structure and organization of our lives and our cultures. They also bring together the complex elements of the psyche and assist us to reach for deeper meanings.

This understanding of myth helps to illuminate the power of sacred stories. Of course, we can take the position that the sacred stories of our own traditions are "true," and those of other cultures are "just myths." However, the literal truth of these narratives, whether written into scripture or carried forward in other ways, may be the least significant issue to consider. These sacred narratives are true because they reveal the divine and, through the power of hierophantic symbols, assist humanity in making direct contact with the power of the sacred. The well-known cultural historian and religious scholar, Thomas Berry, claims that myths not only provide us with "the interpretative patterns of our existence," but also link us to the universe and to the sacred. Our contemporary critical analysis and pragmatic realism have cut us off from the world of the sacred, once available to humanity through the mythic imagination, and left us suffocating in "consumerism and the excitement over the instant communication of the trivial." In order to recover meaning, we must recover the sacred through "a return to the depths of our own being."*

* * *

The Hymn of Creation (X. 129)

*1. Non-being then existed not nor being;
There was no air, nor sky that is beyond it.*

*What was concealed? Wherein? In
whose protection? And was there deep
unfathomable water?*

*2. Death then existed not nor life immortal;
Of neither night nor day was any token.*

*By its inherent force the One breathed
windless: No other thing than that beyond
existed.*

*3. Darkness there was at first by darkness
hidden; Without distinctive marks, this all
was water. That which, becoming, by the
void was covered, That One by force of heat
came into being.*

4. Desire entered the One in the beginning:

*It was the earliest seed, of thought the
product. The sages searching in their hearts
with wisdom, Found out the bond of being in
non-being.*

*5. Their ray extended light across the
darkness: But was the One above or was it
under?*

*Creative force was there, and fertile power:
Below was energy, above was impulse.*

*6. Who knows for certain? Who shall here
declare it? Whence was it born, and whence
came this creation? The gods were born
after this world's creation:*

*Then who can know from whence it has
arisen?*

*7. None knoweth whence creation has
arisen; And whether he has or has not
produced it: He who surveys it in the highest
heaven, He only knows, or haply he may
know not.*

* * *

EMERGENCE OF MYTH

Many myths depict creation as emerging out of the unfathomable abyss of chaos. In the Babylonian creation account, called the Enuma Elish, the first gods emerge from a primordial state in which the great sweet water ocean (Apsu, called the begetter) is commingled with the great salt-water ocean (Tiamat, the mother of all) in one body. It is a state described as prior to any constructions, when no gods were named and no destinies determined.

In the Genesis creation story, believed by many scholars to be related to the Babylonian account, this is tehom—the deep upon whose face is darkness—understood as formless waters over which moves the spirit or breadth of God (Genesis 1.2). The Hebrew terms that are translated "without form and void" can also be translated as unseen and formless. This concept of the void parallels the Greek concept of Chaos, understood as a great gap or abyss at the beginning of the world.

In fact, there are hundreds of creation stories that involve emergence of creation out of water. This is not surprising. Water is an obvious symbol for the unformed, commingled state before creation, since water has no shape of its own. It is also an obvious symbol for the emergence of life. Not only are humans completely dependent upon water for life, but water (in the form of amniotic fluid) is also our first home. Our human birth is the fundamental paradigm for this emergence theme, as the mother's water breaks and new life emerges from her womb. The womb itself reflects the primordial condition, "the dark, hidden, chaotic, watery cavern from which life emerges."

In some emergence myths, however, life comes not from the waters, but from the center of the earth. In these myths, the earth is viewed as a cosmic mother who brings forth the world. This motif is often associated with the creation of humans who emerge from the womb of the earth mother and pass from one world into another until they arrive on the surface of the earth. Long observes that by associating creation with the earth, this theme contains within itself "all of the potencies of life." These myths depict the process by which humans progress from incompleteness to completeness, a conversion in which there is no immediate or violent transformation. "A certain type of harmony is present within the creative act."

The creation that emerges may take many forms. In some myths, creation emerges out of chaos in the form of a cosmic egg. In others, deities emerge directly from the primordial realm as cosmic parents. However, creation cannot become complete until this initial union of creative forces is transformed. Therefore, these emergence themes are typically accompanied by motifs of separation or division as discussed below. *[1]

IDEAS IN RELATION TO ULTIMATE REALITY

As mentioned earlier, every religion is concerned with the notion of "ultimate reality." It asks who or what is the Absolute? Who or what is the ultimate power that holds, directs, and governs our destiny and to whom or which we are obligated? The diversity of religious views and beliefs are often expressed in

---

[1]*From *Living Myth* by L. J. Tessier. Copyright © 2011 by Kendall Hunt Publishing Company. Reprinted by permission.

their understanding of the nature of the ultimate reality. The expression may be in theistic or nontheistic form. Religions can be classified as theistic or nontheistic. Theistic religions (from the Greek *theos* meaning god) are those that are God-based or divine-based faiths. If it is not, it is termed nontheistic religion. Even nontheistic beliefs like Confucianism may appeal to nature (or Nature) as its ultimate reality.

Theism:	god- or divine-based belief
Nontheistic:	non-god- or divine-based belief; this is not the same as atheism
Polytheism:	the belief in many gods
Monotheism:	the belief in the existence of only one god
Henotheism:	the belief in hierarchy of gods of which one is elevated as the head
Pantheism:	the belief that god and the material world is one
Monism:	the belief in a single principle of existence; that all reality is ultimately one
Deism:	the belief that God created the world but does not intervene in its day-to-day affairs (God as the noninterventionist creator)
Stoicism:	the belief in nonemotional, pantheistic philosophy
Agnosticism:	the belief that there is not enough evidence or knowledge to accept or deny the existence of God
Atheism:	the belief in nonexistence of the divinity of god

The ultimate reality is sacred, that it stands apart from the ordinary and is not subject to our mere consumption. The sacred is considered transcendent and for some the divine is both transcendent and immanent as found in Christianity. On the one hand, the term "transcendent" refers to the superordinary realm, a Spiritual Reality (God) who is completely outside or beyond the world or the material. On the other hand, the term "immanence" (divine presence) refers to some divine being or essence that manifests in and through all aspects of the material world. Such manifestation is what Mircea Eliade (1961) calls "Hierophany."

It can manifest itself through both natural objects and human artifacts such as sacred persons, icons, and at a sacred time and space. In Judeo-Christian traditions, the term "revelation" is used to explain the manifestation of the divine to an individual or a community like the one that was given to Moses and the people of Israel on Mount Sinai and to the Apostle John in the Island of Patmos in Book of Revelation.

In theology it is a disclosure of divine will or truth; something not known before. There are two types of revelation: *general revelation* and *special revelation*. General revelation refers to the disclosure of divine will and truth or mystery through nature or creation. This type of revelation is innate and is available to all rational being who desire to know by virtue of reason. Special revelation, on the other hand, is the divine's self-disclosure to a selected people or an individual for a special reason at a certain time and place. It may involve mystical or supernatural experience of the Holy.

The sacred evokes awe, reverence, and fear on one hand, and on the other, fascination and

©jorisvo/Shutterstock.com

© Michael D. Brown/Shutterstock

attraction. Rudolf Otto calls this the *numinous* experience. The sacred is characterized by power, which can be ambiguous. In Emile Durkheim's seven distinctiveness of the nature of the sacred, he draws attention to the power and the nature of the power of the sacred that elicit intense respect. The sacred can be good and evil and the profane can also be good and evil. He goes on to describe the ability of the sacred to impinge on human consciousness, moral obligation, and ethical imperatives (Durkheim, [1915?]).

Finally, a word about religion and spirituality: What is the interconnectedness between spirituality and religion and where do they also diverge? Spirituality is an essential dimension of religion. It can be viewed as the fluid, flexible, permeating, overpowering, persistent, mystical facet in religious practice where the transcendent and the human meet, and transcendence becomes immanence producing a deeper self-awareness and transformation of the human person. Spirituality is something much more internal like a meandering stream in the forest (Swenson and Nelson) but exhibits an overwhelming influence on its surrounding.

Religion is often looked at from the institutional dimension that comprises the doctrinal or confessional, rituals, the arts and artifacts, and the structural elements. These elements make people consider religion as static, rigid, ceremonial, and routine—a way of life. But religion and spirituality to a larger extent share common ethos and needs each other. Religion without spirituality could be a mere institution overseeing dead rituals and broken symbols. Likewise, spirituality needs religion to check the former's probability of engaging in excesses.

In this chapter we have examined variety of definitions of religion, why we have religions, basic constituents of religion, and theosophical ideas that describe people's understanding of the nature of God or Ultimate Reality. To conclude, let us look at the global religious landscape as it exists today.

KEY WORDS

Essentialist	Functionalist	Ultimate Concern
Mysterium Tremendum	Theism	Scientific Materialism
Henotheism	Pantheism	Monism
Deism	Agnosticism	Cosmic
Primordial	Nontheistic	Stoicism
Positivism	*Enuma Elish*	*Numinous*
Hierophany	Spirituality	Metaphysical
Transcendence	Immanence	Rationalism
Experiential knowledge	Revelation	Myth
Mystical experience	General revelation	Special revelation

QUESTIONS FOR FURTHER STUDY

1. How will you respond to the materialists' explanation of the reason why religions exist?

2. How will you define religion?

3. What is the relationship between culture and religion?

4. Explain the notion that "religion is a social fact" from the functionalists' perspective.

5. Discuss the viewpoints of functionalism, essentialism, and scientific materialism as pertains to faith and religion

6. "Religion matters." Present argument for and against this proposition.

7. What will you say to someone who claims to be a spiritual person but not religious?

8. Identify these persons and their contributions to religious understanding:

    a. Emile Durkheim

    b. Mircea Eliade

    c. Rudolf Otto

    d. Clifford Geertz

e.   Ninian Smart

f.   Paul Tillich

g.   Karl Marx

h.   Sigmund Freud

i.   George W. Russel

j.   Immanuel Kant

The Study of Religions

Why do we study religion at all? What is the academic study of religion? What approach or approaches do scholars use in studying religion? These are the subjects we will explore in this chapter.

WHY DO WE STUDY RELIGION?

Religion has always been something we do. That is, religion is a practicing matter rather than an intellectually scrutinizing stuff. There are many reasons. We study religion to understand human beings and to overcome our ignorance. Religion is something that adherents *do* rather than just know creating a dissonance between intellectual understanding of religion and the practice of religion. From experience we know that many students and even church people lack a sophisticated understanding of the history and doctrines of their own faith, let alone other religions. Also, religion is important to history, literature, political philosophy, and other disciplines, thus making it an essential part of the liberal studies. Studying religion helps us to understand our culture. Societies and cultures cannot be understood without considering their systems of beliefs. Furthermore, studying religion helps us formulate our own religious beliefs or philosophy of life. We come to appreciate the religious response to the primordial questions of life: Why are we here? Where do we come from? Where are we going? What is the end of all this we call existence? What happens when we die? Finally, comparative study of those beliefs draws attention to common ethical values shared across cultures though expressed in different ways. In this way, like the owl, our perspectives become global.

WHAT IS THE ACADEMIC STUDY OF RELIGION?

The academic study of religion, which is a recent development, is whereby religious scholars, and anyone interested, engages in critical examination and analysis of religious traditions by using certain specific methods. There are basic rules to follow in order for it to be regarded as scholarly. James C. Livingston says one of the rules is to make available to all interested parties or persons the evidence or criteria upon which religious claims are made. Second, the study must involve critical analysis. Third, the study must deal with "explanatory question" instead of merely "describing and transmitting" (Livingston 2008, 16). A religious study as a discipline in the social sciences or humanities is a science. Propositions, assertions, and evidences are to be interpreted. An interpretive model must be utilized. The term "hermeneutic" is used to describe this model. Hermeneutic in the modern sense means the science of interpreting scripture or sacred scripture using critical tools.

The history of hermeneutics is embedded with a genuine concern to maintain the integrity of sources that are foundational to religious phenomena. On the one hand there is an interest in the humanities that includes religion and distinguishes them from the natural sciences. On the other hand, there is the quest for openness in examining these sources or texts handed over to us without reducing them into something else. According to Friedrich Schleiermacher, "understanding other cultures is not something we can take for granted. Understanding others involves an openness towards the fact that what seems rational, true, or coherent may cover something deeply unfamiliar. This openness is only possible in so far as we systematically scrutinize our own hermeneutic prejudices" though the method may not be without flaw. Schleiermacher calls it "an indispensable aid" (http://plato.stanford.edu/archives/win2014/- entries/hermeneutics). Augustine, the first to claim the universality of hermeneutics asserted that there is a connection between language and interpretation and that "interpretation of Scripture involves a deeper, existential level of self-understanding" (ibid). Hermeneutics therefore seeks to avoid reductionism while showing disinterested openness demanded by scholarship so far as the human sciences are concerned. Understanding the value of hermeneutics "is fundamentally a matter of perceiving a moving horizon, engaging a strand of dialogue that is an on-going re-articulation of the dynamically historical nature of all human thought" (ibid). It is rightly stated that in *the academic study of religion,*

> Scholars use evidence from authoritative texts, history . . . studies, and other concrete sources to make arguments . . . the arguments made about a given religion are designed to convince readers who [don't] practice that religion. Whether [it] is written by an "insider" or an "outsider," the intended audience always explicitly includes "outsiders" to that religion. (Christine Kraemer, www.patheos.com, January 3, 2013)

The academic study of religion is cross-cultural, multidisciplinary, and polymethodic. With these methods of religious study in mind, I find Wikipedia's definition of religious studies fascinating when it says, "Religious studies is the academic field of multi-disciplinary, secular study of religious beliefs, behaviors, and institutions. It defines, compares, interprets and explains religion, emphasizing systematic, historically-based, and cross-cultural perspectives."

THE STUDY OF RELIGION IS DISTINCT FROM THEOLOGICAL STUDIES

Many religious practitioners confuse the study of religion and theological studies and think the two are the same. Though theology is not completely separate from the broad field of religious studies, the former has a distinctive objective that cannot be endorsed by religious studies as an academic inquiry. Theological study is a specialized study of religion which examines "the nature of God and religious truth." Theology, from the Greek, *theologia,* simply means "the study of God." A theologian is an apologist, an intellectual defender or champion of a particular faith. Apologetics is a defense of faith with reasonable argument and persuasion. There are varieties of theology; hence contemporary scholarship speaks of "theologies" as well as diverse theological objectives. A few will suffice here: Christian theology (general) and Christian theologies (particularities); Islamic theology (general) and Islamic theologies (particularities); Judaic theology (general) and Judaic theologies (particularities). Also, the term "theology" is used widely to include all religions that have theistic beliefs and speak or reason about God (*Theos*). Theology asserts, validates, and protects the truth of a faith tradition. Unlike religious studies, theological studies carry with it a presupposition or a kind of biasness and rightly so.

For theology to achieve the status of critical inquiry, it is argued that, first, it must open itself to critical investigation by applying critical tools to its beliefs and practices. Second, it must expand the inquiry to include outsiders, but not limit it to insiders and sympathizers only. Third, it must treat its assertions or claims as hypothesis without seeking solution based on privileged beliefs. Finally, in spite of its presupposition, which we know is not peculiar to theology alone, it is required of theology to strive for objectivity without negating its commitment and faithfulness to the faith tradition it represents. For this reason, theology claims to be normative.

Having laid down the scientific academic requirements demanded from theological studies, there is the need to point out that religious and theological studies share certain common characteristics. First, both of them are rational critical studies because it makes use of the same principles and methods as science. The scientific method, which also becomes then the theological method, may be defined as "that method for describing and explaining the revelations of God that incorporates the principles of verification, operational definition, statistical generalization and confirmation" (www.theology.edu/theology.htm). In addition, both are open to new truth. Lastly, an authentic holistic definition of religion, like theology, needs to include a belief in a non-ordinary transcendent reality, what Rudolf Otto called the "Wholly Other" (Otto, 1950, 26) though theology, on the one hand, claims, is normative, and religion, on the other hand, asserts its empirical stance.

DIVERSE APPROACHES TO THE STUDY OF RELIGION

The study of religion depends on the use of diverse methods and disciplines. It is multidisciplinary and employs other academic fields of study such as history, philosophy, sociology, anthropology, psychology, cultural studies, and archaeology in the process (Livingston, 17–25). Moreover, the polymethodic study of religion has as its key components the literary critical method, phenomenology, and the comparative method. Liberation theology has also gained popular standing in religious and theological investigation. This approach qualifies the studies regarded as academic. Let us briefly examine the features of the methods—literary criticism, phenomenology, comparative method, and liberation theology—and some of the academic disciplines mentioned above.

The Literary Critical Method

The literary critical method involves two approaches: textual or lower criticism, and documentary, or higher criticism (also called "form criticism"). *Textual* or lower criticism investigates whether our text is from the original or authentic source and therefore uses a number of methods and procedures. It examines grammatical constructions, original language(s), syntax (relationship of words), etc. by comparing texts particularly to the most original.

Documentary or higher (Form) criticism, a method of biblical criticism that classifies units of scripture by literary pattern (such as parables or legends) and that attempts to trace each type to its period of oral transmission, deals with issues of authenticity, interpretation, and historical evaluation of the text so as to arrive at the original intent of the author and how it was understood by the recipients or hearers then.

Phenomenological Method

Phenomenological approach attempts to maintain balance between the outlook of an insider and the outlook of an outsider. It also must show empathy, that is, "the capacity for seeing things from another's perspective" (Brodd et al. 2013, 24). This method provides a description of conscious experience in all its varieties without reference to the question of whether what is experienced is objectively real. In short, it is a practical investigation of religious practices from the perspective of the practitioners to understand

their meaning for their adherent. The method employed includes data gathering, analyzes of the data, identification of a structural pattern, and formulation of a general conception of the religion(s). It is essentially descriptive.

Comparative Method

The chief proponent of comparative study of religion is said to be Friedrich Max Mueller (1823–1900) who is regarded as the founder of the modern field of religious studies. Based on Mueller's notion, "He who knows only one knows none," comparative method studies religion cross-culturally and multitraditionally. With an empathetic heart and objective mind, the method observes the similarities and differences in religions (*Encyclopedia of Religion,* vol. 4, p. 25).

Liberation Theology Method

The hermeneutic principle of the theology of liberation includes the revelation of God in Christ as the liberator of the oppressed from social, economic, and political oppression, a recognition that their fight against oppression and injustice is not only consistent with the gospel, but *is* the gospel of Jesus Christ, and an assertion that Western theological assumptions must be viewed with suspicion for all theological discourses.

Multidisciplinary Approaches

Aesthetic: Religious study encounters cultures and an important aspect of culture is art—how beauty is described and appreciated. Many religious symbols are meant to show the beauty of the religion or the divine. Islam, Hinduism, Roman Catholicism, and Orthodox Christianity, for example, are infatuated with arts, sculptures, or icons that speak of the essence of the faith. The Quran is considered artistic that portrays the nature of Allah. Understanding the philosophical principles of aesthetic in a particular religious culture such as the "Love Songs" called "The Song of Songs" of King Solomon in Jewish culture helps us appreciate the importance of women without attributing such description to extreme sexism.

> *Behold, you are beautiful, my love,*
> *behold, you are beautiful!*
> *Your eyes are doves*
> *behind your veil.*
> *Your hair is like a flock of goats*
> *leaping down the slopes of Gilead.*
> [2] *Your teeth are like a flock of shorn ewes*
> *that have come up from the washing,*
> *all of which bear twins,*
> *and not one among them has lost its young.*

[3] *Your lips are like a scarlet thread,*
and your mouth is lovely.
Your cheeks are like halves of a pomegranate
behind your veil.
[4] *Your neck is like the tower of David,*
built in rows of stone;[a]
on it hang a thousand shields,
all of them shields of warriors.
[5] *Your two breasts are like two fawns,*
twins of a gazelle,
that graze among the lilies.
[6] *Until the day breathes*
and the shadows flee,
I will go away to the mountain of myrrh
and the hill of frankincense.
[7] *You are altogether beautiful, my love;*
there is no flaw in you.

(Song of Songs 3:1–7)

Anthropology: Anthropology also helps religious studies by providing resources dealing with human culture or human development in all dimensions. We met quite a number of cultural anthropologists such as Clifford Geertz and Edward B. Tylor in our quest for definition of religion. Cultural anthropology or sociocultural anthropology examines cultural or social differences among humans and therefore aids in the study of religion.

Archeology: Archeology as "the scientific study of ancient cultures through the examination of their material remains such as buildings, graves, tools, and other artifacts usually dug up from the ground," is one of the most useful tools or disciplines that have contributed to our new understanding of religion and theology. Through its scientific method ancient sites, buildings, mummies, texts, human and animal skeletons, have been discovered that have helped to clarify, support or heighten doubts on ancients religious texts, beliefs, and practices. The discovery of the Egyptian Book of the Dead, Pyramids or Tomb Writings, the discovery of the Dead Sea Scroll, and the Hindu Tombs writings are a few examples.

Geography: Geography provides a resource for religious study to identify places, physical features, climatic conditions and distribution of plant, animal, and human life.

Historiography: Religious and theological studies employ the principles, theories and methods of historical research and writing by analyzing source material and asking questions pertaining to dates, place, recipients, and authorship, and comparing them to other historical materials or data of the same time frame.

Isa Khan's tomb, New Delhi

©Darko Vrcan/Shutterstock.com

Linguistic studies: Understanding of the languages used in the religion under review is a useful tool. For example the Vedas in the Sanskrit language, the Quran in Arabic, The Christian Bible in Hebrew and Greek (koine), Egyptology or hieroglyphics, and expertise in oral traditions.

Philosophy: Philosophy is the discipline that is closest to the field of religion and theology. It questions sources and kinds of knowledge and deals with basic concepts such as truth, reason, reality, existence, causality, freedom, fate, and destiny. As we noted in chapter 1, these concepts are essential to the study of religion. Classical philosophers such as Plotinus, Plato, Aristotle, Augustine, Aquinas, and modern philosophers like Rene Descartes, Immanuel Kant, Zera Yacob, Søren Kierkegaard, Karl Marx, Henry Thoreau, William James, and Friedrich Nietzsche are among a few that have significantly influenced religious and theological thought. The philosophy of religion is a branch of philosophy that is concerned with

> The philosophical examination of the central themes and concepts involved in religious traditions. It involves all the main areas of philosophy: metaphysics, epistemology, logic, ethics and value theory, the philosophy of language, philosophy of science, law, sociology, politics, history, and so on. Philosophy of religion also includes an investigation into the religious significance of historical events (e.g., the Holocaust) and general features of the cosmos (e.g., laws of nature, the emergence of conscious life, widespread testimony of religious significance, and so on). [*The Stanford Encyclopedia of Philosophy*]

Psychology: It is a scientific study of the human mind, mental state, and temperament and associated behavior of a person or group, an animal(s), or those engaged in an activity. Psychologists have been a source of strong criticism against religion. Cynics like Sigmund Freud and supporters such as William James, Gordon Allport, and Carl Jung made impact on religious studies. It has also been used to validate religious practices in relation to the benefits religion offers to the human person or the group. Psychology has been used to explain certain religious phenomena.

Sociology: Sociology is concerned with culture, social structures, and, in relation to religion, the social function and analysis of religion. Scholars like Auguste Comte, Max Weber, Emile Durkheim, John Bowker, and others have made tremendous contributions to the study of religion from the standpoint of sociology. Sociology of religion has explored, on the one hand, the influence of religion on society, social norms, and survivability, and, on the other hand, the effect of society on religious beliefs and practices.

Science and Religion

Human beings want to know the answers to the most essential questions of life such as the question of the origin of humans (where did we come from? Where were we before coming on this earth?); the question of death/afterlife (does life continue after we die? Where do we go when we die?). Discovering the answers to these ever deeper and broader questions bring joy, personal meaning, passionate purpose, and a dynamic peacefulness that transforms life. When it comes to explaining the essential questions of origins and afterlife, modern people appeal to science *or* religion (or science *and* religion) for answers. These two positions can be categorized into three discovery groups or viewpoints: the *evolutionist* group, the *intelligent design* group, and the *creationist* group.

Evolution (also known as Darwinism or natural selection) is the process by which different kinds of living organisms are thought to have developed and diversified from earlier forms during the history of the earth. The theory of evolution, according to Charles Darwin who developed it states that "all species of organism arise and develop through the natural selection of small, inherited variations that increase the individual's ability to compete, survive, and reproduce" (www.intelligentdesign.org). Humans, it is argued, evolved from lower animals into the humans they are today.

In the 1980s, some scientists revealed that intelligent design of the universe could be shown empirically based on the same argument made by William Paley over 200 years ago. Paley argued that "some pieces of organic machinery are too complex to be explained as anything but the work of an intelligent designer." This effort turned into a movement that is also known as the "intelligent design community," sometimes referred to as ID. Intelligent design was supported by the Seattle-based Discovery Institute. The institution created a center for the study of ID, which was endowed with over a million US dollars.

Intelligent design is the theory that life cannot have arisen by chance and was designed and created by some intelligent entity. It asks the question "How did we get here?" The two are related in the fact that they deal with a higher being. Intelligent Design refers to a scientific research program that consist of scientists, philosophers, and other scholars who seek evidence of design in nature. Certain features of the universe and other living things are explained by ID, not natural selection.

Intelligent design requires the use of the scientific method to determine structures, analyzing DNA, and the complex physical architecture of the universe. There are four steps involved in the scientific process that include observation, hypothesis, experiments, and conclusion. Observation is the first step that intelligent agents use to make complex and specified information.

The next step is to hypothesize if the object was designed. Then, scientists perform experiments on the natural objects to determine if the object has complex and specified information. The results of their findings lead to their conclusion. Intelligent design deals with the idea of a higher power such as God. It explains how God or the gods created humans and the world for a purpose.

Creationism is often compared and contrasted to ID. It is a religious belief that the universe and life originated from specific acts of divine creation. Creationism starts with a religious text or story and attempts to make a connection to science. Intelligent design, on the other hand, begins with evidence of nature. The purpose is to seek what inferences can be drawn from the evidence.

Educators, philosophers, and the scientific community have demonstrated that ID is "a religious argument, a form of creationism that lacks empirical support and offers no testable or tenable hypotheses." They consider ID a "pseudoscience" (Shermer 2011). There are, however, critics of ID who have analyzed creationism and ID and have acknowledged the difference between the two. For example, Ronald Numbers, a historian of science at the University of Wisconsin, who is not a friend of ID, is critical of Darwinists who link ID with creationism. In his opinion, many Darwinists try to combine the two because it is the easiest way to discredit ID, ("Explaining the Science of Intelligent Design," www.intelligentdesign.org, April 15, 2016).

While ID tends to support the religious argument of all the powerful and omnipotent entity, without necessarily resorting to biological supernaturalism, the evolutionist theory is radically against religious beliefs and prefers to rely on the empirical methods of science only. Differentiating between authentic science and pseudoscience in reference to evolution and intelligent design respectively is problematic according to Michael Shermer. For Shermer such demarcation should be based on "the pragmatic usefulness of an idea" to the scientific community. He states:

> [A] practical criterion for resolving the demarcation problem [is the] pragmatic usefulness of an idea. That is, does [the idea] generate any interest [among] working scientists for [their own use]? If not, [it's probably] pseudoscience (Shermer, 2011).

In this chapter we have examined the diverse ways religion is studied. We saw that the study is rigorous, wide-ranging, challenging, interesting, and a necessity. Many students come to this study unprepared for one reason or another and may be overwhelmed by the amount of materials to cover. Some, however, assume that because they are active believers they already know. Still there are those who are curious about the subject matter of religious studies or world religions and therefore approach the study with greater expectation of not wanting to lose holy curiosity.

KEY WORDS

Aesthetic	Religiocultural	Destiny	The Book of the Dead
Temperament	Polymethodic	Empathy	Cultural Anthropology
Metaphysics	Phenomenon	Vedas	Archeology
Causality	Hypothesis	Modernity	Liberator
Fate	Nihilism	Reality	Conscious experience
Historiography	Predestination	Linguistic	*Hermeneutic*

QUESTIONS FOR FURTHER STUDY

1. Why is the study of religion both difficult and necessary?

2. Name and describe some of the approaches used in the study of religion.

3. Describe the three things that academic study of religion requires.

4. Explain the effect of modernity and science on religious development.

5. What are the key principles in the theology of liberation?

6. Name and explain the steps used in the phenomenological method in studying religion.

7. What are some of the challenges that modern science pose to religious studies?

The Sacred and the Practice of Religion

Religion is practiced by observing or performing rituals. Religious rituals are actions performed in relation to the sacred or the holy, at least most of them are. They could be motivated by a sense of obligation, as an expression of devotion and gratitude, or to honor the Holy. We will later look at the nature of holy rituals. Meanwhile let us turn our attention to the notion of the Sacred.

IDEAS IN RELATION TO THE SACRED

The term "sacred" is common among people of diverse cultures and traditions. Everyone has something they consider sacred: from the bedroom to the compound of Hollywood. Some use it to refer to something exceptionally special, not for common or everyday use, or someone distinct from all others—somebody or something of a different kind. Though "sacredness" has acquired common usage, it does not mean that its significance in the minds of the users is devalued. In the minds of the users, that which is sacred is thought of as something non-ordinary, non-common, or non-utilitarian. So, what is the meaning of the term "sacred?" *The American Heritage College Dictionary* defines sacred as: "Dedicated to or set apart for the worship of a deity"; "worthy of religious veneration"; "worthy of respect"; "devoted exclusively to a single use, purpose, or person"; of or relating to religious objects, rites or practice." We can infer from this definition that sacredness has both religious and nonreligious usage. What is also clear about sacredness is that it refers to a particular thing or being that is set apart for special usage; that sacredness commands respect or worship and is purposeful.

Another feature of the sacred is that it can manifest itself through both natural objects and human artifacts; the ordinary is transformed from a common use to a sacred presence. This means anything can become the means of disclosure of the sacred. Individuals have their sacred spot, families have their sacred spot, religious organizations have their sacred sites, and societies or nations have their sacred locales. Sacred space is where some people go to rediscover themselves, attain self-realization, find their purpose of life, or engage the Transcendent. The first time I stepped on the seminary campus of my faith tradition as a young seminarian, I felt as someone walking on a holy ground. I sensed something like what Moses might have felt when the voice told him to remove his sandals for he was standing on a hallowed ground. I felt a stronger connection with the One who is The Holy.

The *desacralization* of modern society, however, has caused a revocation of certain places previously regarded as hallowed and special. In spite of the revocation, there are many sacred spaces of great importance. Mircea Eliade (1961) refers to such places as *axis mundi* meaning "the center of the world"—the point around which, in symbolic concept, the world rotates. Sacred places abound in religion. Buddhism's Bodhi Gaya, site of Gautama's foundational experience of enlightenment; Christianity's Church of the Nativity; Islam's city of Mecca, particularly the *Kaaba*; and Judaic city of Jerusalem are among many examples of sacred places regarded by their religious traditions as axis mundi.

In theistic religions like Judaism, Christianity, and Islam, the Sacred is identified with the Creator as the one and only God who is relational, personal, transcendent, and immanent. Judaism and Christianity speak of Him as Father. In Hinduism the divine, Brahman, is known as the cosmic force or energy of whom the world emanates. The Sacred is the essence of religion and anything or any person that have direct contact with the sacred acquires a degree of sacredness depending upon their particular role and significance. Another term that is used as a synonym of sacredness is "holiness," that the Sacred is the Holy One. Holiness, from the word *qadosh,* basically means separation or to set apart and denotes purity and cleanness in ceremonial observances. In biblical usage it expresses the absoluteness, majesty, and awfulness of the Creator in His distinction from the creature. There is also an ethical concept of holiness that ascribes a distinct character of God ("be ye holy; for I am holy"). Holiness can be applied to objects, persons, seasons, and events in direct relationship of their attachment or association with the Divine. For example, Judaism talks about the holy temple, holy water, holy men (priests), Seder, and the Sabbath. The entire book of Leviticus describes holy things and persons as they relate to the worship of God. The sacred and the holy are thus used interchangeably.

The sacred does not only manifest itself in space, but also in time. Time as the moment (*kairos* in Greek) is "the right or opportune moment ('the supreme moment'), a qualitative experience without any reference to its timeline or timetable" (*chronos*). 'The ancient Greeks had two words for time, *chronos* and *kairos*. While the former refers to chronological or sequential time, the latter signifies a time lapse, a moment of indeterminate time in which everything happens" (*Wikipedia,* "*Kairos*"). In religious quest, any time is an opportune moment when dealing with the sacred. Kairos acts like the spirit (life-force) of the time and chronos, the letter (strict accounting) of time. Mircea Eliade mentions the Judaic innovation of time as linear, which has a beginning and therefore an end contrary to the cyclical notion of time. The significance of it is that it made God a participant in history.

Both Eliade (1961) and Durkheim (routledgesoc.com, 2016) wrote on the distinction between the sacred and profane. The term "profane" is not vulgar or debase. It is just a reference to a common use or something ordinary. Eliade explains that the sacred provides access to the ontological reality for which *"homo religiosus"* thirst. *Homo religiosus,* he argues, thirsts for being. In terms of space, the Sacred delineates the demarcation between sacred and profane and thus locates the axis mundi as center (Eliade 1961). For Durkheim, the *profane* is the realm of routine experience; the secular; everyday world of work, toil, and domestic duties. It is the sphere of adaptive behavior and is essentially utilitarian, whereas the "sacred" is the realm of human experience other than this work-a-day sphere. The sacred, he argues, lays somewhere beyond the profane sphere and evokes an attitude of awe and reverence. The sacred denotes "those collective representations that are set apart from society, or that which transcends the humdrum of everyday life" (Durkheim, Reprint], 1995, *278*). For Durkheim, "the division of the world into two domains, the one containing all that is sacred, the other, all that is profane is the distinctive trait of religious thought" (ibid, 37). He argues that the two fundamental categories of religion, which are beliefs and rites, have their significance in the sacred–profane distinction. Religious beliefs, he explains, are the "representations which express the nature of sacred things and the relations which they sustain," and religious rites are "rules of conduct which prescribe how a man should comport himself in the presence of sacred objects" (ibid, 41).

There are some characteristics of the sacred that distinguishes it from the profane. They include, first, a recognition of a belief, power, or force. The idea of a belief or power that can make things happen or can affect and control things, and humans sits at the center of religion. This is what religion identifies as the realm of the supernatural or superordinary. What on earth would command obedience if there is not an inherent authority and power that is found to be not under any human control or order? Also, the sacred is "non-utilitarian." The sacred is not there just for our mere consumption. The value of the sacred is beyond its usefulness to us. Our labor and its fruits are for our own usage and manipulation. The sacred is beyond the everyday or the ordinary.

Moreover, the sacred is non-empirical. That is to say the sacred is beyond empirical nature. It means the knowledge that people have of the sacred is not the kind of knowledge based on the senses. Empirical knowledge is sense-derived knowledge obtained through observation and experimentation. In addition, the sacred is "supportive and strength giving"—it raises the individual above himself or herself and impinges on human consciousness a sense of moral obligation and ethical imperatives. The sacred elicits intense respect. Also, the sacred is determinative of various aspects of human existence—the sacred requires the ordering of our ways in a certain manner. Lastly, the sacred is ambivalent. It is physical and moral; it is positive and negative; it is helpful and dangerous; it evokes both celebration and mourning; and, according to Durkheim, the sacred can be good and evil in the same way that the profane can be good and evil. Therefore, the sacred–profane dichotomy must not be equated with good–evil dualism (ibid, 37).

WHAT ARE THE MEANS OF COMMUNICATING WITH THE SACRED OR THE DIVINE?

There are basically two forms of communication with the Divine: verbal expression and symbolic expressions. Though other forms of communications are listed below, they can broadly be placed under one of the two. Verbal expression, often termed "linguistic communication," involves the use of words or speech. For example, the young boy, Samuel, was serving Eli in the temple when he heard someone calling his name. He thought it was Eli who was calling him and for three times ran to Eli in response. Eli realized it was the LORD who was calling Samuel and instructed him that if the voice called him again he should respond by saying "LORD, speak for your servant is listening." For the fourth time the voice called, and Samuel answered, "LORD, speak for your servant is listening." The LORD spoke to Samuel about the calamity He was going to bring upon the house of Eli for their misconduct and failure (1 Samuel 3:1–16). The Islamic proclamation *"Allahu Akbar"* is the Muslim's verbal acclamation of God's greatness par excellence.

Symbolic expressions are also human's unique ways of communicating with the Divine. These involve images, art, and gestures. They are used to express the experiences a person or a group has had with the Sacred. The use of symbols as forms of communication is not limited to the field of religion. They are found in every human community and in all sectors of life. It is said that the whole universe or nature is symbolic. In Christianity and Judaism, the whole world and the universe is described as "an expression of the glory of God" (Psalm 19:1–2; Romans 1:19–20). In ancient Hinduism, the world is viewed as the image or physical manifestation of Brahman—the cosmic force or power. Even both spoken and written languages could also be considered symbolic. The offering of physical objects (material) in the form of sacrifice is also symbolic expression of devotion to the Divine.

In Judaism, it is believed, certain symbols or images are derived from something that existed somewhere in the spiritual realm and were revealed to the people. Such a model is referred to as an archetype or prototype. An archetype is defined as "an original model or type after which other similar things are patterned; a prototype, form, or instance serving as a basis or standard for later stages" (Merriam-Webster Dictionary). It is believed that physical things are a replica of original things or ideals—a shadow or copy of the ideal forms. So an archetype is often understood as "a perfect example of something." For instance, Moses' tabernacle and its artifacts were a replica of the archetype (or prototype) revealed to him on the mountain. The type or copy, the Tabernacle, also became the model upon which King Solomon built the permanent and enlarged Temple.

Symbols are special kinds of signs pointing or directing us to something that is in absentia or something that is not here. One must understand and appreciate the significance of religious symbols. But to gain understanding and see their usefulness and significance, one needs to have access to their spiritual codes to unlock their meaning and significance. Herein lays the importance of religious language, culture, and traditions. The tools we learned about in chapter 2 are meant to help us uncover the hidden meaning and significances of religious forms and message. There are some symbols that represent things that are distinct, and people become connected to their usage because of custom or habitual practice. They are understood by their cultural context. Such symbols are called "*representational symbols*" (Livingston 2008, 60). Other symbols do participate in or are similar to the thing they represent. They make the thing they symbolize present. In other words, they manifest or make present the sacred or the holy. These symbols are referred to as *presentational symbols* (ibid, 60). The Christian *Eucharist (Lord's Supper)*, the Hindu's *mudras*, or the Buddhist *mantras* are examples of presentational symbols, whereas the Buddhist's *Eight-spoked Wheel*, the Jewish *Star of David* or the Muslim's *Crescent Moon* are all representational symbols.

Other forms of communication are intuition, visions, dreams, spirit possession, and divination. Intuition, according to *Merriam-Webster Dictionary*, is explained as "a natural ability or power that makes it possible to know something without any proof or evidence." It is "a feeling that guides a person to act a certain way without fully understanding why;" a kind of "direct knowledge or cognition without evident rational thought and inference." Much is said about dreams, visions, spirit possession, and divination in chapter 4 in African indigenous religions.

Other forms by which religious experience are communicated are religious myth, storytelling or parables, and doctrines or creeds. A "religious doctrine" is a propositional language, a codification of beliefs, or a body of teachings, taught principles, or positions presented to adherents as religious truths for acceptance or belief. Doctrines appeal more to rational thinking than to the emotion. In short, a religious doctrine is an interpretation of religious symbol, parable, story, or myth.

Ritual

A ritual is the hub, the heartbeat, of religion. Religion is something people do. That is why religion appears to be a newcomer in scholarly pursuit. In his *Anatomy of the Sacred,* Livingston provides the following characteristics of sacred rituals:

- Rituals are forms of symbolic expression.
- Rituals are found in every human community; they are universal.
- Rituals are primordial (very ancient).
- Rituals appeal to the whole person.
- Rituals are primary means of social communication and cohesion.
- Rituals can be described as "significant" actions.

The word "ritual" comes from the Greek word for "rite," which is derived from the word *dromenon,* which is explained as "'a thing done' to achieve a specific end." That's the meaning of "rite." Livingstone says a religious ritual is sacred and defines it as "an agreed-on and formalized pattern of ceremonial movements and verbal expressions carried out in a sacred context" (Livingston 2008, 98). A ritual is simply an intentional and often formal activity that is performed at a specific time and/or in a specific place. When it is performed in a sacred environment, it acquires sacredness and therefore is intended to have a sacred meaning and/or a sacred result. Generally, there are three types of sacred rituals: life cycle rites or rites of passage, life crisis rites or healing rites, and calendar or seasonal rites. Also, ritual can be designated as private (domestic) or public and corporate rite. Furthermore, it can be described in relation to historical or mythological event that it commemorates.

Life cycle rites (rites of passage): This is a non-periodic rite. Associated with the transitional stages in a person's life, like birth, initiation into adulthood, marriage, consecration or induction, and death, life cycle rite have three distinct elements in their observation: separation, transition and reincorporation (reentrance). In separation stage, a person is removed from their old status. The transition stage is marked by some form of social isolation and by a condition of statelessness. The reincorporation stage is marked by passing into a new status, symbolically represented by something. In birth and death rites, the person of the occasion is a non-active unconscious participate.

Life crisis ritual (also called healing ritual): This rite, which can be periodic or non-periodic, is meant to meet a specific crisis in an individual's or community's life. It can apply to a whole nation or a world-wide event to bring healing and comfort to them. A typical example is the memorial service held after September 11, 2001 (referred to as 9/11) atrocity that had world-wide effect. This rite is an attempt to heal or promote wellness among people and to ward off evil spirits, danger, or death. It is also meant to restore a balance or harmony between the spiritual and the physical—to mediate between, on the one hand, divine anger and punishment and, on the other hand, human unfaithfulness and repentance.

Calendar or seasonal ritual: This is a periodic ritual that may be connected with the seasonal changes like planting and harvesting; routine changes of winter, spring, summer, and autumn or the sun or moon; or historical events like Good Friday/Easter (Christianity), Passover and Hanukkah (Judaism), Ramadan (Islam), Holi (Hinduism). This rite secures the well-being of an individual or society. The celebration follows what is called "four principal movements." They are, first, the principle of *mortification* that ends a period or season. Second, the principle of *purgation* by which defilements are gotten rid of. Third, the principle of *invigoration* renews, restores, and empowers the community or an individual. Finally, there is the principle of *jubilation*. This rite indicates relief and celebrates victory with joy and merry-making, giving hope and aspiration to the whole community. Some typical examples are the *Homowo Festival* of the Ga-Adangbe people of Ghana, the Akuapem *Odwira,* the Asante *Akwasidɛ Kɛseɛ,* the Islamic *Hajj,* or the Jewish Day of Atonement.

Sacrifice

The ritual act of sacrifice has intention. Livingston citing E. B. Tylor states that sacrifice evolves around three important stages: gift giving, homage, and renunciation (Livingston 2008). For Tylor the rite of sacrifice functions as *propitiation, expiation,* and *atonement.* As propitiation, the offeror's purpose is to cause the deity to become favorably inclined to them, a kind of appeasement. As expiation, the offeror seeks to make amends or restitution, and in atonement the offeror petition for the removal of sin and defilement and a restoration of fellowship as understood in the Judaic and Christian rite of atonement. Generally, all religious ritual is sacramental, which means, they manifest the sacred or holy. Sacrament makes use of temporal or material things for a spiritual purpose, and may be generally defined as an outward sign of an inward spiritual grace (*The American Church Dictionary and Cyclopedia* 1901 online). It is concerned with the presence of the Divine. Examples are baptism and the Eucharist shared by all streams of Christianity. Roman Catholic and the Orthodox traditions, however, observe seven sacraments: baptism, confirmation, repentance, Eucharist (Lord's Supper), marriage, holy orders or ordination, and last rite (prayer for the sick or dying).

In conclusion, in this chapter, we have considered the ideal of the sacred and its nature and connectedness to religious practice in the form of rituals. Sacred rituals are not easily changed, but it is important that they be reevaluated in relation to a new understanding as well as our contemporary context. Symbols and rites that no longer speak to the tradition become dead symbols and dead ritual. To conclude, I would like to restate the spiritual, psychological, and social significance of these religious rituals. Sacred ritual transforms status and being. It provides a means of dealing with defilement or bad things in society. Also, it not only heals individuals and community or a whole society but also renews, invigorates, and empowers people and society. Sacred ritual strengthens the bond between individual and community and among family members and enhances intercommunity relationships. While it reinforces cultural traditions and customs, ritual also instills corrective moral consciousness in people and checks behaviors.

KEY WORDS

Desacralization	Propitiation	Anti-structural	Initiation
Axis mundi	Sacrament	*Communitas*	Reincorporation
Profane	Expiation	Ritual	Representational symbols
Hierophany	Atonement	Homage	Presentational symbols
Defilement	Sin	Baptism	Archetype/Prototype
Sacrifice	Eucharist	Rites of passage	Intuition

Name: _____

QUESTIONS FOR FURTHER STUDY

1. What are some of the characteristics of the sacred discussed in this book?

2. Give a definition of sacred symbol and sacred ritual.

3. Why are symbols pervasive in human cultures?

4. What are the means by which religious experiences are communicated?

5. Explain E. B. Tylor's ritual act of sacrifice and its functions.

6. Discuss the notion of the ambivalence of the sacred.

7. What are rites of passage?

8. What is a life crisis rite?

9. What is calendar or seasonal ritual? Explore the *Homowo Festival* of the Ga people of Ghana. How does it fit into this ritual?

10. What role do sacred rituals play in people's or society's life?

Indigenous Primal Religions

THE NATURE OF INDIGENOUS LIFE: GENERAL FEATURES

Indigenous life is also called primal life, and indigenous religions called primal religions. This means the terms are often used interchangeably. In such understanding, indigenous or primal may be defined as "having existed from the beginning; something in an earliest or original stage or state. It denotes a primordial life, being first in time, original, or primeval" (www.vocabulary.com/dictionary/primal). Examples of indigenous religions are African traditional religions, Native American religions, Shintoism, Shamanism, Zoroastrianism, religion of the Aborigines of Australia, Chinese traditional religions, *Sanatana Dharma* (now called Hinduism), and many more.

Who are indigenous people? Indigenous people are deeply rooted in a given place. Indigenous things are considered "home grown." They have not been significantly altered or influenced by external inputs. Indigenous religions are akin to indigenous life. Their life is their religion, and their religion, their life. Generally, indigenous life exhibits the following characteristics: *kinship, lifeway and vision quest, divination, myths, storytelling, ancestral veneration*, and *rites of passage*.

Kinship: Social relations where people share common brotherhood and sisterhood which can be blood-related or non-blood-related lifts a person from blood ties to a level where human beings transcend race, ethnicity, or tribe. Thus, indigenous cultures have a strong sense of universal brotherhood. Indigenous religious life has a resilient devotion for the family, clan, or tribe to whom they share collective life and identity. By extension, indigenous life carries within its psyche an indomitable commitment to the well-being of others in the interest of universal brotherhood—*onipa nua ne onipa* (literally means, "Man's brother is man"). For this reason "strangers" or "foreigners" (no one is actually a stranger in their philosophy) are accorded special treatment and care. Also, in Native American religions, every head of family is the spiritual head or leader. This is due to the belief that sacred rituals prescribe the right thing to do, and the head of the clan has the responsibility of teaching and leading in the performance of the sacred rituals and traditions.

Indigenous religions coexist peacefully with other faiths since they do not proselytize. Instead by their beliefs, practices, and worldviews, they serve as a bedrock of the major world religions. For example, Egyptian religious' ("The Book of the Dead") beliefs in the afterlife, final judgment, and paradise influenced Judaism and Christianity; religions of Rome impacted on Catholicism in iconography and sainthood; Tibetan indigenous religions shaped Tantric Buddhism (Thunderbolt); Japanese indigenous religious culture swayed Zen Buddhism; and many other indigenous religions' influences.

Lifeway and Vision Quest: These are other religious views that emphasize the unity of all life. The spiritual and material, physical and the unseen, are all connected and inseparable. This is called "lifeway." Indigenous people pursue personal spiritual guidance called a "vision quest," which is a solitary practice undertaken to seek spiritual guidance about one's mission in life. Visionary experiences, dreams, and their interpretations are considered revealing and guidance tools, and opportunities for worship are open to all. Fisher calls this "democratized shamanism" (Fisher 2011, 61). As a healing religion, primal faiths stress healing as a way to restore harmony between humans and their universe, between people, and for individual persons. True healing is holistic. It involves all dimensions of life—body, emotions, mind, and spirit or soul. Hence, music, drumming, and dancing as arts and forms of language for the purpose of transmitting tradition, expressing love, virtues and authority, and for entertainment—all play major parts in these religions.

Divination: Primal religions practice divination as a medium. Divination is the art or practice that seeks to foresee or foretell future events or discover hidden knowledge usually by the interpretation of omens or by the aid of supernatural powers. The diviner is able to read and interpret cards, leaves, cowries, or any other elements used to solicit information from the spirits according to the way they are randomly arranged. Spirit possession and exorcism are common. In ecstasy a person communicates with spirits or ancestors or with the dead and demons; the spirits are messengers of the gods and are known as "helping spirits" and always under the control of the head priest (the *diviner* or *shaman)*, who experiences minimal ecstasy. The head priests possess authority and power and are adored and feared as well. The community supports the priest's living since the office is a full-time profession and allows him or her not to do business activities for a living. In this practice the ancestors are venerated as the medium provides the link between the three members of any given indigenous society: the living dead (those in the afterlife), the living, and the yet to be born (posterity).

Other important features are *myths*, *storytelling*, *ancestral veneration*, and *rites of passage*. These four dimensions of indigenous religions serve as anchors that keep the traditions alive. The power that they wield on the identity, way of life, psyche, and actions of the adherents cannot be overemphasized. By them, the narrative is kept, explained, feared and reverenced, obeyed and practiced, transmitted and passed on. It is a common saying among traditionalists that "these are traditions and customs we came to meet; if you cannot add value to them, leave them as they are; don't dare to destroy or devalue them." This is not to suggest that indigenous religions are static, because they are not. They are adaptive to social change or to the time.

* * *

MYTH

Human beings may be hard wired for narrative. Not only are our brains designed to think symbolically, but recent studies regarding the structure of our thinking also suggest that our entire conceptual framework is fundamentally metaphorical. We use the power of the metaphor to bring reason and imagination together, to comprehend partially what we can never understand fully—our emotions, our artistic and moral values, and our spirituality.

The first story at the core of our thinking is always our own story. We attach our memories, the story of where we have been, to the present in an unfolding narrative that not only tells us what is happening but also helps us know who we are. That narrative then extends into the future as we build the story from what we next intend to eat to what we plan as our most ambitious and far-reaching goals. We are comfortable with stories. They are organic to us.

In contemporary culture, the term "myth" is typically used to refer to a common belief that is not true. However, the expression, "It's just a myth," indicates a serious loss of connection and identity in our culture. This notion that myth is false completely misses the vital connection to story upon which a healthy mind and a sturdy culture depend.

To begin with, then, myths are true. They are fundamentally, eternally, ultimately true. The key to understanding that myths are true is realizing the sorts of truths that myths tell and the language that myths use to communicate.

These mythic truths are our most profound guides to understanding ourselves as individuals, as communities, and as cultures. First, they help us understand who we are. As Karen Armstrong points out, myths are true because they are effective—they enable us to find a psychological and spiritual path and guide us toward effective action along that path. However, this issue of identity is more than an individual matter. Identity is a relational concept. We do not really know who we are until we come into contact with others, and our identity, our personhood, is formed in relation. Therefore, myths also tell us truths about our most fundamental relationships—first with ourselves, but also with those we love, with those who surround us, with all living things, with our planet, and finally with the entire cosmos. Myths are always about these relationships. Many scholars point out that myths are also about origins—they help us know who we are by helping us understand where we started and where we have been.

In order to access these truths and unfold the secrets of myth, we must also understand the language of myth. All language is, of course, symbolic, but the symbolic language of myth is of a different order. Joseph Campbell observes that the living metaphors of myth deliver not only ideas, but also a sense of actual participation in the world. "Indeed, the first and most essential service of a mythology is this one, of opening the mind and heart to the utter wonder of all being," Transcending the false idea of "material things as things-in-themselves," mythic metaphors have both psychological and metaphysical connotations. "By way of this dual focus the psychologically significant feature of any local social order, environment, or supposed history can be transformed through myth into transparencies revelatory of transcendence." Campbell's work forcefully illustrates that the symbols in myth carry their truths metaphorically, pointing beyond themselves to greater underlying truths.

Because of this language, myths have the capacity to reach beyond ordinary narrative and to communicate what could not otherwise be expressed. They extend beyond our rationality and take us places we could not otherwise reach.[1]

Tate's mentioning of Paul Ricoeur's well-known definition of myth provides additional insight into the power of myth in human culture. He describes myth as

... a traditional narration which relates to events that happened at the beginning of time and which has the purpose of providing grounds for the ritual actions of men [sic] of today and, in a general manner, establishing all the forms of action and thought by which man understands himself in his [sic] world.[2]

* * *

The rest of the chapter will focus on African indigenous religions (AIR), Native American religions, and Chinese Shinto religions.

---

[1]Excerpt from *Living Myth* by L. J. Tessier. Copyright © 2011 by Kendall Hunt Publishing Company. Reprinted by permission.
[2]Ibid.

AFRICAN INDIGENOUS RELIGIONS

"To be human is to be religious; to live is to be religious."

An African maxim

Mr. Anthony, a devout Roman Catholic, came home after church on one hot Sunday. His wife, who could not go to church that day, had prepared his favorite fufu and palm nut soup for him. Mr. Anthony took off his church clothing, put on casual attire, and came to the table. He then said grace before meal as devoted Christians often do. He washed his hand and dipped it into the bowl of fufu and palm nut soup. But, before any of the balls would get into his mouth, he dipped a small bit onto the floor (earth). When asked what he just did, he responded, "Oh, I did that? Well, it seems this tradition will never go away," implying he did that unconsciously. The tradition he was referring to was a form of prayer or practice in the traditional religion or culture that acknowledges the source of the food and also invites the ancestors to have a share of the meal.

African people, it is widely observed, are stubbornly religious. By that they mean African people are spiritual. One other aspect of spirituality is the evocation of sacred power—the power of the divine. From the African perspective, religion or the Supreme Being or God and His associated spirits are revered because of the power they exhibit. Power is that which gets things done and manifests the presence of God or the divine. Power commands obedience, respect, and fear. Thus, Mircea Eliade (1961) is right when he says, sacred power is ambiguous for it can build and tear down, heal and destroy, embrace and dispel. And Rudolf Otto will say it is mystifying, an overwhelming, and yet fascinating and inviting at the same time.

For Africans, religion should be serviceable. It is for our usage, service, and benefits. That's the reason the spirit beings (the messengers of the Supreme Being/God) are there. If these divine entities cannot deliver, then they are incompetent messengers or assistants, and they must be abandoned or replaced by those who can deliver. What do the worshippers expect them to deliver? Things that make life worth living: productivity, longevity, material progress (wealth), continuity of the family, clan or society, victory over evil, good health (well-being), peace, and harmony. Africans are very careful not to show any disrespect to the Supreme Being or God and nothing incompetent or bad can be ascribed to Him.

Africans are religiously traditional—to preserve what has been inherited from the tradition or ancestors so as to pass it on wholesomely and fittingly to the generations to come. To be traditional is not necessarily to be out-of-date as the literal meaning of the word "traditional" suggests. These religious customs and norms are said to have been given by the divine who knows, a priori, such matters must be carefully observed and be understood from the point of view of the forbearers. It is like exploring the original intent of that tradition. It is worth to note that these traditions act like our modern constitutions as the fundamental norms for the peoples' way of life—spiritual, economic, social, and political.

Speaking about African religions, contemporary African religious scholars and theologians argue that there are three religious traditions in Africa. They are the *indigenous religions, Christianity, and Islam.* There are some Asian religions on the continent, but they are not as yet permeated into the African psyche or way of life. Christianity came to the African continent, specifically North Africa, in the first century at the beginning of Christianity. The North African churches became exemplars of Christian churches in the development of Christian doctrines, church structures, gospel narrative, church conflicts and splits, habitat of biblical texts, and canonization. The African church did not penetrate into the sub-Saharan regions, and, with the emergence of Islam on the continent in the late seventh century, the Christian church lost its power, influence, and presence in Africa, except for the Ethiopian Orthodox Church. Christianity reemerged in Africa south of the Sahara through Western Christian Missionaries vis-à-vis the political and economic expedition of European imperial powers and adventurers. Christianity in African today is vibrant, pervasive, diverse, indigenized, and populous and has acquired the status of a traditional religion in Africa.

Islam entered Africa in the mid-seventh century by Caliph Umar's general, Amr Ibn al-As', who is believed to have led as many as twelve thousand Islamic soldiers across the "Red Sea" to conquer the city of Fustat. This city was renamed "Cairo" in the middle of the 10th century CE (http://bak.whyislam.org/muslim-world/cairo-egypt-3/). Islam was soon after became established in North Africa and made inroads into sub-Saharan regions mainly by trade, social engagements, and cultural tolerance.

However, the bedrock of these two "foreign religions" (as some Africans describe Christianity and Islam) is the indigenous traditional religion(s). The African indigenous religions (AIR or ATR) have also been designated as "nature religion" by sociologists. Nature religions are kinship- or tribal-based; they are nonconversional and nonconfessional; they have no particular founder(s), and the narratives and teachings are communicated or transmitted orally. In brief, the following are general features of indigenous African religions.

Diversity of beliefs and practices: It must first be stated that African indigenous religion is not monolithic, hence African indigenous *religions*. There is multiplicity of beliefs and practices. There is a complex system of divinities and ritual practices. AIR is pluralistic. Yet we can still identify a common pattern, structure, and practice that are shared across the diverse people groups. African indigenous religion is a macrocosm.

A belief in and worship of the Supreme Being: AIR believes in a transcendent, eternal Supreme Being who is the creator and sustainer of all creation. The Supreme Being can be related to directly and also indirectly through His assistants or a medium. This Supreme Being is all knowing, wise, and providential, who dispenses good (reward) and evil (punishment) to people according to what they do.

A belief in spirits or divinities: Spirit beings as messengers, intermediaries, or divine assistants of the Supreme Being. They could be messengers of goodwill if from the Supreme Being, or messengers of bad things if from the devil (*bonsam* in Akan). Evil spirits, magic, and witchcrafts meant to cause harm and malevolence to people and society are believed to be agents of the devil. These spirits, both the good and evil, can inhabit in a person or any material object, like plants, stones, rivers/lakes, the sea, hills, etc. For this reason, Africans believe in and practice spiritual warfare. Spiritual battle or warfare is a kind of spiritual attack and defense mounted against evil spirits, witchcrafts, malevolent spirits that seek to distort, disrupt, and change a person's good destiny or to hinder and destroy a community's progress. In the effort to conquer the forces of evil and destruction, the diviner or medicine man or woman displays their powers.

A belief in Earth as "mother": The Earth, from whose space (womb) comes life-sustaining elements and into whose bosom the dead are entrusted (buried), receives homage as "Mother Earth." Among the Akans, the Earth day is Thursday, and in the time past, no work on the land is done on that day. The Earth is feminine and is associated with productivity or fruitfulness, an encompassing protective space, compassion and caring, regeneration, and comforting. The sky is masculine. Traditional prayers in the form of libation make reference to "Mother Earth' and the Supreme Being.

Ancestors are venerated. This is a well-known practice in Africa that honors the living dead and signifies the holistic perspective of community in African thought. It also demonstrates African belief in the afterlife. African community, it is believed, comprises the living, the ancestors, and the yet to-be-born. Ancestors are men and women who have played their part on earth and have left the physical scene, exist in the spiritual realm, and yet have interest in the ongoing life of the living. They could be consulted by spiritualists and traditional rulers (kings, queens, chiefs, and the elders). Ancestors are mentioned or referenced in libation—traditional modes of prayer where petitions are made to God, Mother Earth, and divinities and strong drink or water (in some cases) are poured on the ground. An ancestor may be reincarnated. The living have a special responsibility toward the yet-to-be-born if the society will continue to thrive. This explains the unique significance of women (reproduction and nurturing) as the means of continuity in African societies.

Art and artifacts are mediums of contacts and expressions. The world, to the African, is symbolic. Symbols are a window into reality. They point to something beyond themselves (representational symbols) and can also make the transcendent or hidden present (presentational symbols). Materials designed to communicate spiritual reality are called "artifacts." They can express the peoples' story (myth or narrative), their beliefs, prohibitions *(taboos),* relationships and community, mystical experiences, ethical norms, and many more. Art includes paintings, sculptures, carvings, weavings, designs, etc. African indigenous Religion asserts that any natural object can manifest the divine and that every living thing has a spirit—a kind of life force, hence the concept of *animism.* In African philosophy the universe is filled with spirits. The universe as well as other living organisms manifests the divine or the divine's presence. The world is a sacred environment. To ignore this presence is to live a life of purposelessness and peril. That being the case, humans beings must respect nature and live in harmony not only among themselves but also with nature. A civilization of this kind that embraces harmony among all living things is described as *lifeway.*

Medicine, Healing, and well-being: Medicine and medicine men and women are special agents in African societies. Their sole purpose is to forestall well-being. Among the Akan people for example, well-being includes good health, material prosperity, reproduction, peace of mind, and social harmony. Kelvin Onongha says factors that influence wellness (and for that matter well-being) are right relationship, right living, and right worship (Aderibigbe & Medine 2015, 63–64). The practice of rites of passage, vision quest, seasonal rituals, festivities, and worship in the form of blood, food, or monetary sacrifice, singing, drumming and dancing, libation, and declaration of attributes and praises are to forestall well-being in its holistic sense.

A belief in predestination or destiny: Predestination is the concept or belief that everything that happens has been decided in advance by God and humans cannot change it. Destiny is "a predetermined course of events often held to be an irresistible power or agency" (Merriam-Webster Dictionary) or "the force that . . . controls what happens in the future, and which cannot be influenced by people" (Cambridge Dictionary Online). Fate is defined as "a power that is believed to control what happens in the future" (Merriam-Webster Dictionary). Based on the meaning, "destiny" and "fate" are used interchangeably. Is predestination, therefore, the *plan* and destiny or fate the *agency* or *power* that pushes the button of the plan? Some Africans such as the Akan and Yoruba believe that people choose their destiny while coming into the world. In a Yoruba or Akan predestination narrative, "Man kneels down to choose his lot before the presence of God and Orunmila (divinity) and God sanctions it." With that "man's destiny is unalterable except by the deities, [spiritually] wicked people, what man does on his own free-will, bad head (lot), and man's character" (Dopamu 2014, 343). The destiny is then sealed and the person does not remember it, but it will begin to unfold once the person is born. Some Asante songs speak about destiny or predestination:

> Dεε Onyame de me besi biara
> Mapene so, mapene so

Meaning: Whatever God will bring to me / wherever God will place me
              I've accepted it, I've accepted it.

Another says: *Nkrabea yεmmɔ n'adane* (destiny cannot be changed). Also, they say, *Obi rekra ne Nyame na obi nnyina hɔ* (when a person was saying goodbye to God in relation to his destiny no one else was standing by).

The foregoing thought shows that there is a harmony between predestination and freewill. God destines, human beings choose among the destinies, and destiny or fate enforces it, or perhaps, destiny has a built-in capacity to enforce itself. The question of unchangeability of destiny is complicated by the belief that wicked spirits, a person's own character, and freewill are among the agencies that can thwart a good destiny. If that is the case, then predestination is not absolutely sealed. There is always a window that allows for a breakthrough or alteration.

As an example of African indigenous religions, let us examine a little closer the African religion of *Santería* known in many parts of North and South America. It is a well-known version of the indigenous Yoruba religion of modern-day Nigeria transplanted in the Americas that exhibits many of the features described in this chapter.

HISTORICAL BACKGROUND OF SANTERÍA

Santería is believed to be the best known religion among the Afro-Cuban religions. Other influential Afro-Cuban traditional religions are Regla de Palo, Mayombe, the Abakua, and Secret Society (Rutz and Korrol 2006, 699). Enslaved Africans were brought to Cuba from Haiti in the early 1600s to replace the weak and diseased natives of Cuba. The successful endurance of this labor force led the Spaniards to seek more of the Africans to work on their plantations. In the early nineteenth century, hundreds of thousands of men and women of the Yoruba people, from what are now Nigeria and Benin of West Africa, were brought to Cuba to work in the island's booming sugar industry (that would be the second wave of the movement of enslaved Africans to the Americas). For about 350 years (from 1511 to 1886), this enslavement and forced labor continued until it was abolished in Cuba in 1886 (Lefever ""1996, 319). Harry Lefever argues that it was the enslaved Africans brought to Cuba in the early nineteenth century from Southwestern Nigeria and the Bantu of Congo, rather than the earlier ones of the sixteenth century from Haiti, "who were the major carriers of the religious beliefs and practices that contributed to the development of the Santería religion" (ibid, 320). Of course, the major carriers were the Yorubas. These Yoruba people brought with them their African religion, the worship of *Oludumare* (also spelt *Olodumare*, the Supreme, High God), manifested in lesser gods or spirits called *orishas*. For instance, *Obatala* (meaning king of white cloth) is the *orisha* that was entrusted by Oludumare with the creation of the human being; *Ogun* is god of iron, and *Shango* represents fire, thunder, and lightning. As the practice was in those days, the enslaved Africans were not allowed to assert their culture or their religion. As a result the religion became secretive. The followers, mostly of the poor lower class were persecuted by their slave masters. The media also misrepresented the faith and embarrassed the practioners (Vicky and Virginia, 207). For these and other reasons, it went under-ground, and since religion is a spiritual experience and a social fact that cannot be completely eliminated, the Africans found a way of living their religion and preserving its unique identity for over 500 years. The religion became attractive to and popular among the non-Yoruba enslaved people in Cuba, too.

The name "Santería," meaning "the way of the saints" is the most common Spanish word used to describe this religious practice that venerates the ancestors or the spirits of the tribe called orisha (Murphy 1987, 66). Santería is also referred to as *Iyalocha* and *Manalocha,* which is basically a reference to the priestess of the religion. This is an indication of the role women play in Santería. The terms *"santero"* (masculine) and *"santera"* (feminine) refer to the initiated devotee. Later initiated generations of santeros and santeras would construct elaborate systems of correspondences between orishas and saints. According to Harry Lefever, Santería emerged as a new form of religious tradition as a result of the encounter between the Yoruba religion of orisha, Roman Catholicism, and French spiritism (Lefever, 319). French spiritism involves the belief that spirit beings exist in hierarchical structure and are seeking enlightenment after their bodily existence. Through the efforts of a medium, a spirit can receive light and once enlightened can ascend to the next spiritual level (ibid, 319). In effect, the religion's devotion to the orishas was expressed through the iconography of Roman Catholic saints, leading observers to see this Yoruba religion as a model for understanding religious syncretism and cultural change (Murphy 1987, 66). Indigenous faiths do bor-row from other indigenous traditions and, as mentioned earlier, adapt to the time or social change. Despite the numerous faces of Catholic symbols in Santería rites and the attendance of santeros and santeras at Catholic sacraments, Santería is essentially an African traditional religion's way of worship drawn into symbolic relationship with Roman Catholicism. Lawrence Levy in his unpublished doctoral research paper argues that "[t]here is no mixing of Catholic beliefs, only a use of Catholic symbolism to mask the African [religion], as a protective camouflage. And, Santeria Saints, more properly called *Orisha* can be propitiated, but never controlled" (Levy 2000, 10).

The orishas are spirits or divinities that assist Oludumare, the all-powerful supreme God of the universe. The orishas act as intermediaries between the people—worshippers—and the supreme deity. Oludumare, unlike the Judeo-Christian and Islamic God, is far removed from the day-to-day business of the world and has entrusted these affairs to the intermediary spirits. Initially, there were as many as four hundred orishas, and some put the number in the thousands, serving both the interests of Oludumare and the needs of the community or tribe. In the course of time, the number of orisha went down to sixteen, and today it is be-lieved to be only seven, now referred to as "the Seven African spirits or powers" (Canizares 1999, 31–33). Each orisha is unique from the others. Raul Canizares lists the Seven Orishas as (1) Obatala—son of Oludumare, creator of humankind, highest among the orishas and typically associated with white cloth; (2) Shango—orisha of thunder, lightning, and fire, and known as the warrior and healer; (3) Ogun—orisha of the mountains and minerals and who paves the way for humans with his tools and is associated with the colors green and black; (4) Orula—advisor to humans, tells fortunes, and interpreter of events in the community; (5) Yemaya—orisha of the sea, mother of all orishas, and the extinguisher of the fires used in the creation of the earth; (6) Oshun—orisha of love and all things feminine, protects pregnant moth-ers, and associated with the color of yellow and all things of beauty; and (7) Eleggua-Eshu—two orishas bound together, who deal with issues of humanity and how to overcome them, and is the first orisha that people must go through to contact the others (ibid, 31–33).

Each Orisha is unique from the others and are not strictly speaking hierarchical in structure, though some, like Obatala and Yemaya, appear to occupy positions of prestige. Also, it appeared some orishas were more powerful or had more authority than others; hence the number of orishas has declined from thousands to only a few saints. This suggests that some orishas were discarded or their roles and jurisdiction incorporated into that of the more powerful ones. What are the orishas' counterparts in the Roman Catholic sainthood? Cathy Smith says Santerianism developed a system of "equating each one of their *Orisha's* to a Catholic Saint in order to 'stay true' to their [Catholic] faith: *Elegba* (also *Eleggua*) became St. Anthony; *Ogun* became St. Peter; *Ochosi* was equated with St. Norbert; *Obatala* represented Our Lady of Mercy; *Babalu Aye* became St. Lazarus; *Orula (also Orunmila)* represented St. Francis of Assisi; the ultimate supreme god *Ororon (also Oludumare)* was equated with Jesus Christ and so on" (2011, 3). As mentioned above, each *Orisha* controls an aspect of nature and human life. The religion has a strong social, supportive system, and what anthropologists would call "magical" aspects. In reality, Santeria is a religion of life.

ADHERENTS

Santerians can be found in many countries associated with Afro-Cuban and Afro-Asiatic cultures such as Cuba, Argentina, Brazil, Colombia, Mexico, France, the Netherlands, Caribbean countries, and the United States. Santeria is growing rapidly in the United States because of the rapid growth of the Latino population. It is now seen in the urban areas of Miami, Tampa, New York City, Atlanta, Savanna (Georgia), Detroit, Chicago, Philadelphia, many cities of California, and other unnamed urban places. Santerianism has also spread among the African American population in an effort to reclaim lost ethnic identity. It is also widely practiced in Puerto Rico, and there are practitioners in other Latin American countries including Panama, Venezuela, and Mexico. In addition, many non-Cuban, non-Puerto Rican Hispanics have also embraced Santeria (Levy 2000, 10). The devotees are mostly secretive and would not easily disclose that they are in the religion. For instance, in the Cuban American population, it is not certain how many practice a form of Santería because many of those who might use the services of a Santero as folk therapist identify themselves as Catholic and do not identify themselves as being part of the religion of Santería. In addition, there are many levels of affiliation to Santeria. Someone might be initiated or have undergone the ceremony to receive what are called *collares* (beads), or Warriors. Some people are merely clients who go to the santero for divination when a crisis arises in their lives and have no interest in Santería as a religion. These people do not identify as being part of Santeria and are most likely to identify as being Catholic. It is also not known how many people are in Santeria from the black, non-Hispanic population. In all it was estimated as of 1994 that there was at least five hundred thousand members, but that number, it is believed, has skyrocketed by now with the boom in the Latino population, and some say they number in the millions (Lefever 1996, 319).

BELIEFS AND RITUALS

The purpose of Santería, like other religions of Africa, is "to assist the individual regardless of their religious background or affiliation, to have harmony with their assigned destiny by ensuring they possess the necessary rituals to navigate life's difficulties" (De La Torre 2004, 4). The root cause of human problem is spiritual disharmony. The physical world emerged out of the unseen spiritual world. Therefore, spiritual disharmony occurs when there is imbalance between the physical and the spiritual realms. Santerians believe that there are essentially four elements of physical existence: (1) Air (fresh air) resolves ethical dilemmas for spiritual growth; (2) Fire that burns spiritual impurities making way for spiritual transformation; (3) Water, which cleanses or washes away dirt and bad or evil energy. Fresh water symbolizes fertility, salt water as the maternal of all life, and stagnant water for spiritual death, which is a prerequisite for new life; and (4) Earth, which provides resources and nourishment for survival (De La Torre 2004, 5).

The religious tradition of Santeria is having a hard time being understood by mainstream America. Worship in Santeria is quite complex and involves incantations, spirit or trance-possession, visions, and animal sacrifice (mostly chicken). The rituals carried out in Santeria are not common to the modern Western world. One of such rituals is animal sacrifice. In sacrifice, natural and human-made items are offered to the deity as expiation (to atone for wrongdoing or appease the divine), propitiation (to be favorably inclined, to seek divine favor), or thanksgiving (for favors received). In some cases animal sacrifice is involved. In such circumstances, specific animals are offered to each saint or orisha. For instance, the orisha called Oshun needs a sacrifice of a female white hen, goat, or sheep. In spiritual cleansing or healing, it is believed that "such animals absorb the problems and negative vibrations of the person being cleansed. In such cases, the animal carcass is disposed of without being eaten." Except for spiritual cleansing the meat of the sacrificed animal is eaten. It needs not be mentioned here of the many controversies associated with the religion's ritual of animal sacrifice in the United States. One vivid example was the legal suit pursued by the Church of the Lukumi Babalu Aye of Hialeah in Florida in the early 1990s to assert its constitutional right to practice its ritual of animal sacrifice. The church won the case. Much importance has been placed on the statement of Justice Anthony Kennedy: "Although the practice of animal sacrifice may seem abhorrent to some, religious belief need not be acceptable, logical, consistent, or comprehensible to others in order to merit First Amendment protection." The decision of the Supreme Court helped to shred the cloud of acrimony associated with the religion and helped bring it to the public domain.

NATIVE AMERICAN RELIGIONS

Native American religions are among the primary indigenous religions of the Americas. Native American lifestyle was more spiritual and less technological in that they view the world not in divided segments but holistically. Contrary to European culture where money or possessions determined status and power, the Native Americans lived in small communities where community and care for one another determined power and status. The strength of the community was derived from strong interpersonal relationship and everyone playing their role. Their religious beliefs nourished their social, economic, and political life. Because of the vast amount of tribes that occupied the Americas, the religious beliefs were very diverse and differed from tribe to tribe, but they collectively shared general principles and worldviews.

Native American religions are a form of spirituality passed from generation to generation by oral tradition instead of written text. Similar to the Egyptians, they used a sort of hieroglyphic symbolism instead of an alphabet system, so stories were reiterated through word of mouth. The very many Native American tribal communities have significant differing qualities among their customs. Their creation mythologies provide one example about their differences. For example, the Iroquois longhouse elders talk about the Creator's "Unique Instructions" to individuals, utilizing male sex references, and ascribing to this holiness as well as the arranging and sorting out of creation and the characteristics of goodness, shrewdness, and flawlessness that are reminiscent of the Christian God. However, for the *Koyukon,* hunters who lived on the Koyukuk River in Alaska, the universe is quite decentralized. . The raven, whom *Koyukon* legends credit with the formation of individuals, is one among the numerous powerful elements in the *Koyukon* world.

He shows human shortcomings, for example, desire and pride. Generally, the raven in many mythological traditions was often reported to be the creator of the world, and the Koyukon tribe tied it to the flood many thought once overtook the earth. *The Koyukon believed that the great raven Dot-son-paa made the world, and that when the great flood came he placed two of every animal, bird, and insect upon a raft so that they would survive. To this day, the Koyukon people treat all wildlife with the courtesy that they accord to human beings, but make a special point of showing particular respect to the raven.* (Tate 2008, 111–117).

A "Creation Story" was present in most if not all early Native American tribes. Two well-known creation stories are those of the Inuit and Seneca tribes. The Inuit were a group of people native to modern Canada and Alaska. The Inuit creation myth says that a race of giants existed before humans. The giants gave birth to a sea goddess. The sea goddess in turn gave birth to the human race. Thus the Inuit believed humans arose from sea.

The Seneca people lived in what is today New York and Pennsylvania. Their creation mythology involved two nonhuman brothers who lived on an island. One brother sought evil while the other had good intentions. They both agreed more life (humans and nonhumans) needed to exist on the island. The "good" brother created humans while the other brother created destructive animals that wanted to harm others.

Many Native American tribes believed in an immortal soul. One example is the Sheepeaters (also Sheep Eaters), a subgroup of the Shoshone tribe, whose name described their primary source of food—bighorn sheep. Some other tribes, depending upon where they were at a given time, were also designated by their food source such as *Salmoneaters, Camaseaters,* and *Bufallo Hunters.*" The Sheepeaters believed that three forms of the soul exist. The first is the *suap* or "ego-soul," which is embodied in the breath. The second is the *navushieip* or "free-soul" that is able to leave the body during dreams, trances, and comas. It is the *navushieip* that encounters the guardian spirit that becomes one's ally during life. Finally, there is *mugua* or "body-soul," which activates the body during the waking hours (*Idaho State Historical Society online, April 20, 2016*). Sheepeaters would have a shaman who is able to directly access these spirits. The Shaman also conducts spiritual ceremonies as well as medicinal practices and uses both for healing. They believe that the soul is the strength of the body and continues to live after death or physical demise.

Another tribe called the Huron believed that all human beings have two souls: one of these souls animates the body and the other extends beyond physical activities or physical life. In sleep, one soul communicates with spirits and with other human souls. Both tribes believed that plants and animals also have souls that can communicate with the outside world. Immortality of the soul is still one of the essential beliefs of Native American religions and way of life and undergirds their sense of ethics and morality.

The belief in the immortality of the soul is directly linked to their common belief in the afterlife. Some believed the soul reincarnated into another human or other form of life (plants and animals). Another belief was that humans return as spirits or ghosts. They could be benevolence or mischievous and may help or haunt the people depending upon their behavior and response to traditions or rituals. Others believed that another world existed for the soul to travel to. The Native Americans viewed the world as a spiritual place that existed simultaneously with the physical realm.

Essentially, all Native American tribes believed in one all-powerful deity. Whether one looks at their beliefs as encompassing pantheism, polytheism, henotheism or monism, many of them insist in the existence of "The Great Spirit." This spirit is also known as the "Master Spirit." It is believed, the Great Spirit created the universe. Some tribes associate the Master Spirit with the Sun or the "father" and the Earth as a goddess or mother. Along with the "father" and "mother," a group of lesser deities act as agents of the Great Spirit. For Native Americans, the worship of these divinities does not contradict their ultimate allegiance and reverence to the Great Spirit. These lesser deities were believed to have an effect on certain things in the physical realm such as weather, crops, health, and other matters that are out of the hands of humans.

Native American religions exhibit hearts of gratitude expressed through unique ceremonies and celebrations. The purpose of the ceremonies and celebrations was to tighten and create bonds with the spirit world, precisely the Master Spirit and his agents who were closely associated with the tribes.

The Native Americans are deeply imbedded in their tradition and culture. They believe that everything natural is sacred whether it is land, humans, plants, or animals. They find life lessons with everything they come in contact with. The Native Americans see themselves as egalitarian communities of people or tribes and relate equally to everything including the land, water bodies, plants, and animals they come in contact with. To Native American individuals, life is spoken to by the circle, a powerful metaphor for equality and involvement. In the circle, there is space for everyone. Nobody is last, everybody is alike or equivalent. Every individual is seen as having something remarkable to add to the list. There is a worth of mutuality which fosters a feeling of solidarity, security, and agreeableness.

In Native American religious cultures, the self is seen as an indispensable part of the universe and aggregate workings of the world. Overesteemed characteristics of self instill guilt and a continuance of agony. However,

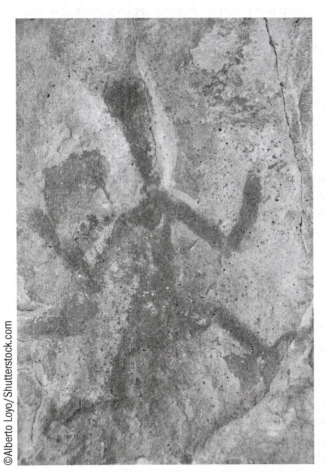

Examples of Native American symbols and their meaning

enduring with tolerance and quietness, controlled feelings, genuineness and excellence, a sense of pride and self-esteem, regard for others, and individual flexibility is the kind of life that Native Americans pursued in fulfilling their life quest. The length and breadth of it all is to be in harmony with nature and oneself. Ties to the family and the environment are, additionally, a key portion of Native American life. Liberality is highly esteemed, particularly in helping other people who are less fortunate. Demise is an acknowledged certainty of normal life, not to be drawn nearer with trepidation. They knew from early ages that death from hunger, disease, or enemies was never far away. The spirit is accepted to be undying in the feeling of encountering a "changing of universes"—a moment of transitioning into another form or state of existence even if the soul will eventually cease to exist ("Native American Religion" in *Encyclopedia of Death and Dying*).

SHINTO RELIGION OF JAPAN

Introduction

The Shinto religion, which is also known as "the way of the Gods," is the indigenous religion of the Japanese people and as old as Japan itself. It is still Japan's major religion alongside Buddhism (specifically the Zen branch). The name *Shinto* was formed from the combination of two Chinese syllable: *shen,* meaning "divine being" and *tao,* meaning "way." In ancient Japanese writing, the characters for Shinto is translated to *kannagara no michi* or *kami no michi,* perhaps meaning "the way which accords to kami," (The Concise Oxford Dictionary of World Religions, 1997) or, according to the anthropologist Rosemarie Bernard "the way of the deities" (New World Encyclopedia, 2003). "Kami" refers to the indwelling spirit or the spirit that dwells in nature, animals, creationary forces, and the spirit of the ancestors, or Gods. It is believed that when humans die they become kami and are revered by their families as ancestral kami.

The Shinto religion does not have a founder, established deities, or sacred scriptures like the Bible, Quran, or sutra, although modern Shinto has developed a text called *Kojiki* meaning "records of ancient matters" (Encyclopedia of Science and Religion, 2003). Shinto was made a state religion of Japan during the Meiji political revolution, referred to as Meiji Restoration of 1868, until 1945 (World War II) when it was abolished (Encyclopedia Britannica). Other tribal religions that arrived in Japan probably through earlier Korean invasion were all integrated into Shinto. Over 100,000 Shinto shrines were erected and patronized.

A Kagoshima Shinto shrine (outside and inside)

Concept of Kami

Ancient Japanese people, like other indigenous cultures, practiced animism, a word derived from the Latin *anima*, meaning "breath," "spirit," or "life." Animism is the worldview that nonhumans, such as animals, plants, and inanimate objects like rivers, lakes, seas, rocks, and mountains, possess a spiritual essence or life force. In the case of Japanese religions, these were the *kami* found (or "hidden") in all humans and everything that exists. Therefore, the central theme in Shinto is that all reverence is to be given to the *kami* or "that which is hidden." Also, the *kami* can refer to many different things such as the followers of Shinto, the qualitative attributes of those followers, and the essence of their existence (Encyclopedia of Science and Religion, 2003). A Shinto statement describing what it calls "the children of kami" says,

> *Shinto regards that the land, its nature, and all creatures including humans are children of Kami. Accordingly, all things existing on this earth have the possibility of becoming Kami. Nevertheless, revered status as Kami is limited to those that live quite extraordinary lives beyond human wisdom or power and that have a profound influence, for good or ill, on human beings. As to natural elements or phenomena that have such enormous power, there exist Kami of Rain, Kami of River, Kami of Thunder, Kami of Wind, Kami of Mountain, Kami of Ocean. All these Kami are involved in the life of a rice-cultivating agricultural society* (Faith in Conservation, 2003).

The presence of kami in all things points to the needed reverential treatment for and harmony of everything that exist. Throughout their lives, beings have their kami domiciled within them, and it is not until death that the kami is released. These spirits are then a part of the spiritual world and have the power to affect nature and alter landscape. While many of the kami are believed to be innately good in Shinto, negative occurrences such as natural disasters, crime, poverty, and other unhealthy phenomena are believed to be caused by evil spirits. Such evil spirits are dealt with through the ritual of devotion and prayer and sacrifice of appeasement. By the same ritual they offer respect and love to the good kami who may be the spirit of their loved ones.

Most kami are classified into three subgroups: the Japanese clan ancestors (*the Ujikami)*, kami of nature, and the souls of deceased human beings who had had a great life by following the ways of a kami (Honcho 2003). Kami are neither perfect beings nor all powerful beings; they are simply considered to be on a higher tier of life than humans. To discern good from evil definitely, Shinto followers use the concept of *musubi* and *tsumi*. Musubi is the overall good harmonizing power of kami, whereas tsumi is the power that drives humans into evil, pollution, and sin. Both can have serious influence on humans physically, spiritually, and morally.

Types of Shinto

Shinto can be classified into four major types: Shrine Shinto, Sect Shinto, Folk Shinto, and State Shinto (New World Encyclopedia, 2003). Shrine Shinto is the oldest, most pervasive, and popular form of Shinto that has been a part of Japan's politico-cultural tradition. It has been the enduring form of Shinto in Japanese history.

Sect Shinto denotes the thirteen sects in Shintoism, which emerged in the nineteenth century perhaps in response to the religiocultural and political revolution. They do not have shrines and meet in halls. They include mountain-worship sects, faith-healing sects, purification sects, Confucian sects, and Revival Shinto sects (ibid).

Folk Shinto expresses the common traditional beliefs and practices that might have come from Taoism, Buddhism, or Confucianism. Their beliefs involve deities and spirits, and their practices include divination, spirit possession, and shamanic ritual of healing.

The fourth, State Shinto, was the outcome of the Meiji dynasty's restoration of 1868, which made Shinto the official religion of Japan and introduced imperial worship—the cult of the emperor. The religion was sponsored and administered by the state. It was meant to purify not only Shinto but the entire sociocultural and political spheres of the nation from external influence and ideas. Shinto became the most popular and most influential channel to carry out that mission. It was believed that by instilling Shinto ideals of kami on the people and state machinery no external force could penetrate and overpower the nation.

Major Moral and Ethical Concepts

Wa (benevolence and solidarity): Shinto moral and ethical norm emphasizes group harmony, collectivism, or group identity. The idea of *Wa,* which means "kind, benign, and harmless harmony" and "is inherent in nature and social relationships" (New World Encyclopedia online, 2015). Critics of indigenous cultural and value systems often think that these cultures that allow group solidarity to take precedence over the individual are anti-individual rights and that the individual is regarded as less important than the community. However, an agrarian culture would cherish group harmony more than the individual, me-alone type of social order. Group harmony does not negate individual diversity and progress. It is not either-or but rather both-and. The group exists because of the unique identity of the individual and the individual finds its worthiness within the group. The concept of kami reinforces social and environmental harmony, which in turn nurtures growth.

Sense of awe: The notion that the nature and all existence, including mountains, storms, and wind or air, embodies kami, which anyone can have access to encounter a deity and that every follower is surrounded by a host of deities, provides an atmosphere of wonder and curiosity. Such is the feeling carried by those who enter a Shinto *jinja* (shrine)—a sense of awe.

Afterlife: When a child is born, the child is inducted into the local shrine by declaring him or her *ujiko* meaning "named child." After death he or she becomes *ujigami,* which literally means "kami." Being named "kami" signifies that person has transcended this life. Children who die before their names are added to the list, like stillbirths and aborted babies, are called *mizuko*, literally, "water child." They are believed to cause troubles and epidemics. As such, they are also worshipped to appease them and to ward off all evils. Other than that, every ujiko will transcend to become an ujigami after death.

Torii (Sacred Gateway): Before the arrival of Buddhism, Shinto ceremonies were held outside with no icon of the kami, since it was believed kami is formless. There were no enclosed shrines. However, they erected what they called *torii* as a sacred gateway to the area of the ceremony. Every attendee must pass through this sacred gate as a symbol of purification. Now, every shrine or temple, and even many public places and roads in Japan, have this sacred gateway by which worshippers enter the shrine or under which the general public pass.

People passing the tori gate in Kyoto, Japan

Impurity and Purification: In Shinto, there is concern for purity and impurity or dirtiness for the purpose of maintaining a balance between nature, humans, and deities. Wrong attitudes and deeds if committed must be cleansed. Eating anything involves taking the life of a living being. But this is a necessity. Some lives must be given or sacrificed to enhance other lives. Therefore, it is the custom that all food must be received and eaten with gratitude by acknowledging the life given for one's life to continue. It is impure and ingratitude to ignore this custom and could bring ruin on oneself. Others around will be offended for the person's insensitivity to life or living beings. Purification rites are taken to placate an evil spirit or to seek the favor and blessings from a good spirit. New cars made or bought are purified; purification is done at groundbreaking ceremony to build new houses. Often water is used either by washing or sprinkling. There are certain habits such as cursing or placing a taboo on somebody that should be avoided to prevent impurity.

Sacred Places and Festivals

Sacred places include shrines, and there are thousands of them in Japan. Almost every space is a sacred place because of the presence of kami. However, there are very important shrines that attract lots of tourists and worshippers alike such as the Grand Shrine of Ise, which is dedicated to the Sun Goddess Amaterasu, Meiji Shrine of Emperor Meiji, and Heian Jingu in Tokyo dedicated to two emperors. Mount Fuji is also a worshipful place of importance. Women are not allowed to climb it so as not to cause impurity. There are normal days and good or festive days called *matsuri*. Festive days are held accompanied by music, dancing, wrestling, drinking, and eating. The term "matsuri" expresses an occasion for praises and thanks giving to a deity at a shrine. It also means to "entertain" or "serve" (BBC 2011). Some of the festive days are *Seijin Shiki* (Adult Day), which is a celebration on January 15 that recognizes a young man or woman as an adult at age 20. During another festival, *Aki Matsuri* (Autumn Festival), people ask for good harvest or productivity. The annual *Oshogatsu* festival (New Year, January 1) is when the kami is carried in a divine palanquin during a street parade and offers blessings to the community. This is a festival where the people also ask for kami's favor in the coming year (Encyclopedia of Social Sciences, 2008).

CONCLUSION

From its earliest time Shinto has been influenced by Chinese Taoism, Confucianism, and then Buddhism in both beliefs and practices. However, Shinto has also had influence on Buddhism leading to a new version called Zen Buddhism of Japan. Zen Buddhism uses meditation to expand the mind outward to experience the reality (kami) beyond the limits of reason and the spoken word. Zen Buddhism believes that there is universal reality, which is the Buddha nature in all things. What Zen Buddhists call the Buddha nature is kami in Shinto.

Let me conclude with the words of Rosemarie Bernard: "Today, with the numerous scattered Shinto shrines all over the Japanese archipelago, deities are worshiped and rituals are still performed according to the general patterns established by the state for all shrines in the late nineteenth and early twentieth centuries. Yet this is carried out in keeping with localized tradition and regional or community preferences. Regionality of Shinto religious practice accounts for great diversity in Shinto, while those different instances share certain basic beliefs and values" (New World Encyclopedia, 2009). One cannot underestimate the profound influence of Shinto religion and the indigenous religions of Africa and Native Americans on the environment and ecology. In spite of the challenges these religions had faced and continue to face, they have had a powerful impact on the modern religious landscape, and there are many lessons to be learned by today's technological world if the harmony needed between nature, humanity, and spirituality will be realized.

KEY WORDS

Sacred myth	*French spiritism*	Kinship	Healing ritual
Supernaturalism	Rites of renewal	Shaman	Spiritual universe
Divination	Spirit possession	Sacrifice	Exorcism
Ancestral veneration	Animism	Lifeway	Vision quest
Mediums	Incantation	Magic	Lukumi Babalu Aye
Santerianism	*Oludumare*	*Orisha*	*Obatala*
The Great Spirit	*Soul immortality*	*Koyukon*	*Sheepeaters*
Shintoism	*Kami*	*Shen*	*Tao*
Musubi	*Purification*	*Tsumi*	*Meiji Restoration*

QUESTIONS FOR FURTHER STUDY

1. Discuss the role of music, drumming, and dancing in indigenous religious life.

2. Explain the role and importance of storytelling and orality in indigenous religions.

3. Examine the actions of European invasion on the resistance and survival of the Native Americans.

4. Watch the video "The Egyptian Book of the Dead." From the video, list the key features of ancient Egyptian religion (beliefs, rituals and ceremonies, deities, cosmogony, religion, and society).

5. Why in the Yoruba religion are temples not erected for the High or Supreme God?

6. Discuss the concept of "democratized shamanism" in Native American religions.

7. Explore and identify the locations of the Native American religious communities in the United States.

8. Explain the symbolism of the concept of "the circle" in Native American cosmology.

9. Explain the notion that in Shinto religion all reverence be given to the kami.

10. Describe the ethics and morality of Shintoism and its role in promoting ecological harmony.

Hinduism

INTRODUCTION

The religion now called Hinduism is a broad range of religions in India. Hinduism, the name given to this religion in the nineteenth century, was derived from the Persian word "Hindu." The word "Hindu" means "river" and had nothing to do with religion but originally referred to the people who lived in the Indus River Valley. It later came to be used for all people who lived in India. About 80 percent of India's one billion people regard themselves as Hindus. Hindu became a reference to their way of life including religious life and religious philosophy (religious worldview). Hindus

regard life as an ongoing force of the larger cosmic whole. At any moment, a person will always be in the process of becoming—more than the person was the moment before.

Theosophy is wisdom about that which is divine. Theosophy, in its normal way of use, is religious philosophy. In Christian circles, the use is normally referred to as theology, and all theology is Christian theosophy. In Judaism, theosophy is expressed through what the Rabbis teach and the way that they construct their understandings of God and Judaism, etc. It is the same with the Hindu thinkers. Their theosophy includes the different elements of their religious thought.

The problem with Hinduism is that there is no single theosophy that is standard for the whole religion. Hinduism defies being reduced into a few principle concepts or ideas or theosophical categories. There is no one set of writings that is basic to all religious practices. There is not even universal agreement on what all the gods are in the religion. And there is far from universal agreement about how to go about fulfilling religious obligations. Expressions of Hinduism vary from near naked ascetics wandering from one holy site to another, to private in-home rituals, to festivals that are attended by Indians from all over India, to extremes of meditation, even to goat sacrifices (though at most quite rare). Furthermore, sacrifice in Hinduism, which existed even in its early classical period, has been replaced today almost universally by ideas of honor and worship of the Hindu gods. In Hinduism, outside of agreement on reincarnation and the need to achieve moksha by overcoming the effects of Karma, there is little agreement. Each god has a role of its own, and each god has his own theosophy.

For Hinduism the fundamental question is not sin and righteousness. The question is duty, order, and Karma. Basic to Hinduism is the idea of "dharma," the idea that there is a natural order in the universe that should be maintained. Still further, one's religious obligation is to maintain that order. In other words, doing one's duty involves knowing what the right order is and then doing it or maintaining it. When you do what is right for your caste (your level in society), you are not accumulating Karma. When you don't do what is right for your role/level in society, you accumulate Karma. In the Hindu theosophy, as conceptual understanding developed, the futility of getting rid of this Karma through trying to live a good life was increasingly realized. In Hinduism, the very best that a person can do is to live the very best life possible within one's own caste. But a farmer, for instance, or a merchant, can never become a nobleman in this life. So, the idea is that one should become the best farmer or the best merchant that one can be. Focusing on the merchant, one might say, perhaps, that making a great deal of money is an evidence of being the best merchant possible. But to do that, one may have to either violate some religious tenants (such as compassion) or have to "step on" other people. In either case, bad Karma results even when trying to fulfill one's dharma. And that Karma is going to remain, forcing the merchant into the transmigration to another life.

For Hindus there are a variety of beliefs and an even wider variety of practices. There are about a billion Hindus who worship some 330 million gods and goddesses (Fisher 2011, 73). In different areas of India there are regional variations in the way that the religious tradition is practiced. Go to a place in Northern India, and there may be some very different religious traditions than in a place in Southern India. There is another complicating factor. A Hindu need not follow just one god. There may be several gods, in which case each one will have its own different practices, and the individual has to integrate all of these into the way the religion is practiced. Many of the localized gods are identified with the great gods of Hindu tradition: Brahma, Vishnu, or Shiva. So when a person is worshipping a traditional god, the person may at the same time think of it as worshipping one of these greater gods. Thus, the gods overlap and form cross-identifications.

According to ancient tradition of the people of the Hindu Valley, Hinduism developed from three sources:

1. the rural people of the Hindu Valley (2500–1500 BCE),
2. the more developed Tamils of the Dravidian (aborigines) culture, and
3. the Verdic religion of the Aryans who invaded the northern part of India (c. 1500 BCE) and brought their oral text called Rigvedas ("Vedas" means "eternal truth").

Many Hindu scholars and nationalists dispute this claim and refuse to accept that their traditional religion was foreign-born. Hence they prefer the alternative name of "Sanatana Dharma" (eternal religion).

THE DRAVIDIANS AND ARYANS

It is believed that the Dravidians were a very sophisticated civilization. They lived in large cities with crosshatched streets and were surrounded by a large, well-built wall. The houses were brick, sometimes two stories in height. They had a canal system, sewer systems, indoor plumbing, and because of their location they carried on trade up and down the Indus River valley. There are terracotta and stone sculptures, especially of the male animal and the female human, which are suggestive of their religious system. Seals (like signet ring seals) bear animals in trees (seals of ownership). There are also female figurines, donuts (stone or ceramic round things), and phallic stones. These suggest that the people were simple agriculturalists who practiced what is called a nature religion, probably one that focused on the creative powers in nature. Included in this was probably something related to the cleansing role of water, and it's possible that some form of meditation may have been practiced. This is really all that can be said, even on a suggestive level, about the lifestyle and religion of the Dravidians.

The Aryans were a nomadic or seminomadic, tribal, and wandering people. Anthropologists believe that the Aryans were the ancestors of Indo-Europeans who migrated to the shores of the Atlantic Ocean and Western Europe all the way through Central and Eastern Europe, across many areas of Asia and Southeast Asia, perhaps all the way to the Far East. The basis for this concept is that they seem to share similar elements of society, language, and religious tradition.

One of these groups of people is believed to have swept into India about the year 2000 BCE. Aryans, in spite of their nomadic or seminomadic lifestyle, used chariots in warfare and bronze weapons. The chariots and bronze weapons allowed them to hold military superiority over the Dravidians. So, whenever they moved into India, they were able to move in quickly and with a superior military force. When they came into India, they brought their oral scriptures with them—the Rigveda. Even to this day, there remains an emphasis on this oral aspect in Hindu scripture. That is to say that the verbal transmission not only transmits the text and preserves it but also helps the one who is memorizing it to absorb it into their own lives and follow its teachings. About the year 1000 BCE, these oral scriptures were actually committed to writing. Thus, Hinduism is derived from an ancient scripture known as a "veda," and as a religion is referred to as Vedantism. *Vedantism* in India is essentially the revealed knowledge of god or of eternal truth.

The Aryans preferred male gods to the female gods of the Dravidians. The Aryans had no tradition of temples, but they seem to have made sacrifices to the Aryan gods at temporary altars. There were a number of deities (gods) that they worshipped. One was impersonal power. Another was the god of human obligations. There were the gods of contracts, fire, sun, and the national deity among others. The most important thing about the Aryans cosmology (how existence is perceived) was that there is a divine order to the universe, and human responsibility is to discover and to live in accordance with the divine order and to preserve that divine order. Sacrifice was commonly prescribed for maintaining the relationship between the human and the divine realms. The most important of these was the *Soma* sacrifice, which involved the use of intoxicants. The idea of the sacrifices was that they were essentially to keep order in the universe, the cosmos and to prevent it from becoming chaotic. If the proper sacrifices were not presented at the proper time in the proper way by the proper people, the world might essentially explode in chaos. The priesthood included people specifically trained to do those required things at the proper time, in the proper way.

HINDU CONCEPT OF DIVINITY

For Hinduism, their cosmology involves everything that is an extension of divine substance. Among the millions of divinities, who were the primary deities in Hinduism? What is the Hindu notion of divinity? The primary deities are:

Brahman: Brahman is the Supreme Deity (God), the creator god. Brahman basically creates out of

himself. Thus, everything is an extension of the divine substance. Therefore, everything created is in some sense divine. He is normally represented with four heads and also as a ball of fire out of which the universe originated.

Vishnu: Vishnu, also known as the Pervader (the one who takes many forms), is the sustainer and provider god. He has preserving, restoring, and protecting power. When he sleeps, creation is withdrawn to a seed and rises again when he wakes up. He is blue in color signifying infinity. His followers are one of the largest Hindu groups and are called Vaishnavites. Vishnu has, according to Hinduism, appeared on earth in nine, some say ten, different incarnations or manifestations. Buddha is one of those incarnations. Rama is another.

Shiva: Shiva is the god that judges and destroys and is generally thought of as the Destroyer god. Essentially he judges behavior, but the idea of judgment is not for punishment but for cleansing and purging so that ultimately all of created existence will ultimately be drawn back into the divine substance. In this sense, he offers salvation. Because of this notion, for Hinduism, ultimately everyone will be saved, because, ultimately, all will be purged away and all that was created will be drawn back into the divine substance. Shiva is associated with the Ganges, with its cleansing and purging just as the power of Shiva to cleanse and purge becomes a life source. A popular cult associated with Shiva is called Shaivism. In the Hindu concept, the ultimate religious goal is to return to Brahman—a return to ultimate reality, a restoration back into the divine substance.

Two fundamental ideas that we need to understand at the outset is, first, the unity of the gods in the Hindu notion of divinity. Vishnu explains the unity as follows: "Only the unlearned deem myself (Vishnu) and Shiva to be distinct; he, I and Brahman are one, assuming different names for the creation, preservation and destruction of the universe. We as the triune Self, pervade all creatures; the wise therefore regard all others as themselves." The second idea in the Hindu notion of divinity is that Brahman is the ultimate god, the highest god, but this is ultimate reality rather than personal being. It is on the order of a force or a power rather than in the personal terms found in Christianity, Judaism, or Islam. The distinction is extremely important. If God is an impersonal power or force, it makes a difference in the cosmology of its followers. What separates a person's soul from Brahman is Karma. Fundamentally, all Karma is bad. So-called good Karma is too inadequate in comparison to the bad to wipe away bad Karma. Basically, the state of Hindu thought today is you will never achieve moksha—reabsorption into the divine essence—through trying to get rid of Karma. You have got to find some other way.

THE CASTE SYSTEM

First of all, there was a divinely ordained structure in society that in some sense mirrored the structure in the divine realm. And therefore, if human experience reflects such an order, it means that one must keep that same order in the human realm. This is done by what is known as the major occupational groupings or the caste system. What is the caste system? It is a very highly structured type of society in which there is no movement between one level and another. The Aryans seemed to have had a caste system of four levels.

- The highest level in the caste system was the priest—*Brahmins*. The Brahmins or priests were the ones responsible for seeing that religion was carried out in the proper way and so forth.
- The second level is the *Kshatriyas*. These were the warriors or nobility.
- The third level was the *Vaishyas*, what you could call the peasants, farmers, small-time independent farmer, maybe even the middle class when they reach the point where they have a middle class.
- The fourth level is the *Shudras*. They are related to the Aryans but in this system, they are at the very bottom level. They were the artisans and manual laborers.
- Still, below these original four groups are the *Pariahs* or *outcasts*. When the Aryans came into India and took over the territory of the Dravidians, they had a whole new group of people who are outside the caste system entirely (the "outcastes"). Hence, the term *outcast*.

  Under the Aryan system, there was no place for them (the Dravidians). They become the ones who clean out the sewers and pick up the cow dung off the street, etc. They are what are also known as the *untouchables*. There is no place for them in the society. They must do the work and the jobs that nobody else wants to do and nobody else is willing to do.

What is especially significant about the caste system is that it determines nearly everything else about a person's lot in life—what will be eaten, clothing that will be worn, type of vocations pursued, possibilities for marriage, places of residence, etc. Even though since Gandhi in 1948, officially the whole caste system has been outlawed, it is so fundamental to the lifestyle and religious system of Hindus that it continues to survive in an "underground" manner.

RELIGIOUS OBSERVANCE AND THE RISE OF REVIVAL MOVEMENTS

As the Aryans invaded India, they did not do so in a single large invasion or a sweeping conquest over an immense geographical area. Rather, they conquered a section of territory, settled, assimilated the region into their rulership, and then continued to another section, as Dravidians fled before them. The impact was to create a vast number of slightly different regions, all at different levels of assimilation, and lacking in social, political, and even linguistic universality. This has resulted in a society and culture today of many different languages, customs, and even different personal religious beliefs. In different regions or towns of India, different gods are considered most important, and there are many localized religious observances. There are, however, a few aspects of the Hindu religion held in common across India, and it is these that we will focus upon.

Ritual observance in the Aryan system was primarily aimed at assuring a materially happy life in harmony with all of the cosmic order. It was the Veda that provided the knowledge for this to happen and around which the religion centered. Rituals, sacrifices, and day-to-day experiences through the caste system were to be in harmony with the universal cosmic orders. If successful, then material happiness and eternal happiness for the individual was found.

The Vedas: (1) The oldest of the Vedas is known as the *Rigveda* and essentially consists of praise (like a hymnal). This existed before the Aryan invasions. However, as assimilation and a broader area over which the Aryan world ruler began developing after the beginning of the conquests, the priests became even more concerned with preserving the rituals and sacrifices according to the ancient system. This led to two additional sacred scriptures: (2) the *Yagurveda* and (3) the *Somaveda,* which are closely related. Both of these are primarily associated with instructions for sacrifice. The Somaveda is focused primarily on the Soma sacrifices, the most important of all the sacrifices. (4) The *Atharvaveda* was developed later. It was primarily composed of spells and magic by which worshippers could obtain what they wanted in this world from the divine realm.

The Brahmanas (priestly sacred texts): With the additional Vedas, and with the political and social and religious worlds becoming more diverse due to the expansion of the Aryan world, the role of the priesthood became even more important. This resulted in the development of an almost "divine" priesthood and a body of commentary known as the Brahmanas. These commentaries were prepared basically by the priests to instruct other priests in carrying out the sacrifices. The Brahmanas began to emerge or develop around 1500 BCE and they continue to be compiled until about 1000 BCE.

By the year 1000 BCE, the role of the priest had become very sterile and routine. They were still an important element in society, but by the year 1000 BCE, whatever personal involvement there may have been to religious experiences was gone, and the religion was becoming very methodical and ritualistic. There is not any personal application. It is all what the priest does and nothing else.

The Revival Movements: New groups of writings were developed as reactions to the priestly ritualism and religious sterilization to revitalize inner devotion and to help develop a personal approach to sacrifice. These writings were the *Aranyakas* by the Kshatriya clan. A new movement began to develop among the Kshatriyas (the warriors and nobility group), in part as a counterweight to the immense role in society that the priests had assumed and in part because of the desire for a more personal religious experience. This was formed out of the notion of sacrifice as something more than just what the priest did. The resulting idea was one of inner or personal sacrifice. Through inner sacrifice, it was thought that one could do mentally what the sacrifices that the priests perform intended to do in a physical sense. In other words, it would bring a right relationship with the whole universal order. It would not then be just the "priest's religion" any longer. This transformation was so dramatic and thorough that whereas thirty-five hundred years ago the priests performed blood sacrifices to maintain the order in the universe, today no Hindu performs blood sacrifices for anything. Now the only sacrifices are internal sacrifices.

The Aranyakas (literally, "forest books") were written to help people who wanted to follow this path of inner sacrifice to do so when they would go into the forest for meditation (personal retreats). They would take these books and they would meditate upon them. This meditation would help them not only then but also in the future to understand and appropriate the meaning of the sacrifices of the religion. The other line of action was the emergence of ascetic life. The goal of this movement was to seek personalization of the religious experience through ascetic activities. Ascetism is forsaking this world and everything having to do with it for the purpose of religious devotion. The ascetic life assumed four major forms or paths: Ajavikas, Jainism, Buddhism, and Upanishads.

The Ajavikas (ascetic) path: This ascetic life, based on the notion that everything in the universe is absolutely predestined, maintained that no one can do anything to change either the present situation or the course of future events. Whether by inner sacrifice or presenting sacrifices, none of that does anything to change the present or the future. Therefore, the only thing that a person really can do in a religious sense is to try as much as possible to keep from being involved in this world so as to accumulate as little Karma as possible. Essentially this means doing nothing or being nothing. This brought about the practice of what is called "extreme asceticism." The Ajavikas were the extreme ascetics. Their asceticism involved eating, drinking, and wearing as little clothing as possible (usually nothing); living in the least quality housing as possible (usually no house or residence but wandering naked and eating when and where food is found). They have nothing to do with sex, forming relationships, politics, vocations, etc. While this movement didn't really last or grow and was not self-sustaining, it influenced the development of the practice of self-denial in Hinduism. It also fostered a certain degree of cynicism in religious beliefs (the notion that there is nothing one can do to influence the present or the future, so all study, inner sacrifice, priestly sacrifices, and pilgrimages, are of doubtful value). They became fatalists in the sense that the only thing that they could do was to avoid accumulating, as much as possible, any bad Karma.

Jainism (the Jains): Jainism arose out of the teaching of Prince Vardhamana and became one of the paths to liberation. Though it arose from Hinduism and shares similar teachings and values of Hinduism, Jainism differs significantly from its parent religion and thus it is not considered a sect of Hinduism. Prince Vardhamana rejected the idea of physical sacrifice as well as the worship of the myriads of gods associated with Hinduism. Instead, he chose a path stricter than that of the traditional Hindu as we shall see in the next chapter.

The path of Siddhartha Gautama (Buddhism): Gautama was the son of a minor nobleman. He also rejected the notion of sacrifices in Hindu religion but the Vedas as well as they basically prescribed the sacrifices and dictated the social structure that became the caste system; he also rejected the caste system. As with the Jains, he believed that the Hindu gods were generally uninvolved with humanity. He also believed in the necessity of a personal search and a reliance on oneself to achieve whatever it was that a person would achieve. He focused on one issue, the concept of suffering (the idea that being separated from the divine essence is suffering, and therefore life itself is suffering). If one could overcome suffering, then one could achieve, in a single lifetime, that reabsorption into the divine essence. Buddhism was probably the single most important movement, other than Hinduism itself, that came out of the development of Hinduism. We will deal in much more detail with these concepts separately.

The Upanishads: Still another approach was that which was set forth in the Upanishads (a volume of essays and religious reflection compiled between 500 BCE and 100 CE), and would eventually develop into mainstream Hinduism. It would be about 100 BCE when Patanjali would set forth the first major approach to modern Hindu religious practice. In the Upanishads, the Hindu triad, Brahma, Vishnu, and Shiva takes shape. For them Brahma is absolute, mystery, and unknowable. Upanishads is more contemplative in practice and also philosophical and speculative in thought. The Upanishads sets forth the notion of moksha as the goal of the religion, as absorption into the divine realm from which one was taken at creation. It identifies the *Atman* with Brahman as well as being the divine essence within a person. Atman is the eternal soul that is reborn millions of times and in many modes or forms. The Karma–Samsara cycle, however, prevents the Atman from being released, whereby one attains moksha. Also, in the Upanishads, certain religious disciplines are suggested as methods for dealing with what is otherwise an impossible human situation. For instance, contemplation focused on the Atman empowers people to cope with the caste system.

THE SOUL AND INCARNATIONS

Hindus believe that all existence—in fact, not just human existence, but all existence such as animals, plants, all living things—have a soul (Atman plus Karma); that soul has been in existence since beginningless time; in other words, since eternity past. That soul passes through an innumerable number of rebirth/redeath cycles—as it goes from one form of existence to another (plants and things like that, to animals and eventually to a level within the caste system)—seeking its real self—the Brahman that is within. In this process a person will gradually climb up through the caste system until eventually reaching the level of a Brahmin, that is a priest. And what lies beyond the priesthood is achieving that unity with the divine essence, called moksha.

Once a person achieves the level of being born into a human existence, then it is the merit or demerit that determines whether when one is born the next time as a Brahmin, a nobleperson, a Shudra, etc. It takes many lifetimes for a person to discover their true inner self. So, a Hindu just simply expects not to do it in one lifetime. That doesn't excuse one from doing what can be done in one lifetime toward that end. However, Hindus see no reason why they should be penalized, for instance, in hell, for being unable to achieve the goal of finding their real inner self (which is the basic religious focus for Hinduism) in just a single lifetime. This is an important distinction from monotheistic religions.

What happens to the soul, which is the Atman plus Karma, between incarnations? That is, between death and rebirth? Each one of the Hindu gods has their own heaven, and one's soul goes temporarily to the heaven of one of these Hindu gods before the next lifetime. In order to do that, though, one has to have done a special deed or good action to that particular god, for instance, having built a temple to that god, having endowed a monastery on behalf of that god, or supplying the priesthood with their needs—some special, major act of good or kindness. Then that person's soul is believed not necessarily to go immediately to another lifetime but rather, in a sense, enjoys a "vacation" in-between in the heaven of one of these gods.

As Hinduism developed during the centuries, the religious situation was increasingly perceived as virtually insoluble. Religious actions alone could not overcome the effects of Karma, whether the practices involved responsible living according to one's position in the caste system (Dharma), offering of sacrifices (as priests might do), use of rituals, or going on pilgrimages. During any individual lifetime, a person accumulates Karma, which surrounds the Atman like the layers of an onion. This Karma prevents the release of the Atman, and forces the Karma–Samsara cycle, resulting in reincarnation into another lifetime. However, in each subsequent lifetime, rather than successfully overcoming one's Karma, one accumulates more Karma, making release of the Atman even more remote. This continued existence of Karma forces even more lifetimes of reincarnation (remember *all* Karma is regarded as bad by Hinduism—even the so-called good Karma—because any Karma forces reincarnation and makes achieving moksha more remote). Therefore, some other way had to exist in order to achieve moksha and to overcome the problem of Karma accumulation. The traditional Vedic religion more or less indicated that it was done by the priests, the sacrifices, maintaining order in the universe, etc. But this approach had become increasingly remote and sterile to personal involvement in the religion. What is the way out? And is there a way out?

CLASSICAL HINDUISM: THE WAY TO MOKSHA (THE FOUR MAJOR PATHS OF YOGA)

By the year 500 BCE, along with various movements to personalize religious experience and to find a non-priestly path to religious success, mainstream Hinduism began to focus on the practice of Yoga (which means religious discipline). By this time, the essential ideas (above) of Hinduism had emerged. Also developed were the basic elements of Hinduism: the necessity of intellectual or mental sacrifice—inner sacrifice; the importance of control over the world's forces (that was what the sacrificial system was all about, control over the world's forces); and finally, meditation, yoga, religious disciplines to achieve success. Between humans and the divine realm no relationship really existed, nor was there any clear connection between the gods' heavens and moksha. The gods are there to assist one on the way toward moksha—and to give rest between one incarnation and the next. The idea of gaining the benefits of being like a priest were sought through inner sacrifice, an approach based on self-effort, which might be called Karma Yoga (the way of action).

Karma Yoga emphasizes the performance of proper deeds and actions. In an earlier time, this was more or less the primary way in which Hinduism was practiced. Today Karma Yoga is regarded as the conjunction of two other forms of Yoga: Jnana Yoga (yana yoga—the way of knowledge or logic) and Bhakti Yoga (bati yoga—the way of devotion). For a Bhakti devotee, Karma Yoga says that in all that you do, do it as unto the Lord rather than for self-interest or gain so that everything that you do is sacred. For Jnana Yoga, Karma Yoga says to do what is required because it is required; concentrate on fulfilling each duty as it arises, accept loss, pain, or shame with equanimity considering that these are teachers whereby one achieves calmness, even in the midst of intense activity.

Jnana Yoga: After 500 BCE, a spiritual and bodily discipline based on self-knowledge, known as Jnana Yoga, developed. The practice of Jnana Yoga was thought to succeed in achieving moksha because, through contemplation, one could cut through the layers of Karma to discover the real self that is within (Atman), which can then be released. Though the Atman (one's inmost being) is considered virtually identical with Brahman (divine essence) and since divinity is not personal, Jnana is not perceived as self-absorbed. The idea in Jnana Yoga is, via meditation, to climb into yourself and walk around finding the divine person that is there. It is like taking an onion, running a knife through it and then pulling it back to expose the inner essence that is there. That is what Jnana Yoga intends—to release the inner essence that is there, to open it up, and let it out. There are four stages in the process of Jnana Yoga. The idea is that you do this not just one time in one situation but throughout your life:

- Introduction of the idea of an Atman within
- Distinguish between one's persona or personality (surface self) and the true inner being—the Atman.
- The Atman becomes the outer self, known as detachment. There are two stages in the detachment:
  - During reflection, meditation, quiet moments.
  - While an event is actually occurring.

Bhakti Yoga: By 300 BCE, there developed yet another approach known as Bhakti Yoga, which is something on the order of devotional discipline. Instead of a discipline of the mind through self-knowledge, it is a discipline of the heart. The idea is that through intense devotion to a god or manifestation of a god, one can overcome the effects of Karma and achieve moksha, just as the manifestations of that god were able to do so. In essence, one seeks to become, through devotion, a manifestation of a particular Hindu god. From this approach, moksha is thought by many today to be achieved primarily by the gracious love of an adorable one (the god or manifestation of a god one chooses), a reward that is bestowed upon worshippers. Moksha then, in modern Hinduism, is not primarily achieved through a specific, prescribed set of actions but rather is achieved largely through the devotion of a worshipper to an adorable one. Devotion in Bhakti includes prayer; personal acts of devotion; ritual and ceremony; pilgrimages; and may involve myths, symbols or images (aids on which to focus and with which to identify). Another form of devotion is meditation. Meditation could be done by repeating the name of the god chosen to follow over and over and over. Another focus of meditation might include the ways in which a person can relate to another. The Greeks identified four forms of love: parent/child, friend/friend, lovers, self-sacrificing. So meditation and practical devotion might involve the various ways that one can love god through these different types of love.

The choice of which manifestation to which one will practice devotion is an individual one. Today, some of the better known possibilities include Rama, Krishna, Buddha, and Jesus. Christianity is regarded by modern classical Hindu religion as one "brilliantly lit Bhakti highway to God." The thing is that where Christianity would say it is THE way to God, the Hindu would say that it is not the only way. One interesting aspect of Bhakti is that in Bhakti, those that follow this approach draw a distinction between Brahman and Atman. They do not see the Atman as identical to Brahman. Rather they see divinity in a personal way, as totally other, as personal, and as one to be adored and loved exclusively for himself.

Bhakti Yoga is the kind of yoga that allows one to go about the regular routine of daily life while becoming increasingly devoted to a god. Jnana Yoga is generally monastic because, fundamentally, it is necessary for one to withdraw into intense, protracted contemplation. One needs a guru that helps lead in the process, or at least it is very helpful to have a guru to lead to discover the inner self and let it out.

Raja Yoga: A fourth Yoga, more difficult to understand, is Raja Yoga. Raja Yoga perceives four layers to human existence, proceeding from the exterior to the interior. The outer layer is the body. Then comes an inner layer of the mind. A still deeper inner layer is the subconscious (soul). At the very center of the individual lies the Atman, which also is identified as Brahman. The aim in Raja Yoga is to practice prescribed mental exercises and to observe their subjective effect. This action proves the validity of the four-part notion. To follow this approach requires a guru who prescribes these exercises, each validating that the body, or the mind, or the subconscious, or the Atman is really there. This is thought to lead one into a deep sense of self-knowledge and concentration whereby one experiences "the beyond which is within," a momentary ecstasy in which one is in unity with the divine realm.

Today, it is common practice for faithful Hindus to use all four types of Yoga to some degree or another, but generally whatever best suits their personality is going to be the one that they tend to follow more than the others. Any one of these four is equally okay. Not only that, but the individual Hindu is free to create a hybrid of these four. This means any combination and in any degree. Whatever works for an individual is acceptable. Furthermore, this combination might change over the course of a lifetime.

Whatever Yoga or combination of Yoga practices a person chooses, there are some general aspects of religious practice that apply for all. First of all there are some moral preliminaries which apply regardless of which Yoga a Hindu follows. The moral preliminaries are in two parts, positive and negative. On the negative side, one is to abstain from injuring any one or thing and also to abstain from falsehood; from stealing; from sensuality; and from greed. On the positive side, one should observe cleanliness and also, contentment (peace in whatever circumstance one is in); self-control; studiousness; and contemplation of the divine (meditation).

THE GOAL OF YOGA AND STEPS OF MEDITATION

In seeking liberation of the Atman, the whole idea of cleansing becomes important. In Hinduism, cleansing also has both a negative and a positive sense to it. In the negative sense, cleansing is denial and death to self. It is the god Shiva to which the Hindu worshipper turns for this. Shiva is the destroyer god, which destroys the finite to enable the infinite to come forth. In the positive sense, cleansing in the Hindu concept is enlarging one's view of life, its events, and its problems, from the perspective of divinity. This involves detachment and training oneself to step back and view the world as a third party. For instance, pain would be viewed as a detached observer rather than one who is experiencing it. The way in which one learns to do this is through discipline—Yoga. It is training a body and mind, ultimately, toward absorption with the infinite/divine/ultimate reality. As such, the ultimate goal of yoga is to release the Atman from the finiteness of life (flesh, mind, Karma).

The practice of meditation is perhaps the feature most connected with Hindu religious tradition, though for the Bhakti practitioner, meditation may play little, if any, role in religious life. Meditation involves a number of steps:

1. Centering down, which is simply withdrawing from the world and settling the mind, heart, thoughts, emotions, etc.
2. Assume and practice using the lotus position.
3. Practice controlling respiration. The idea is that control of respiration helps focus attention away from the outer world.

4. Concentration. The moment one's eyes are closed there are dozens of things that start going back and forth across the mind. The idea here is to focus on one thing—to eliminate the distractions.

5. Meditation upon the object of focus—meditate so completely that there is no longer an awareness of separateness from that thought, a state which is known as samadhi. This is to have achieved moksha on a momentary basis, though it is not full moksha. In this stage of absorption, the mind continues to think but as if seeing and comprehending what is invisible, totally caught up into the subject of contemplation.

Finally, the personal devotion of Bhakti has a particular form which is commonly followed: Before rising, utter sacred sound "Uhmmm," then utter the name of one's god or gods. Proceed before the sacred shelf or shrine room where there are pictures or images of each god. Mark the forehead with ash or paste as symbol of submission to god(s). Present offerings (flowers, lit candles, food) on the altar. At dawn, midday, or sunset recite the most sacred of Vedic verses. Repeat these acts, sitting barefooted and facing east—then meditate. Bathe at midday, meditate, and make an offering. Finally, worship in the evening before retiring. Daily, act to honor parents and ancestors; give shelter to guests or alms to the poor; and feed animals, especially cows (incarnation of the god Brahma). Practitioners of Bhakti might be found routinely at a temple service.

WRITINGS IN ASSOCIATION WITH THE YOGA: THE EPICS AND THE PURANAS

This Yoga emerged in association with a new era of writing, which included accounts contained in what are known as the Epics and the Puranas. Taken together, the Epics and the Puranas urged a sense of devotion on the part of the Hindu toward one or another of the gods. These books established something like a hierarchy of the deities. Behind everything is Brahman, which is in and around and permeates everything. This is the divine essence—the divine life force. Then there is the triad of Brahma, Vishnu, and Shiva. These are the great gods—the creator god, the sustainer god, and the destroyer god. Then come all kinds of lesser deities, the other 330 million, organized in a hierarchy in regard to each of them. Each has different roles and different relationships to humans and different relationships that they play in society. Hindu reflection established a very strong association between Brahman and the god Shiva. The god Shiva destroys—for redemption, for re-creation, for making anew. It was not just destruction for the sake of destruction, but destruction for the sake of re-creation.

In addition, the Epics and the Puranas discuss divine incarnation or manifestation. Embedded in the Epics and Puranas are commands essentially to worship, to devote oneself, to give oneself to this god or that god or this goddess or that goddess, whatever the case may be. The notion represented here is much more emphatic than just devotion, however. It is to be so devoted that one's own identity is lost in the identity of the gods and goddesses, to become, as it were, that god or goddess. In so doing, one overcomes the effects of Karma just as the god or goddess is not subject to the effects of Karma. To jump ahead, a Hindu today tends to utilize what is known as Bhakti Yoga, almost exclusively, with the belief that if one is faithfully devoted to the gods in this life, then at death, that person will achieve moksha and be united with the divine realm.

On the one hand, the *Puranas* deal mostly with such things as creation and the end of the universe, devotion, why a particular temple existed or why a particular god was venerated there. These conveyed a sense of divine presence to Hindus and developed the association between local gods and goddesses and their relationship to the greater gods of Hinduism. The Epics, on the other hand, deal with manifestations of the god Vishnu as a human in order to guide humans toward right living and achieving moksha. Together, the Puranas and the Epics help convey the sense that the Hindu deities are not just remote and uninvolved with humanity. Rather they are very real and are personal. Corporate devotional activity, in fact, often focuses on these gods through the use of dance, drama, and storytelling. The Puranas weave the varieties of localized religious belief and practice into an overall Hindu religious tradition. The Epics are foundational for devotional practice. There are two main epics. One is known as the Mahabharata. The other one is known as the Ramayana.

The Ramayana is a short book that recounts the life of the next to the last incarnation or manifestation of the Hindu god Vishnu. Rama must rescue his wife when she is kidnapped, and through the story, he is regarded as the example of the perfect man, husband, father, son, in all things: the way he treats women; the way he treats other people; the way he interrelates with the government, etc. Rama is a divine manifestation that comes and lives among humans successfully achieving moksha during his lifetime. By devoting oneself to this manifestation, one thereby may also overcome the effects of Karma.

The Mahabharata is the story of the struggle for "world" (i.e., a part of India) domination between two ancient Indian families. The important passage that is regarded as scripture for many Hindus is the *Bhagavad Gita* (meaning the "song of the Lord"). In this passage, the warrior Arunja is a young man but a proven warrior. He is heading toward the field of battle in a chariot. The chariot driver is Krishna—a manifestation of the god Vishnu. As the chariot proceeds toward the battle, Arunja suddenly is gripped with the fear that because some of his brothers are fighting with the enemy, it is possible that he could find himself fighting with one of his own family. This would incur great Karma, he supposes, and directs his chariot driver to turn aside from the battle. Instead, Krishna continues directing the chariot into the battle and counsels the young warrior concerning truth. He indicates that there is a deeper issue of living up to responsibility and that failing to do so is where Arunja would incur Karma. It deals with religious discipline (Yoga), specifically identifying Bhakti Yoga as the highest form of Yoga, and personalizes Brahman as a loving god (rather than the usual impersonal force). The Bhagavad Gita makes reference to the idea of an adorable one (a Bhagavan or Avatar—the earthly incarnation of a deity). This adorable one is the divine manifestation to whom the worshipper chooses to commit himself in Bhakti (devotion). The Epic thereby encourages Bhakti commitment and devotion to a Bhagavan or Avatar.

WRITINGS THAT SUPPLEMENT THE VEDAS

Some of the written sources for Hindu religious tradition and practice have already been mentioned. The Vedas, the Brahmanas, and to some extent the Aranyakas, all focused on things outside of individual religious experience. But as people wanted to become more and more personally involved in religious practice, a series of writings developed providing prescriptions of how to do that.

Vedas: These dealt mostly with sacrifice but also with other things about the universe that were believed to have been handed down from the divine realm, according to the Aryan tradition, to ancient wise men who then passed them on to others. In a nutshell, the Vedas were believed to be divine revelation of truth. The believer who accepts these notions of truth contained in the Vedas is called an Astika. Priests are all Astikas. The Jains and the Buddhists, who reject the notion of truth in the Vedas, are Nastika. Today the Vedas are still important for Hinduism, though other texts have been added to as supplements.

Sutras: One supplement to the Vedas is the Sutras, which also supplement the Brahmanas. The Sutras prescribe sacrificial acts and ceremonies for individual households—not priests—to carry out. The focus is on the individual and individual households—religious acts, sacrifices, offerings, ceremonies, which each individual household carries out as devotional acts.

Sastras: Another supplement to the Vedas is the Sastras. These are instructions for human conduct and human relationships. These provide the ethics of Hinduism. The Sastras are instructions on how to act and on relationships between people generally. Among the things covered are not just relationships between people but also issues of law, relationships between the individual and the government, and the way the government ought to be constituted (the way it ought to operate, the responsibilities it ought to have toward the people it governs).

TEMPLES, PILGRIMAGES, AND OTHER HINDU RELIGIOUS EXPRESSION

Hindus from all walks of life, regardless of caste, Yoga, or where they live (inside or outside of India), maintain a home shrine. The idea of the home altar is to reinforce the relationship or presence of the one worshipped in the home and to aid in personal acts of devotion. In addition, there are village temples and great temples, and Hindus often go on pilgrimages to holy sites in India.

Temples are regarded as residences of the deities. Usually a temple is erected at the place where it is believed a particular deity was manifested to humans in some very apparent and powerful way. Local temples are especially accessible to the local population. The local gods are frequently identified with Vishnu or Shiva, or with Rama or Krishna, but then Rama or Krishna are manifestations of Vishnu. This means that for a Hindu, the major Hindu gods are essentially localized for them to worship. As one worships the local deity, it is also understood that the worship is also directed toward the greater Hindu gods as well.

Structurally, temples and shrines are usually surrounded by a wall that encloses a courtyard. Within that courtyard, there is a tank of water for ritual cleansing (whether it be for washing the feet to cleanse oneself or for cleansing an offering). In the courtyard there also will be a small sacred room or building containing an image of the particular god or goddess venerated at that site. The priests perform daily ceremonies and activities related to that god as if they were servants in a royal court. On a daily basis they wake the god up, bathe it, clothe it, feed it (offerings), and present offerings of flowers and incense. They oftentimes chant a mantra (a brief syllable like "uhmmmmm"), singing it over and over as they are going through the entire day's activities.

Pilgrimages to holy sites and festivals are also acts of worship and devotion toward the Hindu gods. These help the devotee to grasp the human/divine relationship. When one goes to a place where it is believed that a god was manifested, or to a place of religious significance such as along the Ganges River where it is believed submerging in the river can wash away Karma, there is a greater sense of identification to be perceived between the worshiper and the divine realm. Pilgrimages may be made to rivers, mountains, coasts, shrines of various gods—anywhere where human/divine contact is believed to have occurred. Before departing on the pilgrimage, one would worship the god *Ganesha*, which is regarded as the one who controls the success of any venture. One of the most popular of the pilgrimage sites is a place called *Varanasi*, which is on the Ganges River. Varanasi is one of the most significant for several reasons: it is a place that Shiva is reported to have lived, and it is said that there are two white footprints of Vishnu that are visible there. It is also said that Rama worshipped at Varanasi. It is the site where the god/human interaction is thought to have been the strongest. One annual festival is celebrated at this site, the *Dussehra* festival. During this festival the whole Ramayana story is reenacted. Other activities associated with pilgrimages vary, but typically may include performing various rites such as bathing and presenting offerings. Offerings of incense and flowers are the most common. Bathing requires certain rites, such as shaving the head, donning a particular robe, or fasting for a certain number of days. Many of these things depend on caste.

At a site called Allahabad, also on the Ganges River, in February a festival takes place called the Magh Mela. This pilgrimage includes performances of religious plays and preaching of sermons by different priests or outstanding religious persons. This resembles, in some ways, an old time camp meeting or revival in American religious history.

Another way in which Hindu worshippers, especially those no longer residing in the land where their temples are located, seek to continue to keep their Hindu traditions alive and vibrant has been through organized groups that would meet together for prayer or singing and for communal acts of devotion. Much of this approach has come out of the Western experience of the prayer meeting. However, there is a practice native to India that in recent years has become popular in America among Christian groups known as Ashrams. The idea was imported from India by Christian missionaries. It is similar to a retreat center. The purpose of the Ashram is to provide the Hindu with a place for reflection and growth as a personal religious retreat. Each Ashram has its own particular goal. Sometimes it might be to discover a deeper sense of spirituality; at other times there is teaching in order to bring traditional Hindu ideas and modern ideas together. The daily discipline at an Ashram includes such things as lectures by various religious leaders, periods for meditation and the facilities to do the meditation, food and lodging (usually with an ascetic emphasis), and group devotion.

THE HINDU FESTIVAL CALENDAR

The celebration of the festivals has social benefits, which include helping to release tension and stress, providing energy to cope with harsh economic and political conditions, and alleviating alienation and degradation due to the caste system. Below are the most important of the Hindu festivals often associated with the divinities and the changes of the season.

January:	*Lohri*—celebrated in the Punjah to mark the end of winter
February:	*Pongal Sankranti*—a feast held in South India to celebrate rice harvest
March:	*Holi*—National celebration of spring and the New Year
	Shivaratri—a national honoring of Shiva; fasting and all-night vigil takes place in temples dedicated to Shiva
April:	*Sri Vaishnavas*—an honoring of Vishnu
May:	*Rathyata*—birthdate of Lord Jagannath celebrated with chariots in Puri
August:	*Jammashtami*—the birthdate of Krishna, a national celebration, a day of fasting
September:	*Dusserah*—a celebration of the triumph of good over evil in honor of Deva or Rama
	Ganesh Chaturthi—birthday of Ganesh celebrated nationwide in India.
October:	*Diwali*—the return of Rama from exile; a national celebration in honor of Rama and his wife

HINDU SECTS

Shaivism: Shaivism was begun in South India around 800 CE. It stressed hermit-like service to Shiva and a belief in one god that represented the energy of life. The spokesman and teacher, Shankara, taught that the soul is an essential part of the godhead and Brahman is the only deity. In other words, Shiva is a manifestation of Brahman and the one god, Brahman, is life-giving energy. He also emphasized that humans should spend their life seeking their soul via Jnana Yoga. This sect continues in India still today.

Brahmo Samaj: It's also called in Sanskrit, "Society of Brahma" founded in the nineteenth century. The goal of Brahma Samaj is to modernize Hinduism for an urban middle class. Throughout most of India's history, there were very few cities and the caste system had no place for a middle class. The goal of the Brahma Samaj was to modernize Hinduism for a new urban population. The movement arose in the late 1700s and early 1800s when the British East India Company was increasing its control over the country. The British presence brought a good deal of commerce to India, resulting in a growing middle class. The spokesman for the movement was Ram Mohan Roy. He concentrated on devotional Hinduism rather than its mystical aspects. This was something that the urban middle class could do because every observant Hindu had shrines in their home. They may not have had the time or opportunity to go to a temple or engage in long periods of meditation, but they could perform devotional acts at home altars when they got up in the morning by offering food and drink to the gods, saying some prayers, and offering flowers. These acts of devotion were emphasized in his approach. Idol worship, the caste system, and suttee were all condemned. Suttee was the practice in Hinduism wherein a widow would cast herself on the funeral pyre and be consumed with her husband's body in an act of grief, sorrow, and identification with him. Brahman Samaj was a little too radical for its day and gained only a limited following, but it did initiate some limited social reform.

Rama Krishna: Rama Krishna began as a mission founded in Belur, Calcutta, India, in 1897. It was introduced by Swami Vivekananda. Vivekananda taught that all persons are potentially divine. Everybody has the essence of divinity within as a result of creation itself. Religious responsibility requires that each person should work to unleash the unlimited power of the divine essence that is within. He went beyond just the use of Jnana Yoga to insist that Bhakti Yoga should also be an essential part of Hindu religion in order to gain moksha. He taught that all religions lead to the same goal, which is union or absorption into the divine essence. In the same fashion since all religions lead to the same goal, he believed that all religious figures in history are manifestations of the same divine energy or reality. Whether it be Rama, Krishna, Buddha, Jesus, or any other religious figure, these are manifestations of the same divine reality. Regardless of the religion one chooses, according to Rama Krishna the goal is one and the same end. Therefore, he suggested that Hinduism was really the universal religion for all humanity. It was like an overarching religious umbrella which included all of the different religious expressions of all humanity. An associate of his, Sri Ghose (1872–1950), introduced a slightly different form of Yoga—Integral Yoga. In Integral Yoga, rather than withdrawing from the world either to follow Jnana Yoga or Karma Yoga or Raja Yoga, Integral Yoga was used to unite both the world and religious devotion.

Transcendental Meditation: Based in the Netherlands, the transcendental meditation was an idea propagated by Maharishi Yogi. It required no particular religious belief at all but advocated the use of twenty minutes a day of yoga-style meditation to reduce stress and to "connect" with whatever is transcendent, whether it be God or Brahman or Vishnu or Jesus. *Hare Krishna:* Hare Krishna is actually a modern revival of a fifteenth-century devotional sect named Chaitanya. The sect employs a shaven head, a yellow robe, music, dance, and chanting as a means to achieve ecstatic union with the divine realm in a mystical-type devotion. The devotion service consists of chanting the mantra Hare Krishna while participating in dance movements building into an ecstatic experience. Consistent with traditional Hinduism, this union with the divine essence is believed to be the same as attaining moksha.

Gandhism: This is a movement named after Mahatma Mohandas Gandhi. Gandhi was not really a major Hindu religious leader, nor did he establish a religious tradition. He was primarily a political leader, but he was definitely influenced by Hinduism in his advocacy of nonviolence. And some who followed Gandhi saw certain religious precepts in his approach. He said once, "Those who say religion has nothing to do with politics do not know what religion is." He preached nonviolence (from the Hindu concept of *ahimsa*) for the purpose of understanding the truth (*satyagraha*) and resolving conflict (Livingston 2008, 268). Gandhi regarded nonviolence as an expression of devotion to truth. In a religious sense, truth became the divine essence, and devotion to that truth formed a religious system in some ways.

A HINDU LIFE DESIRES AND GOALS

Four Desirable Goals of Life
1. The pursuit of legitimate and appropriate behavior—responsible living (*Dharma*)
2. The pursuit of legitimate worldly success (*artha*)
3. The pursuit of legitimate pleasure (*kama*)
4. The pursuit of eternal release of rebirth and a unification with the Absolute (*moksha*)

Four Stages of Life a Hindu Will Pass Through
1. Student life—a learner (*brahmacarya*)
2. Householder—family head (*grihastha*)
3. Meditation—one who withdraws for reflection (*vanaprastha*)
4. A world-renouncer—spiritual seeker (*sannyasin*)

* * *

THE INTRODUCTION TO THE LAWS OF MANU

All Hindu scriptures are divided into two main divisions: the Shruti ("that which is heard or revealed") and the Smrti ("that which is remembered"). The *Laws of Manu* or *Code of Manu* (*Manu Shastra*) belong to the Smrti. Being a metrical work of 2,685 verses, the *Laws of Manu* deals with a wide range of religious, social, political, ethical, and legal matters. Concerning its practical orientation, S. Radhakrishan writes: "The book discusses certain philosophical topics and offers solutions based on the Samkhya and the Vedanta, but its aim is not the exposition of a philosophical system." [Radhakrishnan and Moore 1957:172] Of existential interest, the *Laws of Manu* offer what can be called "a philosophy of life." Two key aspects or its philosophy of life are the doctrine of the four stages of life and the four aims of life. These aspects are discussed in this textual selection. These two existential aspects of human life are linked to the "divine" model of society that Manu offers.

The *Laws of Manu* is generally considered to be the product of the Epic Period of Hinduism (ca. 500 BCE–200 CE). The *Laws of Munu* belongs to the category of *Dharma shastras,* and the *Mahabharata* and *Ramayana* belong to the category of epics. The primary objective of the *shastras* is the firm maintenance of the Hindu social order enabling the realization of material and spiritual interests through proper ethical conduct of all social members.

KEY WORDS

Sanatana Dharma	*Dravidians*	*Veda*	*Sutras*
Sastras	*Brahman*	*Brahmans (Brahmin)*	*Brahmanas*
Upanishad	*Krishna*	*Bhagavad Gita*	*Rama and Ramayana*
Dharma	*Karma*	*Samsara*	*Moksha*
Ahimsa	*Satyagraha*	*Gandhi*	*Gandhism*
Diwali	*Pranav*	*Holi*	*Caste*
Theosophy	*Dravidian*	*Hindu Sects*	*Parts of Yoga*

Name: _____

QUESTIONS FOR FURTHER STUDY

1. Discuss some of the social and religious implication of the caste system.

2. What is the concept of divinity in Hinduism?

3. What are the four desirable goals of a Hindu?

4. What are the four stages of life of a Hindu?

5. Typically, what will you find in a Hindu Temple? What is the story or image the Hindu temple portrays?

6. Explain the types and importance of the Vedas and Bhagavad Gita.

7. Discuss the idea of the "cosmic man" in Hindu mythology.

Jainism

INTRODUCTION

Jainism (the Jains) arose out of the teaching of Prince Vardhamana. That he was a prince is a reflection of what was happening in the mainstream of the religion at the time. At the top of the caste system were the priests. A prince is at the second level. This immediately implies that there is going to be some degree of distance between his perception of Hindu practice and the traditional perception primarily involving the priests. As mentioned in chapter 5 Jainism arose out of the revival movements but unlike the Ajavikas or the traditional he asserted that the Hindu gods were uninvolved in the world and that something can be done to change the present and the future, but everything depends upon the individual. They believe that Jiva which is the spark of divine essence has the potential within it to overcome all of one's Karma. The question is how do you do it?

In a manner similar to the Ajavikas, the Jains assert that one must withdraw from active participation in this lifetime. But the asceticism of the Jains is not nearly as extreme as that of the Ajavikas. Rather, the Jains withdraw into a monastic-style community where they live away from the normal cares and occupations of life, but where they continue to provide for their own needs, at least at a minimal level. For those who accept the basic idea but aren't ready to retreat in so severe a fashion should follow those occupations that are most closely associated with what Jainism represents so that they accumulate as little Karma as possible. In a future life, they can then come back and be a Jain when they are more ready to live the more rigorous observance through Jainism.

HISTORICAL DEVELOPMENT

Among the religions of the world, Jainism is among the least known. It has only six million adherents of which half are located in its original homeland of Northern India. Its contemporary is Buddhism, and as a revival movement, it shares common themes with Buddhism as well as Hinduism but may be interpreted slightly differently. Some key beliefs and practices in Hinduism are rejected in Jainism. Jainism started in the sixth century BCE during the time of the emergence of Hindu revival movements. It does not have a single founder but a chain of founding figures called *tirthankaras* of whom Mahavira was the twenty-fourth and the last tirthankara of the present age. Tirthankaras, meaning "conquerors," are teachers who make the way—truth teachers—like what other faiths called "prophets." Who was Prince Vardhamana who came to be known as Mahavira ("great hero")? He was born Nataputa Vardhamana to a raja (ruler) belonging to the *Kshatriya* clan in a province in Northern India. Although a contemporary of Siddhartha Gautama (who became the "Buddha" and was also from the same province), Vardhamana and Siddhartha likely never met each other or studied together, let alone planned together what they would do with their lives in the future. The sixth century BCE was an interesting time period in the history of religions when one observes the religious landscape involving Zoroastrianism, Judaism, Greek religions, Hinduism, and then Confucianism, Jainism, and Buddhism. The period appeared to be a shaking up, a transitional stage for religious movements and establishments.

Vardhamana was brought up in a life of affluence, married, and had a daughter. But the luxurious palace life did not bring him the desire of his heart—something he was not getting from the traditional religion of Hinduism. Then, at age thirty, he sought permission to leave home to become a monk. He joined some Jain ascetic wanderers. Jains are those Hindu spiritualists who had achieved spiritual liberation. His Jain master was Parshva, believed to be the last existing Tirthankara prior to Vardhamana whose symbol is the serpent (Brodd 2013, 214–215). He later wandered alone from the rest of the ascetics in extreme austerity, "naked and exposed. Fasting, going for long periods without sleep, withstanding the verbal and physical abuse from opponents, enduring the bites of insects rather than doing them harm" (214). For twelve years he led this life of renunciation, nonviolence, and nonattachment, thus earning the epithet Mahavira "great hero." On the thirteenth year, Jains believed, Mahavira attained *kevala* (meaning "omniscience."). *Kevala* is the state of perfect knowledge that results in liberation from *samsara* when death occurs. It is reported that before his enlightenment, Mahavira spent two and a half days "fasting in the heat of the sun, squatting near a tree but out of its shade." After his enlightenment, he preached for the next thirty years accompanied by his eleven disciples (*ganadharas*). As tirthankara, his symbol is the lion.

TEACHINGS OF JAINISM

The official symbol of Jainism is a pictogram whose geometric outline symbolizes the world (lok); within the image is a raised hand inscribed with "ahimsa" (nonviolence); a swastika symbolizing the four worlds into which one can be reborn; three dots symbolizing the three jewels of Jainism; and an arc symbolizing the abode of the Siddhas.

Jainism does not accept the gods in Hinduism. Actually Jainism is not a theistic religion because they do not believe in God or gods in the normative sense. It cannot be said to be a completely atheistic either, leading some scholars like Heinrich Robert Zimmer (1890–1943) to describe it as *transtheistic* meaning beyond theism; that is, an understanding "inaccessible by arguments as to whether or not a God exists." He writes, "the supreme orders of Jana contemplation, the tirthankaras, have passed beyond the godly governors of the natural order. Jainism, that is to say, is not atheistic; it is transtheistic. Its tirthankaras . . . are 'cut-of' (*Kevala*) from the state of creation, preservation, and destruction, which are the concerns and spheres-of-operations of the gods. The Makers of the River-crossing are beyond cosmic event as well as the problems of biography; they are transcendent, cleaned of temporality, omniscient, actionless, and are absolutely at peace" (Zimmer 1969, 182). There is no creator God. Souls are uncreated, eternal, and has unlimited power and knowledgeable. Each soul is capable of becoming god. Jainism seeks to address the problem of existence inherent with evil or suffering: "that soul exists, that it is eternal; that it is the doer of karma; that it bears the consequences; that there is liberation (*moksha*); and that there is a way to attain the liberation" (New Dictionary of the History of Ideas. 2005). The Jain teachers (tirthankaras) are those who are completely liberated and exist as Gods and are completely detached from the material world. For Jains, the universe consists of three spheres: the hellish sphere, the earthly sphere, and the heavenly sphere of the liberated souls (*siddhas*). Both heaven and hell have different levels. Hell has eight levels, and each level becomes progressively colder. Jains teachings on Karma, paths to liberation, and ethics will be our focus.

KARMA

There is the notion that every soul or substance of living being (*jiva*) is potentially divine but is greatly influenced by Karma. People's conduct or ethical actions not properly guarded do cause "influx of karma" (*asrava*) putting the soul into bondage (*bandha*). The bondage is expressed in

A Jain Temple in the Kumbhalgarh Fort, Rajasthan, India, Asia

the life–death–rebirth cycle (*samsara*). Karma, therefore, needs to be stopped and its attachment burned out. It is important that one properly understands Karma and its effect on the conduct of living beings or else the proper approach cannot be followed. Jains believe that the Hindu gods are all caught up in the cycle of samsara. But how can attachments be completely exhausted? Like Buddhism, Jainism prescribes a path to follow.

PATH TO LIBERATION

Jainism paths to liberation are threefold: the path of right perception (*Samyak Darsana*), the path of right knowledge (*Samyak Jnana*), and the path of right conduct (*Samyak Charitra*). They are called the "Three Jewels."

Right perception, like right view or understanding in Buddhism, involves having the appropriate outlook or philosophy of the world, existence, and the human condition. In Jainism it is having the right beliefs.

Right knowledge includes the appropriate approach to concentration or meditation. It is imperative to have adequate and correct information or teaching on the path of liberation. The gods in Hinduism were not omniscient and lack having the final say and therefore could not give the right prescription—what to do and how to do it. Jains teach that knowledge is relative and that the disciples should stay alert so as to become aware of knowledge that may come from other sources. In this regard Jains teach in any given statement or idea that there are multiple points of view that are relative to each other. No view is absolutely right, and no view is absolutely wrong. Points of views also depend upon the context, and therefore all dimensions of an issue or idea must be considered.

Right conduct is about behavior, which should be characterized by certain basic values or principles. They include respect for all life, nonviolence (*ahimsa*), an interdependence of all life forms, and a principle that inspires nonviolent disposition to life and invokes humility and carefulness. So, life in Jainism, particularly the *Digambara* tradition, is lived with extreme care not to harm any living creature, including the biting insects—hence, the five *samitis (Rules of Carefulness)*. Right conduct also involves renunciation of luxuries and "comfortabilities" that will increase attachment to the material—physical world. Mental and emotional renunciation and the ability to endure pain and harsh treatment are needed behaviors.

JAIN ETHICS

Ethics or virtues in Jainism consist of the five Great Vows (*Maha-Vratas*) of the ascetics, the five Rules of Carefulness, the three *Guptis* (rules of preservation), the ten Supreme Virtues (listed in this chapter), the twelve *Bhavna* (reflections, thoughts, or *anupreksha*), the twenty-two *Parishaha* (subduing of suffering), and the twelve *Pratima* (Rules for the Lay Householder, listed in this chapter). Many of these rules overlap and can be classified into the classes of disciplines: The newly initiated or to be initiated, lay household, the mendicants (ascetics), and the general universal principles.

The Five Great Vows of the Ascetics (Mendicants):

- Nonviolence (*ahimsa*)
- Truthfulness (*satya*)
- Taking only that which is freely given (i.e., not stealing (*asteya*)
- Celibacy (*brahmachanga*)
- Nonpossessiveness (*aparigraha*)

The Five Rules of Carefulness:

- One should exert one's self-stresses self-control; to hold oneself or to take authority of oneself
- Abstain from pleasures
- Understand the world
- Be impartial like a sage
- And guard one's self

It is carefulness in all manner of life—in thought, feeling, or when walking, speaking, eating, and working—so as not to cause harm or take away the life of living beings because of carelessness.

The Three *Guptis* (Rules of Preservation):

- Geographical restraints
- Consumptions restraints
- Avoidance of purposeless activities

Let us sum up all these rules and statutes with the ten Supreme Universal Virtues and the twelve Rules for the Householder(s):

1. Virtue of supreme forgiveness
2. Virtue of supreme tenderness or humility
3. Virtue of supreme uprightness or honesty
4. Virtue of supreme contentment or purity
5. Virtue of supreme truthfulness
6. Virtue of supreme self-restraint
7. Virtue of supreme austerities or penance
8. Virtue of supreme renunciation
9. Virtue of supreme nonattachment
10. Virtue of supreme chastity

The twelve rules or vows for the householder (made up of the five Great Vows—the first five on the list and the most important, the three rules of preservation, and four disciplinary vows):

The Five Vows:

1. Nonviolence
2. Truthfulness
3. Nonstealing
4. Celibacy (illicit sex)
5. Nonattachment (nonpossessiveness)

The Three Rules of Preservation:

6. Limited area of nonvirtuous activity vow
7. Limited use of consumable and nonconsumable items vow
8. Avoidance of purposeless sins—harmful activities vow

The Four Disciplinary Vows:

9. Meditation of limited duration—meditation and reading scripture for at least 48 consecutive minutes
10. Nonvirtuous Activity of limiting space
11. Ascetic's life of limited duration
12. Limited charity to monks and nuns

BRANCHES

There are two major branches of Jainism: the *Digambara* tradition, which practices extreme asceticism, and the *Swetambara* tradition, which practices moderation with greater proportion of its members being women. The split came as a result of the unacceptable moderate stand that a group that left during a severe famine for twelve years predicted by a Jain master, Bhadrabahu. He led about twelve thousand monks to Southern India to avoid the famine. When they returned afterward, they found out that the group that remained had codified the teachings of Mahavira and had also relaxed some of the teachings and practices they considered very restrictive. The group did not agree to a compromise and therefore split into two orders: the Digambaras and the Swetambaras. The monks of the former group wear nothing at all, whereas the latter group wears white clad. According to Fisher, of the almost six thousand Jain nuns, only about one hundred are Digambaras.

An unidentified group of Digambaras Jain nuns, sadhvis, attend a religious ceremony at the Jain temple during Caturmas in Ajmer, Rajasthan, India.

©Daniel J. Rao/Shutterstock.com

FESTIVALS AND PILGRIMAGE

Both branches celebrate the major festivals in Jainism. One of them is the Mahavira birthday called *Mahavira Jayanti*. It occurs in March/April. Celebrations include community worship, processions, and other devotional and spiritual activities. Another festival is *Paryushana*. Considered by some to be the most important of Jains' festivities, all Jains are required to fast and the spiritual leader reads out and explains in detail the *Kalpasutra* (sacred scripture). The first seven days of the festival are days of attainment, and the eighth and final day is one of fulfillment and achievement.

Diwali: It is also a major Hindu festival. It occurs in October/ November. The whole night of Diwali should be spent in the recitation of holy hymns and mediation. Swetambara Jains believe that on the night of the day of Diwali in 537 BCE, Mahavira achieved Nirvana, or deliverance, and attained to a state of kevala. The day after Diwali marks the beginning of the New Year in their calendar.

Kartak Purnima: It is celebrated in October/November. Thousands of Jains go on pilgrimages on this day to sacred Jain sites. *Mauna Agyaras* festival occurs around November/December. It is a day for fasting and silent meditation.

EFFECTS ON SOCIETY

Jains rejection of the caste system and social order has contributed to the eradication of this systemic injustice and progress made toward equal rights in the Indian society. The concept of *ahimsa* (nonviolence) to all living things seeks to harmonize humans and nature, drawing them closer and fostering their interdependence. Coexistence with other religions has contributed to the practice of religious freedom and, for that matter, world peace. Jainism's emphasis on knowledge as a means to beating Karma instead of sacrifice to the gods fosters learning, stirring up the education of the masses in the Indian society.

KEY CONCEPTS

Nataputa Vardhamana	*Mahavira*	*Jiva*	*Tirthankara*
Principles of renunciation	*Bhadrabahu*	*Satya*	*Satyagraha* G
Five Great Vows	*Ganadharas*	*Ahimsa*	Three Jewels
Five Rules of Carefulness	Truthfulness	*Kevala*	*Kalpasutra*
Mahavira Jayanti	*Transtheistic*	Parshva	*Paryushana*
Nonattachment	*Swetambara*	*Digambara*	*Three Guptis*

Name: _____

QUESTIONS FOR FURTHER STUDY

1. Explain the concept "winner over passion" as an appropriate description of Jainism?

2. Discuss Jains view on salvation and the afterlife.

3. Discuss Jainism notion of the universe.

4. Who or what are the twenty-four tirthankaras?

5. Is Jainism theistic, atheistic or transtheistic? Explain.

6. Describe the meaning of the official symbol of Jainism.

7. How were the two main branches of Jainism formed?

8. What role does fasting play in the life of a Jain, especially in the Digambara branch?

9. Describe any two most important festivals of Jainism.

10. What's the effect of Jainism on Indian and world culture?

Buddhism

Buddhism was founded in North India during the fifth century BCE as a result of Siddhartha Gautama's attainment of "enlightenment." Enlightenment in Buddhism simply means "the ultimate truth by which people are freed from the cycle of rebirth" (www.ifdawn.comesa/timeline.html, August 4, 2016). Thus Buddhism appears to be the goal of Hinduism. Gautama became the Buddha—the "Enlightened One" or the "Awoken One" and teacher of the way to escape constant rebirth and suffering associated with it. Following is the story of Gautama and the founding of Buddhism, as well as the religion's teachings and practices.

RELIGIOUS AND SOCIAL BACKGROUND

In India during the fifth century the religious situation was one of stagnation. The priests had arrogated to themselves a monumental level of importance as the ones who keep order in the universe, conveying to them a position of extreme authority. They used this position to exploit and retain power for themselves. Ritual had become mechanical and devoid of substance; they were going through the motions but nothing more. New sects, such as the Ajavikas and Jains, were developing in association with the idea of inner sacrifice. Thus, the stagnation produced a plethora of different searches for a more meaningful religious experience in India. Religious speculation at the time focused on "hair splitting." (Back in the Middle Ages in the West, there were actually doctoral dissertations written by some theology students on subjects like how many angels can dance on the head of a pin.) In addition, the religion was carried out in Sanskrit, which was the old Aryan alphabet and language. By 500 BC, many people living in India no longer understood, read, or wrote Sanskrit. In a radical response to the whole substance of this Brahministic Hinduism, some began teaching that divine grace was just bestowed upon people as some claimed to experience moksha but had no corresponding evidences of it in their life and no sense of personal responsibility. This undermined the idea of personal responsibility so fundamental to Hinduism. Karma had become fatalistic. In fact, the fatalism of the Ajavikas was common at the time. The mysteries of Hinduism—the stories of the gods, the incarnations of the gods, descriptions of how the gods interrelated with humans—degenerated basically into a focus on miracles, the occult, and the fantastic. Hinduism was in a complete state of disarray in the fifth century BCE.

Politically, the situation was not much better. India had become completely fractured, divided into kingdoms the size of counties. Ruling over each one of these was a Raja/Rajput. There were hundreds of these little kingdoms all over India. In the northwest by 500 BCE, the Persians had already begun to invade India. They brought with them a form of religion known as Zoroastrianism. It is still an existing religion in some remote areas of Iran, but mostly today found in exile in India. Zoroastrianism taught that there are two gods—a good god and a bad god. Salvation lies with living in harmony with the good god. The initiated receive the secrets necessary to do this. At the end of time, the good god will overcome the bad god, and if one has lived in harmony with the good god, that person will live eternally. It taught about the belief in the evil aspect in life, hierarchy of angels, an immortal soul, and the resurrection of the body on the day of judgment. Some of these concepts also began to carry over into Hinduism, or into the thinking of people in India at the time. At the same time, the coming of the Persians created socioeconomic suffering for everybody, most of all for those not considered part of the noble and priestly classes. The Persians themselves never actually penetrated much farther than the Indus River Valley. However, the Persians were pretty good at exploiting the economic resources of all the people they conquered and using it for their kingdom and their nobility.

The Buddha's response to all of this was to create a religion that would be cleansed of those aspects of Hinduism, which, to him, seemed degenerate. In doing so, what he created was a religion that had an intense focus on self-effort. Some people have charged Buddhism with being atheistic. This charge is problematic and is based on the view that, unlike Hinduism, Buddhism understands God, reincarnation, Karma, and the goal of human existence in ways that are quite different than Hinduism. The focus of Buddhism is to overcome suffering.

In classical Hinduism being alive is to be suffering (that is, separated from divine essence). When a Buddhist talks about overcoming suffering, this does not mean just getting over a headache; it means overcoming the limitations of this life. Buddha's response, however, focusing so much on self-effort basically meant that anyone (not just priests), of any caste level, could achieve religious success (what he called Nirvana) by focusing on overcoming suffering. Of course there is one fundamental presumption in all of this—that suffering is antithetical to the divine realm, and therefore one who is in union with the divine realm would not cause suffering for oneself or others, if at all possible. This is not necessarily a notion universally accepted by all religions. There are some religions (for instance, Christianity) where the concept of personal suffering is integrated into the religion itself.

ORIGIN OF BUDDHISM

Life of Gautama Buddha: The first monks emphasized Buddha's humanity. For the first 100 years after Buddha's death (he died in 480 BCE), there was no sense in which Buddha was regarded as divine. During this time, he was neither the founder of a new religious perspective, nor a divine manifestation of a god. This was important, since, if he was more than human, what hope would there be for these monks who were trying to follow his example? For them to achieve Nirvana, it was necessary that Buddha also have been merely human. It is only later on, partly through the influence of Hinduism and partly through looking at things in retrospect, that some concluded that Buddha was an incarnation of divinity.

The oldest Buddhist texts were written in Sanskrit and Pali. These offer fragmentary, minor references to Buddha's life, but there is no single, comprehensive, source for life of Buddha from antiquity. There are only bits and pieces drawn together from the Buddhist manuscripts, and their accuracy is sometimes disputed. However, the life of Buddha, to the Buddhists, was not critical for understanding the inner essence of the religion. An additional source for Buddha's life comes from local traditions in various places of India, especially in areas along the Ganges River where he traveled for over forty years teaching his religious perspective. These references provide some sense of the activities of Buddha.

The Buddha was born Siddhartha Gautama in 560 BCE. His father was a Raja, a ruler of a small Indian province of Kapilavastu in the modern state of Nepal. He was the first son of his father and the apparent heir. As part of the nobility, he was a member of the second level in the caste system. As a young man, he would have been educated in the traditions of a military aristocracy, as well as the traditions of court ceremony. As the son of a nobleman, he lived a life of luxury for that day. At least according to legend, he was purposely prevented from observing any sort of actual suffering: death, disease, pain, etc. He was surrounded by women, and he is believed to have married around the age of sixteen or seventeen. Historians are fairly certain he had at least one son. That son was named Rabula, which means "hindrance." There are reasons to suspect that he may have had other wives or concubines and other children, but there is no certainty.

At the age of twenty-five, he was inadvertently exposed to suffering while on a journey. As he was traveling, he encountered a dead body, a person ridden with disease, some extremely poor people, and a wandering holy man (a priest). Because he had not been exposed to such things before, the sight overwhelmed him. After unsuccessfully struggling to understand what he had seen, he interpreted the four separate incidents, or scenes, as signs worth pursuing if one would understand the meaning of life. At the age of twenty-nine, he left his family, princely life, wife, and child (or children) and began a rigorous quest for religious understanding of the problem of suffering, which is to say also the problem of life. The four incidents that sent him out searching for the answers to the problem of suffering and death became known as the Four Signs; the new life he had taken—abandoning home and comfort—became known as the Great Renunciation. At that time, it was not so uncommon for somebody to do as he did for some religious pursuit. His wife was grief stricken and resentful, but he came from a fairly well-off background so she and the child (or children) were cared for by his family, and tradition maintains that eventually all of them became either monks or nuns within the movement he founded.

His quest followed three stages. The first was intense Hinduism. During this process, he placed himself under the guidance of two Hindu masters (gurus), in an intense effort to gain religious understanding regarding suffering. This involved asceticism, monasticism, the practice of yoga. But in all this he didn't find the answer he sought. He eventually broke from these two Hindu masters and, along with several others (ultimately five disciples), sought together to "break the power of the body," to try to get beyond the physical limitations of the body to some kind of an experience of the divine. At one point, during a period of extreme fasting, he almost died. This convinced Siddhartha that asceticism itself was futile. Since neither asceticism nor the Hindu approach brought the satisfaction that he sought, he perceived that whatever the religious answer was, it had to be somewhere between asceticism and indulgence. This would later be the approach of the monastic community that would form around him.

One day, at the age of thirty-five, while meditating under a Bodhi tree, he went into a trance and went through what became known as the four stages of meditative trance, overcame Maara, the Tempter or Evil One, and finally attained enlightenment, perceiving the solution to the problem of suffering. He was then persuaded by Brahman to leave the place to go and teach others of these things hidden even from the gods. It is at this time that he became the Buddha, which means an "Enlightened One." For the next forty-five years of his life, he itinerated annually up and down

the heavily populated area of the Ganges River, preaching to anyone and everyone who would hear him about how they, too, could find enlightenment. It was not that others received enlightenment from him but rather that each one personally had to find it. Buddha's role was to tell them the path by which to find enlightenment, just as he felt he had done.

Uniqueness of Approach: What was unique about this new religion that Buddha was proclaiming to the people? It was not really a religion, as such, but simply a way of dealing with life. Only later would some of his followers transform it into a religion. It was not that his followers should forsake Hinduism but rather find their desired religious success within Hinduism. Unlike most monasteries which are located in isolated, remote areas where they live apart from people, Buddha and his community of monks dwelt right in the midst of the people, and where they carry on their daily activities. Buddha was the spiritual guide. During the greater part of the year, they traveled along the Ganges River basin. In the morning they would arise for meditation. If there would be preaching, it would come at this time. However, since Buddha's message from the time of his enlightenment onward was basically unchanged, disciplining was the primary focus during meditation. At noontime the monks went out in the midst of the community to beg for their food and drink, and then in the afternoon, Buddha and the monks, but especially Buddha, would teach the multitude, the monks being right there with him. Gautama Buddha is believed to be the twenty-fourth Buddha in the present stage of the world. A future Buddha is inevitable and expected when this world order changes and a new stage of the world appears.

On other occasions, they might rest in the afternoon. This was the basic daily routine of Buddha and the monks for those forty-five years. During the rainy season, the group would withdraw together to a fixed abode, generally for about three months for a more intense time of meditation. Initially that had to be something rented or borrowed, but as the movement became popular, grounds and buildings were donated for them. Everything that monks possessed would be donated. The food would be donated. The buildings were donated. The grounds were donated and usually each monk received one new robe a year.

Division and Expansion: This was, basically, what Buddhism was at the time Buddha died. It was not, as such, a separate religion, but a monastic community. The main focus of Buddhism was on the problem of suffering and the transitory nature of life. It is here, and then it is gone. The approach of Buddha was preserved by his monk disciples, who would continue the same itinerate teaching and meditation activities that Buddha had pursued. They would continue this for the next two or three centuries. Why didn't it stay that way? Part of the answer is that the way that he presented was essentially very, very rigid. Only a select few could really participate in the religious method. During the mid-third century BCE a major meeting was held at which some followers began to formulate a theosophy based on his teachings. A schism arose between the more conservative monks and others advocating a new understanding. The more rigorous, conservative followers of Buddha would follow the Theravada form of Buddhism. The advocates of a new, broader interpretation of Buddhism followed the Mahayana form (the great vehicle). By about 250 BCE, both of these streams of Buddhist thought were established in the Ganges area of India where Buddhism was primarily confined.

About 250 BCE, or a little bit later, an Indian ruler, Ashoka (also known as Ashoka the Great of the Mauryan dynasty), conquered nearly all of India and adopted Buddhism as his own religious persuasion. As a result, Buddhism became an officially recognized religion, not just an ethical system or movement within Hinduism. With political favor, it spread broadly across India and beyond. In modern-day Sri Lanka, it was introduced in the second century BCE. For a time, it became the state religion.

In China (Southeast Asia), it was introduced during the first century CE by the trade routes. The form of Hinduism that spread into Indochina was Mahayana. In the first century CE, it also spread into China by monks going over and around the Himalayas. In China it reached its zenith between the seventh and the ninth century CE.

It reached Korea in the third century CE through Chinese influence and continued to grow through the 1300s. Then it began to decline.

It became firmly rooted in Thailand somewhere between the fifth and the thirteenth century CE. After 1238 AD, it became the state religion and remains so yet today.

In Burma, in the fifth century CE, the Tantric form was established, but later it became Theravada. Tantric is a sensual form of Buddhism radically different from either Mahayana or Theravada Buddhism.

In Japan, Buddhism arrived in the sixth century CE from Korean monks. Between 794 and 1333, it was the dominant religion in Japan, mixed with Shinto to form a hybrid known as Zen Buddhism.

In Tibet, Buddhism spread surprisingly very late to the Himalayan Mountains, considering Buddha was from that area. It arrived in the seventh century CE because of a royal marriage. Rival monasteries developed in the Tibetan region, competing with one another for the leadership of the Buddhists there. The leader of a Tibetan monastery enjoys the title of Dalai Lama, of which there are two monasteries that continue today to compete for supremacy.

THE FOUR NOBLE TRUTHS

Buddhism is a religious technique or discipline more than anything else. According to tradition, it seems as though the first sermon that Siddhartha preached after his experience of enlightenment revealed a relatively full statement of what he had come to understand. Whatever it was that he experienced under the Bodhi tree apparently was a complete and wide-ranging perception of the message. The message dealt with the issue of suffering and there was no further development of the concept from the time he first delivered it until the time of his death. His five disciples became the first monks as they embraced the concept and began striving for personal enlightenment as well.

It is important to realize that Buddhism is an individual path. In Mahayana, many people can take it, but it is still an individual path. It deals with the notion of suffering, but consistent with Hinduism, life itself is regarded as suffering. To be alive is to suffer. The cause of this suffering, according to Buddhism, is a thirst or craving or supreme desire for anything not worthy of that desire. Example: Have you ever been really, really thirsty for a drink? You get that drink and you drink it so fast that it upsets your stomach? That upset stomach is suffering. What Buddhism asserts is if there is anything in life that one just absolutely has to have, once gained it will not really turn out to be worth the intense desire. Have you ever bought something that you just had to have? You worked for it, you got it, you brought it home, and it was the most wonderful thing. Then after a short period of time, you don't even bother with it anymore. That is something that wasn't really worth the desire. You suffered for it. You sacrificed to get it. But then when you had it for a while, you did not really care anymore and cast it aside.

For Buddhism, the cause of suffering is this thirst, this craving, this desire for something that is not worthy. There are, however, levels of desire, and on the human level, there are some things that are worthy of desire so long as the intensity remains in perspective. Lesser desires are okay, as long as the desire doesn't overshadow the inherent value that the thing desired has. Nevertheless, for Buddhism there is only one thing truly worthy of the most intense craving and desire. This is Nirvana.

However, improper desire (that is desire for something that is not worthy of that desire) is both mistaken and morally wrong and causes suffering. This suffering may be to the one who desires it, or it could be to others as well. The evil is not in the thing desired but rather in the individual—that is to say, in the selfishness and pride that is compelling you to desire that particular thing. So suffering is associated with moral failure, selfishness, and pride, but not mental misunderstanding. Such cravings are not overcome by withdrawing from the world or from relationships. That is what the Jains and Ajavikas tried in Hinduism. Rather it is necessary to eliminate that within an individual which causes this desire. When successful, then friendliness, compassion, respect, and similar attitudes are found. According to Buddhism, the way to get rid of these cravings is by discipline of oneself to overcome them.

So, fundamentally, Buddhism is a method of conditioning oneself to look at the world differently so that selfishness, pride, and improper cravings are not part of one's inner being anymore. The extent to which one does this will be the extent to which one progresses along in the path of Buddhism. These ideas are embodied in what Siddhartha called the Four Noble Truths:

1. *Life inevitably involves suffering.* It acknowledges the existence of *dukkha*—a state of meaninglessness and frustration.
2. *Suffering originates in our desires or cravings.* It seeks to answer the question, "What causes suffering?"
3. *Suffering will cease if all desires cease.* Thus, Nirvana is possible to attain and *dukkha* can cease totally. This truth answers the question, "What is the cure for suffering?"
4. *There is a way to attain this state—the Eightfold Path.* This fourth truth answers the question, "What is the means for implementing the cure?"

The first of the Four Noble Truths asserts that life certainly involves suffering making all existence meaningless. Suffering is understood as a spiritual problem associated with a life that is dislocated, unfulfilled, insecure, and filled with interpersonal and intrapersonal conflicts (not only between people but within oneself). This is the meaning of dukkha. It is a moral problem. Suffering is most vividly manifested in events such as birth, sickness, the decline of age (growing old, aging), fear of death, being "chained" to something you don't like, and being separated from something you love. (This is related to what the Hindus believe to be the five components of life: body, sensation [the senses], thought, feeling, and consciousness. These are where suffering is located.) Furthermore, suffering is not only a spiritual problem involved with this life but it also precludes the attainment of true/real happiness until it is overcome. Thus, suffering precludes the attainment of Nirvana until it is overcome.

The second of the Four Noble Truths concerns the source of suffering. Buddhism believes the source is desire for personal fulfillment, happiness, a desire for anything unworthy of that desire. This results from selfish attitudes. The conclusion would be that to be free from suffering and selfish desire would require one to become selfless. Suffering causes a person to seek what is desired even at the expense of others. So the only way to success is at the expense of others, which makes the situation a win/lose scheme. And in almost any personal relationship, there is always this win/lose situation, a relationship built on selfish interest.

The third of the Four Noble Truths deals with the cure for suffering. The cure for suffering is evident: being released from narrow self-interest. In other words, by gaining a different perspective, a different sense of identity, one overcomes suffering. If the answer to cravings and selfishness is selflessness, then the way to overcome suffering is to develop a perspective that becomes so enlarged that it includes others as part of oneself. Ultimately, this means enlarging one's understanding of self beyond the limits of the body to include ultimately all of reality. This approach requires training of one's perceptions. If one's physical self is no longer one's limit of identity, then only when it is good for everything is it good for the individual. The technique of Buddhism is going to be one that focuses on enlarging the sense of self, enlarging one's self-identity to encompass the world around.

The fourth of the Four Noble Truth offers the Buddhist ideas of the *means* to the cure for suffering. This is known as the Eightfold Path. The focus is to teach one to become selfless—this is the fearsome part—to see the person nearby as part of oneself. And only if something is good for everyone else can it be good for oneself. If it hurts anyone, it hurts all. Underlying this is the notion that a person will avoid personal injury if possible. Along with this, if everything is going smoothly a person will probably notice oneself very little or not bother attending to the affairs of life all that much because everything is going smoothly. In such a state, one is free to be more oriented toward other people's concerns and issues. And when desire is diminished, this state is more nearly formed within a person.

THE EIGHTFOLD PATH OR RIGHTS (SAMMA)

The Eightfold Path has a particular understanding of the concept of right. This is, in a sense dharma, but it means something rather different. The concept of right in Buddhism is an intuitive wisdom that recognizes and acknowledges the suffering that exists along each step of the Eightfold Path. Thereby, one knows what to do to not cause suffering. Another way of understanding this is that one cannot control what touches the senses to create passion, greed, and those sorts of things. But one can control the mind and emotions, the inner self and response to these things, to recognize these things for what they are, transitory and part of this world, and unworthy of any inordinate craving. This means that one of the results of the discipline of the Eightfold Path is serenity. Instead of being whipped back and forth by greed or passions, no matter what happens in life there is going to be a sense of serenity. Nothing is really going to shake the individual. For this to be the case, as one embraces one of the stages of the Eightfold Path, it is also necessary to continue fulfilling all of the previous ones as well. In the Christian world sin and overcoming of sin in one way or another is seen as the primary purpose of religious activity or religious direction. In Hinduism, the primary purpose is not to overcome sin. That is not the issue in Hinduism. Doing one's duty (dharma) is the issue in Hinduism. In Buddhism, overcoming selfish desire is the issue. Taking it one step further, in Islam submission is the primary focus. Each of the different religions, has a particular focus, but is the meaning the same for each religion?

The Eightfold Path presupposes what is known as "right association." This means that the best chance to be successful is to be in a monastic community. In a way, this is exactly opposite the manner by which Buddha carried out his forty-five years of teaching. Instead of withdrawing (which is the case for many Buddhist monks today), he went around teaching everyone that would listen, trying to help them begin to move in the direction of enlightenment. But today Buddhism presupposes a right association, which means a monastic community of like-minded, like-seeking other Buddhists. It has gone completely the opposite of the way that it began.

The Eightfold Path

1. Right Understanding or Right View
2. Right Intent or Right Thought

3. Right Speech
4. Right Conduct or Right Action (follow the five precepts)
5. Right Livelihood
6. Right Effort
7. Right Mindfulness
8. Right Meditation

Right Understanding or Right View is an acceptance of the Four Noble Truths. Doing so, however, means adopting the particular worldview of Buddhism, that this life is suffering and suffering is the fundamental issue of life. It calls for the training of the mind to question old assumptions and to enable it to see through illusions such as the notion that lasting happiness can be found in material wealth. If one does not have that kind of understanding that enables the one to endorse the Four Noble Truths completely that person has no chance of overcoming suffering and achieving enlightenment or Nirvana. Does this make Buddhism a very exclusivistic religion?

Right Intent or Motive is a passion to consider the motives underlying our actions and thoughts. It means having right thought and right motive; it means not being pretentious or acting from unguarded emotions. The point in this is to guard against self-centeredness or a deceit of oneself.

Right Speech emphasizes truthfulness and charity or love, in all manner of conversation. Wrong speech might include harsh words, gossip, lying, and cursing. It is anything that hurts someone else in any way. Right speech and the discipline to develop it begin by noticing the untruthfulness and the deceit in what one says. It could even be just tactless, blunt speaking, or barbed wit. In a positive sense, right speech involves finding ways to be more honest with oneself and others over one's own identity, one's thoughts, and less vicious in what is said of someone else or how it is said. The whole idea is to become more aware of what one says and the harm that it causes and then to move to developing a way of speaking that is more honest and less hurtful.

Right Conduct is similar to right speech, except that it relates to one's action instead. One attempts to recognize the things one does and the reasons behind these actions. Associated with right conduct are the *five precepts*, which are part of Hinduism. These are: (1) Don't destroy life, and that means don't kill also. This implies a vegetarian diet. (2) Don't steal. (3) Don't lie. (4) Don't drink intoxicants. (5) Don't be unchaste. This also means celibacy if outside of marriage and even restraint within marriage. The focus of right conduct is both on what one does and does not do, and also the motivations for these things. Ultimately, the motivations become even more significant than the acts themselves. For the Buddha, evil conducts are those "done from the motives of partiality, enmity, stupidity, and fear."

Right Livelihood is one's passion to be liberated from suffering. It is making sure that one's means of livelihood does not violate the five precepts. As such, it varies from one individual to another. For some it means joining a monastic order, forsaking the world, forsaking everything in the world, and intensely following the Buddhist discipline. For others, right livelihood means pursuing occupations that promote life in its fullness but don't destroy life. This suggests there are certain occupations which are inappropriate for Buddhists, such as a butcher, hunter, or commercial fisherman. At an extreme, one could be a gardener, as long as the bugs that came into the garden were not harmed and the food raised was not really harvested, but only gathered when it separated from the plant. Whichever role one chooses in right livelihood one's trade should not destroy others or disrupt social harmony. This fifth state is directly associated with the second and fourth stages of the Eightfold Path. An important corollary to right livelihood is that earning a living is not an end in itself. To a Buddhist, earning a living is simply a means for living. Whether a Buddhist is an engineer, a gardener, or a sanitation worker, the Buddhist labors because it is part and parcel of living itself, but not the final goal. Unlike the person who intensely works to achieve fame or wealth, for the Buddhist these things are not worthy of intense desire. What is really worthy of intense desire is Nirvana.

Right Effort refers to developing virtues, curbing selfish passions, and getting rid of destructive states of the mind. For Western societies, this can be particularly problematic to accept. For the Buddhist practicing this step, it would be inappropriate, for instance, to say "he beat me," "he robbed me," "he harmed me," because that is a selfish passion—a selfish, self-directed thought and inappropriate. Right effort seeks to get rid of the causes of destructive mental states, things like depression, brooding, or feeling sorry for oneself. In a positive sense, right effort represents a personal decision not to be victimized but to claim control over one's existence. Thus, as long as one says someone else did something injurious, that person becomes a victim of the action and passion of another, which is beyond any direct control. But for the Buddhist, right effort removes this victimization by seeking for what was said, done, or thought, which either made the event happen or it is removed by choosing not to succumb to the result, thereby maintaining control over one's responses. Also, beginning with right effort, timing becomes important in that a steady and continuous effort is required. It takes steady, gradual, continuously focused, and concentrated effort to be successful.

Right Mindfulness is a continuous, painfully minute self-examination of every thought, every action, every sensation, every emotion, and every image—everything about oneself. The mind is the means to liberation. Therefore, one is constantly examining what in every thought, image, emotion, or action causes suffering and then seeking ways to avoid or change these thoughts, emotions, sensations, and actions so that suffering does not occur. This results in greater self-awareness, but not guilt, because guilt is an emotion associated with a value system and that is not the focus of the Eightfold Path. The examination is painfully minute in order to discover what sort of suffering is caused, and guilt would only cause suffering. This also includes mind control over the physical self, including refusing pain, slowing respiration and the heartbeat, etc. Buddhists also assert that right mindfulness creates a realization that consciousness is not continuous but is a continuous on–off cycle. To put it another way, life is a chain of constant changes, of constant events. Hence, at any point along the way the chain (of suffering that might be associated with these events) can be broken.

Right Meditation is very closely related to Raja Yoga. It involves very focused concentration, not for the purpose of arriving at a solution to anything but simply for the purpose of forcing the mind to expand so that at some point, suddenly the mind expands out beyond oneself and, at least momentarily, embraces all the rest of the universe. It acquires the skill and stillness needed to see the nature of all things. Normally, in a monastic setting, a Buddhist master will give the practitioner a logical absurdity (for example, "What is the sound of one hand clapping?") on which to focus. The idea is not to solve the absurdity but to let the mind become so enlarged in the process that one's mind expands beyond logic and reason, beyond the self, beyond the present situation so much that it embraces the rest of the universe, and yet remains still. This is the happiness sought.

NIRVANA

The primary goal in Buddhism, originally, was an abiding friendship and intimacy with that which is lovely or good (that which does not cause suffering). Buddha shared with the Hindu world of 500 BCE many religious concepts. However, the religious concepts among the Hindus were extremely varied, and this is related to the rapid fracturing that occurred within Hinduism. Additionally, there were some things on which Buddha had a significantly different perspective.

For Hinduism, the goal of all the religious activity is moksha. In Buddhism, one seeks Nirvana. Nirvana is both a spiritual condition as well as a realm. It represented the serene peace that comes from getting rid of all self-centered desires and attachments. Interestingly, Buddha never described Nirvana. In fact, what he said about Nirvana was that it is profound, incomprehensible, and indescribable. In terms of a positive description of Nirvana, there is none from Siddhartha himself. Theravada Buddhism, especially, accepts the notion that there are two states of Nirvana. A person who achieves Nirvana while remaining alive, however fleetingly and briefly, is said to have achieved Nirvana with a residue. The person is still alive but possesses a unique and widened identification with the universe. Nirvana without a residue begins when that person dies. Moksha is believed to involve an actual absorption into the divine realm. Nirvana is not absorption into Brahman or a union with God. Nirvana is a total blowout of the fires of desires and attachments. It also involves the attainment of the quality of serene peace associated with ultimate being, the absence of individual existence, but a merge with the universe.

Whereas life for both Buddhism and Hinduism is transitory, perishing, and suffering, Hinduism looks at life as a training ground, a preparation for moksha. However, Buddhism perceives life as distinct from ultimate reality. So life is the opposite of Nirvana. Life is impermanent, whereas Nirvana, as ultimate reality, permanent. Life is suffering; Nirvana is serene peace. Life is not a preparation for Nirvana. Life is to be overcome whence one achieves Nirvana. At death the enlightened person has expanded the sense of consciousness to include all of reality, all of the universe so that as the finite person dies but consciousness continues because it has already united with the permanent realm through achieving Nirvana. As the physical body dies, conscious existence continues, which is Nirvana, and there are no "strands of finite desire" remaining to pass into another life.

THE REBIRTH–REDEATH/KARMA–SAMSARA CYCLE

The rebirth–redeath cycle is also understood very differently in Buddhism. At death, the five elements of existence (based on the Hinduism concept), body, sensation, thought, feeling, and consciousness, all disintegrate, but Karma continues. What Buddhism means by this idea is that "strands of finite personal desires," which were not already extinguished, are reborn passed from one life to a new one. When a person dies, everything else dies except this ethereal quality of a person's existence (the Karma of finite desires), and this ethereal quality is visited on the person in a newly born body. So Karma is reduced from substance to a quality, or more specifically a predisposition of the mind and the self. In this sense, a person lives again, but other than for these finite desires, doesn't really have a former existence. Liberation for Buddhists (achieving Nirvana) is what stops this process. The Buddhist, who has achieved Nirvana, at death, merges with the universe, and there remains no Karma to pass on to a subsequent generation.

In the Hindu world of Buddha's time, the idea of god as being personal had not developed. There was the ultimate divine essence that was not personal but rather a permanent, powerful, supreme reality, a divine force. Similarly, the concept of divinity that passed into Buddhism is not of a personal god, but of a permanent, supreme reality, a divine essence. There is a difference, however, between the concepts of divinity. For Hinduism, divinity is active, a force, while in Buddhism, divinity is passive, an essence or state of being. Mahayana further developed this notion into a personal divine being, a Great Buddha, of which Siddhartha was but one manifestation. Mahayana would then use a notion similar to Bhakti Yoga to develop its approach to Buddhism. As the idea of Bhakti Yoga began to develop in Hinduism, so in Buddhism, Mahayana would regard Siddhartha as one who had achieved Nirvana, and a manifestation of divinity, so that devoting oneself to him could similarly be expected to produce successful religious results. In addition to Siddhartha Gautama, it is believed that the Great Buddha was also manifested in virtually any originator of a religion, whether it is Jesus, Muhammad, etc. All of these persons are therefore of religious importance, but Siddhartha is the source of Buddhist thought and practice.

FORMS/TYPES OF BUDDHISM

Under the reign of the powerful King Asoka of India, Buddhism attained a national and international fame as a world religion. It was in the twelfth century, during the Muslim invasion in India, that Buddhism lost its stronghold in its home of origin. As the faith expanded and adapted to local cultures two major forms of Buddhism emerged. They were Theravada Buddhism (the Southern school) and Mahayana Buddhism (Northern school). Each has other divisions or sects.

The Theravada Buddhism: In that first century after Siddhartha's death, the Buddhist discipline of following the Eightfold Path was universally the way to achieve Nirvana. A person sought to achieve Nirvana by oneself for oneself. The person who achieved Nirvana with a residue was known as an *Arhant*. Because of the intense discipline required to achieve this, only monks were believed able to do so. This approach came to be known as Theravada Buddhism. Theravada means "Way of the Elders." Theravada accepts the rebirth–redeath/karma–samsara cycle but believes one can go backward as well as forward. If a person lives a particularly evil quality of life, the next existence might be as a hungry ghost or as a resident of hell, a demon. At the very best, such an individual might end up as an animal, meaning many more lifetimes would be required to reach Nirvana. However, the goal for someone who does not achieve Nirvana in a lifetime is to come back in the body of a person because only in that way can one continue to seek Nirvana.

The Theravada Buddhism, also known as the path of mindfulness, developed something called the chain of causation and the doctrine of dependent origination. This teaches that life consists of a chain of causes and corresponding effects. In this teaching, there are twelve elements in the chain of existence: ignorance, predisposition, consciousness, name and form, the six sense organs (contact, sensation, craving, etc.), and old age. All of life is therefore a process, a chain of causes and effects, moving from ignorance to old age. Only Nirvana is independent. All other existence is dependent on each other. This radical thought rejects the belief in Atman in Hindu teaching on the grounds that nothing is permanent.

All forms of appearances are temporal including the gods. One sequence gives rise to another (cause and effect), and death represents a new form of appearance. Buddha is believed to have said as his last words: "Decay is inherent in all compounded things, so continue in watchfulness."

Theravada Buddhists believe that if ignorance disappears, everything else, including birth, old age, death, also end, because everything else in the chain is related back, ultimately, to ignorance as the first cause, the effect of which, ultimately, is life and death. Getting rid of ignorance involves following the Eightfold Path, by which one expands the sense of existence to include the entire universe. Suffering exists only so long as one is ignorant of how big an individual really ought to be; only so long as one's perspective is inadequate. When one overcomes this inborn ignorance, then the whole chain, which includes the other eleven elements of life and death, is broken. The principle focal point for Theravada, and the place where the religious tradition is really experienced, is within the monastery. To become a monk, the novice undergoes a period of instruction and oversight by a senior monk. In order to even be a novice, one must have reached the age of twenty and be free from certain physical and occupational impediments that would prevent the individual from being able to follow the austere discipline of the monastery (sometimes children of six to nine years of age may begin the process, however, and a person need not be under twenty to become a monk—one can be forty, sixty, seventy years of age as well). The novice does not live at the monastery, but participates in its daily occupation while living out in the community. Buddhist monastic communities are usually all male. There are very few nunneries. It is just not a religion that has a strong place for women. When the novice reaches the age of twenty (or older) and the senior monk who is teaching the novice believes the novice is ready to enter the monastery, then he will request admission to the monastery for his novice. At the time that the request is made, there has to be a minimum of ten monks who hear the request and vote. Three requests are made, and each time, the vote has to be unanimous. Only after the third request and unanimous vote for acceptance is the novice then allowed to go into the monastery and reside there as a monk. At that point, the person must submit to the rules of discipline for the monastery. Generally, the rules of discipline are about the same in every monastery, but each will have its own nuances (like when they arise in the morning, when they have certain prayers or meditation, etc.). When the new monk moves into the monastery, he must also take upon himself a vow to abstain from unchastity, murder, stealing, lies, liquor, and perfumes (aftershaves, cologne, deodorant, etc.). The individual's head is shaved, and the new monk receives a robe. Monks also must agree not to exaggerate any miraculous powers that they feel they possess. And they have to agree to refrain from handling money.

In the monastery, or *Sangha,* monks devote all of their time and energy to pursuing the religious life. Unlike the person who lives in the world where, following morning devotions, life consists of an occupation while attempting to preserve the principles of love and compassion, the monk spends the remainder of the day involved in meditation, teaching other people, or some form of begging or receiving assistance, food, food preparation, etc. The primary focus of the monks' attention in all that they do is the hope of attaining enlightenment through their own effort. And following the example of Siddhartha, who, once he was enlightened, didn't just keep it to himself but spent forty-five years teaching others so that the monks, as they gain wisdom, insight, and understanding, could teach the Buddhist laity. For those individuals in Theravada (including women) who are not monks, there are two principle goals. One is to provide alms for the monks so that they can achieve enlightenment and teach others. The second is to live as cleanly as possible in hope of a good rebirth in order to become a monk in another existence. And by listening to the teachings one learns how to live for this goal.

Theravada Buddhism was a physical replication of Siddhartha's life and practices. The Theravada monks during that first century would go from place to place following the same kind of itinerant ministry. They would withdraw to their monastic housing during the rainy season and would carry on their acts of meditation. This approach was possible only for the few. In 380 BCE, a great assembly, called Mahasanghika, was held in an attempt to create a common understanding of what Buddhism was all about and the way to achieve Nirvana. The result of this great assembly was two schools of Buddhism. Also, different monks increasingly developed different ideas and different interpretations so that by about 380 BCE, there were a number of different interpretations of Buddhism.

The Mahayana Buddhism: Mahayana (great boat or great vehicle) also developed. Mahayana is more devotional in character than Theravada. It makes Nirvana open to many. Mahayana is often known as Great Compassion because of the acts of those who had attained Nirvana, but have chosen to remain active in helping those who are still unenlightened and suffering. Mahayana assumes that everyone possesses a "Buddha nature" capable of achieving Nirvana, possible in a single lifetime. Were this not the case, the religious system would have no relevance since some could never reach Nirvana. However, if all are capable of reaching Nirvana (rather than the few in Theravada), the path to enlightenment

must be easier to follow than Theravada. For Mahayana, the path to Enlightenment is similar to Bhakti Yoga. One must exercise faith and devotion to the Great Buddha, as well as to Siddhartha as Buddha (a passionate homage to him as one who has already achieved Nirvana, making him one's example for living), and practice love and compassion for all living things. One who succeeds in achieving Nirvana by this path is called "bodhisattva." A bodhisattva is regarded by Mahayana Buddhists as perfect in wisdom, one who displays universal compassion in all he says and does, and is self-emptying or self-sacrificing. Such a person sacrificially chooses, after achieving Nirvana, to remain alive for a time in the midst of the suffering of this world to help others achieve Nirvana rather than leaving this world to gain supreme peace.

Because Mahayana is devotional in character, religious acts play a much greater role for the followers of Mahayana than for those of Theravada (who primarily focus on meditation based on following the Eightfold Path). Rituals and ceremonies are generally similar to that found in Hinduism. These include basic acts, such as offerings to Buddha's image of

flowers, food, drink, and candles. Also, bowing before Buddha's image (to touch forehead to the ground three times); removing one's shoes; or uttering devotional phrases/mantras (charms and spells). Objects of devotion may be the common image of Buddha sitting; a stupa (funeral mound of Buddha or one of the early monks); a Bodhi tree; and Buddha's teeth. Magic rituals, mostly for protection from things like accidents and snake bites, are recited from the Sanskrit canon. Certain passages are believed to be empowered to provide this protection.

Mahayana Buddhists don't have corporate worship services, but perform devotions privately, morning and evening, at a family shrine. The shrine is usually a ledge or table holding an image of the Buddha and a vase for offerings of flowers. Ritual acts at these shrines include offering flowers and lighting a candle while uttering a mantra. One finishes by reciting the five cardinal precepts of right conduct: don't kill, steal, lie, drink intoxicants, or be unchaste. Afterwards, there might be personal prayers for protection, a good life, or a particular matter of concern. Devotion is also expressed through festivals and pilgrimages. The Uposatha is a monthly festival common across both Theravada and Mahayana Buddhism. For a monk, it is an intensely rigorous self-examination. The rules of the monastery are recited by the leader of the order and monks must admit any transgressions, for which punishment is immediately assessed—ranging from nothing more than public confession already done, to expulsion from the order, either temporarily or permanently for serious offenses. Participation is optional for laity, against whom no penalty is assessed beyond confession. Another common festival is Buddha Day, observed at the full moon in May. This commemorates Buddha's life and is the first festival of the calendar. The rainy season is also important to the annual religious cycle (especially for Theravada) during which time monks continue to remain in the monastery and meditate. There are other regional festivals as well.

Theravada recognizes a scripture called the Pali Canon. This canon consists of three parts: the Book of discipline, which is open to everyone; the Discourses of the Buddha (his teachings that document the Four Noble Truths and Eightfold Path); and the Higher subtleties of the law (for those learned in the religion).

Celebration of Buddha's Birthday, Seoul, Korea
Unidentified Buddhist people attending the famous annual hot-air balloon festival in Taunggyi, Myanmar, the full moon day in November.

Mahayana recognizes a different canon, called the Sanskrit Canon. This is not an actual canonical, systematic body of literature that sets forth a religious system or discipline. It is a collection of separate texts. Some stress one theme, such as wisdom, while others are speculation about such things as universal salvation. The originals have been lost, and the Tibetan translations are regarded as the closest to the originals; the teachings of Siddhartha seem to be more precisely handed down from their oral sources.

Tantric Buddhism (*Vajrayana*): It is a later approach, which is of considerable controversy. Whereas the other forms of Buddhism tend toward the ascetic, Tantric Buddhism is very sensual in character, believing that by ecstatic union, one can achieve Nirvana in a single lifetime. The channel for doing so in Tantrism is through the physical senses. In the other approaches of Buddhism, one mostly attempts to immobilize the body or get outside the limits of the body. In Tantrism, the body, whether it is in a sexual way or just through words and gestures, is used to unite with the deity. Tantric practitioners think it is the superior form of Buddhism because it requires only one lifetime. The practice is based on esoteric literature (hidden) known as Tantras, which embodies three elements:

1. Mantra—mystic syllables believed to possess great power and that convey one into mystical relations with the divine realm
2. Mudra—mystical movements of the body or sacrificial actions also believed to possess great power
3. Mandala—representation of the beauty of the universe, which carries one into union with the divine

When all three (mantra, mudra, and mandala) are put together, the result is very complex and almost mystical. The ritual expressions can involve promiscuous sexual unions during which the practitioner believes the sexual ecstasy also brings union with the divine realm and therefore achievement of Nirvana. This form is largely found in Tibet, though the sexual aspect has been diminished or repudiated by some sects today.

When Buddhism moved into Tibet, the region was, in many ways, naturalistic in religiocultural practices. Some of the traditional ideas and traditional symbols and occult practices that had been part of the Tibetan religion thus have become part of Tantric Buddhism. Animism is the idea that there is a spirit in every rock, tree, bush, field, etc. These spirits need to be satisfied by individuals who almost become slaves to these spirits. If there is a drought, for instance, it is believed that the spirits are not happy. The concept is oftentimes very closely associated with occultism. The idea in occultism is that through a variety of magical formula, rituals, ceremonies, divinations, etc., one learns to satisfy spirits that may impact one's life. Then the appropriate offerings that are necessary to satisfy those spirits are presented. In an occult situation, only a certain select group of people know the magical formulae and the proper ceremonies. These become not only very powerful figures in the community, nation, but are the ones believed to have the wisdom of human/divine interaction deposited within them. This sort of a practice is what existed in Tibet and it mixed with Buddhism ultimately developing into the practice of Tantrism.

Tantric Buddhism: The Tantric practitioner or monk attempts to visualize the deity as being present by drawing a mandala (a thing of holy beauty) of some sort on the ground. The mandala is considered to be esoteric knowledge possessed by those who are "initiated." They visualize the deity as being present and

Buddhist monks making sand Mandala

through the use of words (mantras) and gestures (mudras), they see themselves as merging with divinity. As they merge, the powers and virtues of divinity are thereby conveyed back to them. The initiation ceremony and, to some extent, the Tantric practices follow a set pattern. It begins with water baptism, after which a crown of sorts is placed on the initiate's head. There is a sacred band placed on one shoulder. The initiate is touched with a bell and thunderbolt, the bell being indicative of the female and the thunderbolt indicative of the male in sexual union. A secret name, known only to the initiate, is taken, and a bell and thunderbolt are received from the master. Following that the initiate participates in an experience of Tantric worship, which involves the mandala and the drama of cosmic evolution and resulting in the merging with that deity through the symbols of word and body movement, as these are carried into an experience of bliss or ecstasy. In that ecstasy Nirvana or enlightenment is believed to take place and one appropriates the virtues and powers of the divine realm. In Tantric Buddhism, this experience is repeated many times to experience it afresh with the same or another deity.

Zen Buddhism: It is a popular form of Buddhist practice in the Western world drawn from Mahayana Buddhism. As Buddhism spread to China, some ideas intermixed with Taoism to create a practice known as Chan. One of the influences of Taoism on Buddhism was to focus on the mental element rather than the physical element or devotional activity. For this reason, such things as ceremonies, rituals, Buddha images, and sacrifices, have nothing to do with the essence of religion in Zen. When Chan Buddhism spread through Korea to Japan, it got mixed with some of the religious practices in Japan to create what is known today as Zen Buddhism. Zen teaches that insight (enlightenment), devotion, and practical charity or compassion are complementary. They all work together to enhance one's experience of Buddhism. One the one hand, deep devotion, which is drawn from Mahayana, reaches a sense of gratitude virtually identical to enlightenment. On the other hand, deep meditation also reaches a sense of gratitude, which is identical with the kind of gratitude that is expressed in devotion, which is the kind of gratitude that also is reflected in enlightenment. Therefore, in Zen, the primary focus is not the steps of the Eightfold Path, nor on devotion, but Zen uses meditation to get beyond the limits of reason and the spoken word, to experience the true reality that these things imperfectly represent. As the mind is thus expanded outward to experience the reality that lies beyond reason and the spoken word, it is believed that one realizes the Buddha nature that is within. This is because the reality that lies beyond is that of universal reality or universal essence, which is the Buddha nature. The experience of enlightenment is called *Satori*.

For Zen, the religious experience is to be found only through the meditation process. The practitioner sits in a lotus position and focuses on what is known as a *koan*, or a logical absurdity. The koan is assigned by a Zen master. It is usually a very simple thing, like what is the sound of one hand clapping. The idea is not to find an answer to the question or koan, but force the mind to move beyond the limits of words, to get beyond the representation of those words to the reality that lies beyond. Sometimes a Zen student may spend a year or longer focusing on one koan. The goal is to present to the Zen master a response that reflects the reality beyond the word, perhaps almost another logical absurdity. The process continues with another koan until Satori is experienced. Then the same process continues, seeking for more experiences of Satori. The way that Satori is described is a perception that life is good and the welfare of others is as important as that of oneself. Thus, when one experiences Satori, some point of selflessness may result.

For a person who is from the Zen tradition, but is not intensely involved in meditation, there is an attempt, through some sense of devotion, to seek the same gratitude, but it is not a very common nor familiar path. Generally, Zen is associated with intense meditation. Some Western music personalities from the

1960s and early 1970s became involved in Zen as they sought deeper spiritual satisfaction. That, plus the Vietnam War, brought some of the ideas of Zen Buddhism into America, primarily the ideas of meditation and monastic life. But the part of Zen that was heard in America was the idea that meditation for the sake of meditation is good, that the practice of meditation was somehow useful in and of itself. True Zen is not oriented at just the monastic life and meditation for the sake of doing it. Rather it is focused on expanding the mind through the koans to achieve Satori. Zen, because it sees Buddhism as primarily something of the mind, jumps to the last stage of the Eightfold Path almost directly.

Rather than being associated with the world through the Eightfold Path, the Zen practitioner, through expansion of the mind in meditation on a koan, feels a sense of becoming infused with the eternal. Thus, the Zen practitioner doesn't have to stay in a monastic community. Where the practitioner goes and in the things that are done or said, having been infused with the eternal, all these things help bring the eternal to wherever they are. Zen practitioners do not necessarily withdraw from life but rather see as part of their mission, their purpose in life, to be where other people are, because, being infused with the eternal, wherever they go infuses the eternal into life by their presence. Even doing simple tasks are viewed, in theory, by the practitioners of Zen as something that involves ultimate or eternal reality, whether preparing food for a meal, cleaning the street, or tending a garden. Whether a simple task or a very intense religious activity, all gradually becomes seen and experienced as part of universal reality. From the outside, observing a Zen practitioner, there appears to be an attitude of general agreeableness with life a serene quietness free from preferences, prejudices, and rejections. There is a sense of contentment in whatever happens, good or bad, whether there is social elevation or persecution, all is part of an ultimate reality and to be accepted as part of life.

WORSHIP AND DEVOTION IN BUDDHISM

There are two major forms of worship and devotion in Buddhism: (1) monastic contemplation, and (2) popular devotion. Each is as important as the other, but different forms of Buddhism may lay more emphasis on one or the other. Monastic contemplation involves some form of asceticism such as a withdrawal from the world and pleasure and focus on mindfulness meditation as Gautama did (i.e., following the Master's steps). Popular devotion may involve visiting burial grounds or mounds (stupas) of the Buddha or revered monks such as those known as the celestial Buddhas, who achieved enlightenment such as the eighteen disciples of Buddha who achieved Nirvana during Buddha's lifetime but were active in helping others achieve theirs; making a pilgrimage to places visited by the Buddha in his lifetime; or participating in a Buddhist festival.

THE BUDDHIST PEACE FELLOWSHIP (BPF)

Buddhism is noted for its absolute adherence to peace and nonconfrontational character. The Tibetan Buddhists' pursuance of peace and nonviolent protests in the face of aggressive political suppression provided a model for others in similar situations. However, a recent event in Myanmar involving Buddhist violent attack on Muslims has raised serious concern and challenge for the Buddhist community worldwide. Is this radical Buddhism a new development or just an exception? Will the attack affect the voice of the Buddhist Peace Fellowship? According to Michele Spuler and Michelle Barker (2003), the Buddhist Peace Fellowship is "a nonsectarian international network of engaged Buddhists participating in various forms of nonviolent social activism and environmentalism with chapters all over the world" (www.buddhistpeacefellowship.

org 2012, March 15, 2015). The purpose among other things includes public education on Buddhist practice and interdependence as a way of peace and protection for all beings, raising peace, environmental, feminist, and social justice concerns among North American Buddhists, bringing a Buddhist perspective of nonduality to contemporary social ecological movements, encouraging the practice of nonviolence based on the rich resources of traditional Buddhist and Western spiritual teachings, and providing platforms for dialogue and exchange among the diverse North American and world *Sanghas.*

SUMMARY

Buddhism is one of the most diverse of all the great religions of the world. As with many very ancient religions, there are all sorts of different streams of thought and all sorts of different practices that have developed. In addition, Buddhism has gone into a number of countries, in most cases, some 2,000 years ago, where it was influenced by local cultures and religious practices. In India, a form of Buddhism persisted for 1,000 years or more and then was driven out of India. Only in the twentieth century has it returned. In China, one strain was close to pure Buddhism, while another was heavily influenced by traditional Chinese Taoism. That which was heavily influenced by Taoism migrated into Korea and eventually Japan, where it was further influenced by Japanese religion, emerging as Zen Buddhism. Wherever Buddhism has migrated, there have also been Buddhist monks, who are dedicated to the practice of Buddhism. These monks do more than just meditate and go through the motions of religious practices. These monks are also involved in the thought processes resulting in the development of Buddhism, which adds to the religious diversity. The result is hundreds of patterns of Buddhism, from the very severe to the very sensual. Sometimes these different patterns are scarcely recognizable as part of the same religion. Yet among all there are common threads related to union with the divine essence, by whatever path such attempt at union may be presented.

KEY CONCEPTS

The Path of Moderation	The Buddha	The Four Signs	Great Renunciation
The Four Noble Truths	Mara the Tempter	Theravada	Mahayana
The Noble Eightfold Path	Mahasanghika	Satori	The Five Precepts
Tantric (Vajrayana)	Zen Buddhism	Pali Canon	Sanskrit Canon
The Three Jewels	Bodhisattva	*Nirvana*	*Zen Koan*
Impermanence	Mandala	*Tantras*	Stupa

Name: _____

QUESTIONS FOR FURTHER STUDY

1. How does one become a Buddhist?

2. Explain the problem that led to the division of Buddhism into two major branches.

3. Discuss Buddhist rites of passage.

4. Examine the similarities and differences between Jainism and Buddhism.

5. Discuss the rite of initiation into the monastic community.

6. What was the contribution of King Ashoka in spreading the message of Buddha to the other parts of Asia?

7. What is the purpose of the Buddhist Peace Fellowship?

8. What are the effects of modernity and postmodernity on Buddhism?

Confucianism

INTRODUCTION

Believed to be more of a sociopolitical and ethical philosophy, Confucianism has gained recognition as a religion of the world. The cultures most strongly influenced by Confucianism include those of China, Japan, Korea, and Vietnam, as well as various territories including Hong Kong, Macao, Taiwan, and Singapore, where ethnic Chinese are the majority. Many idealists and realists of contemporary philosophical culture regard Confucianism as a moral philosophy, ethical principles for living, or simply a way of life that can be appropriated by any religion. The term "Confucianism" itself has no relation to China even though that is the birthplace of this faith. The man who came to be called Confucius was a Master whose actual name was Kong Qiu (or Kung fu tzu). So Confucius was a misnaming or mispronunciation of Kong Qiu. In this chapter we will examine the history, beliefs, and practices as well as major holidays or festivals of Confucianism.

Confucianism is a philosophy developed from the teachings of Confucius. Confucius spent most of his time wandering from various places in China seeking a leadership role as the right hand to a powerful ruler but was unsuccessful. Instead as he went from town to town, he taught the sons of nobles about his philosophy and in-turn had a group of disciples that followed him everywhere he went. Even though Confucianism does not have any deities or a concept of the afterlife, it still has many beliefs and rituals similar to those of other religions. No matter how much good Confucius did, he never really considered himself to be as influential as his followers thought he was. After his death, his followers have been credited with gathering his teachings in a book called the *Analects*, which should be used to guide both the rulers of China and Chinese society as a whole.

HISTORY

Confucius lived during a very poor and belligerent time. A series of ruling families governed China for many years some causing prosperity and others, causing strife. The last of the united families was the Zhou dynasty (771–221 BCE) during which the barbarians attacked and caused the Zhou family to split apart. During that time various small rulers fought for control over the broken country. The Chinese society, culture, and religions were all falling apart. At the same time, the Zhou dynasty continued to decline as it was constantly challenged by smaller militant groups. The Zhou then forced men into their army, raised truces, and left just women and older men to tend the fields, which led to food shortage. With the fate of the country at stake, many philosophers came together to think about ideas to salvage and transform the country. The result was the emergence of what came to be known as the "Hundred Schools of Thought" (Joseph A Adler). The Four most famous schools of thought were *Daoism, Mohism, Legalism,* and *Confucianism.* Confucianism was by far the most influential.

It was only until after the death of Kong Qiu (Confucius) that Confucianism really began. A student of Confucius, Mencius, read the *Five Classics* along with the *Analects* and picked up where Confucius left off. He journeyed from city to city and spoke with many different leaders while sharing his own views on how society could be improved, some of which were completely radical to the thought of Confucius. For example, he thought of agriculture in relation to human needs and even proposed that if a ruler were to act tyrannically the people had the right to kill him. Like Confucius, his teachings were gathered into the Book of Mencius. The book later became another classic work of Confucianism.

During the entire formative period of Confucianism there had been twelve disciple figures, but three are regarded as the leading figures. The first was Confucius the founder of Confucianism. As mentioned earlier, his native name was Kong Qiu, born in 551 BC in the land of Lu and died in 479 BCE. It was the Jesuit missionaries to East Asia that Latinized it to Confucius (Kung Fu-tzu). Master Kong Qiu was known to be an adept learner. He developed concepts of society, education, and government. He had ambitions to pursue a career in politics. His political career never took off due to the loyalty he had for his king at the time. Qiu was placed in a minor position in politics, but when at the age of 56 subsequent attempts in politics failed, he exiled himself for 12 years. For those 12 years he travelled to different states in China, spreading his thought to those who were willing to hear him and join his group of followers or scholars (called *ru*). He struggled throughout most of his life trying to find a ruler who would value his ideals and apply them to their societies, but it was to no avail. He finally returned to the state of Lu at age 67 to teach. In his writing he summarized his life by stating, "At [age] fifteen, I set my heart on learning; at thirty, I firmly took my stand; at forty, I had no delusion; at fifty, I knew the mandate of Heaven; at sixty, my ear was attuned; at seventy, I followed my heart's desire without overstepping the boundaries of right" (*Analects* II, 4). When Master Kong Qiu died at age 73 in 479 BCE, this statement succinctly became the password of the philosophy of Confucianism by which learning is understood as the key to everything. It's no wonder that Confucianism acquired the names "The School of Scholars," "Scholarly Studies," (*Ruxue*) or "Religion of Confucius" (Wertz, www.ibiblio.org/chinesehistory, April 23, 2016).

Confucius was always concerned with how societies should be controlled, how rulers should rule, and how strong relationships can be maintained. Confucius always believed that by studying the past and returning to old rituals it was possible to heal the wounds in society. Confucius was the driving force and creator of the basic principles of what is now known as the religion of Confucius or Confucianism. His ethical principles or mores of how people and rulers should govern themselves still hold a strong place in Chinese society to this day even though it came under severe attacked in the Cultural Revolution of the People's Republic of China in the 1960s.

How is Confucianism a religion? As explored in chapter one, religion has many dimensions and definitions. If we go by Clifford Geertz's definition that says religion is "a system of symbols which acts to establish powerful, pervasive and long-lasting moods and motivations in men by formulating conceptions of a general order of existence and clothing these conceptions with such an aura of factuality . . ." (Geertz 1973, 90) or Matthew Arnold's which says, "Religion is ethics heightened, enkindled, lit up by feeling" (Arnold, 1965), then Confucianism could fit any of these definitions. An article by the Asia Society, states that Confucius created a kind of religious system equivalent to what Robert N. Bella calls "civil religion" in America. Its features, the article claims, include "(1) the sense of religious identity and common moral understanding at the foundation of a society's central institutions. It is also what a Chinese sociologist called a 'diffused religion'; (3) its institutions were not a separate church, but those of society, family, school, and state; its priests were not separate liturgical specialists, but parents, teachers, and officials.

Confucianism was part of the Chinese social fabric and way of life; to Confucians, everyday life was the arena of religion" ("Confucianism", asiasociety.org, April 19, 2016).

The second leading figure in Confucianism was born a century after the death of Confucius. He was called Mencius (also Latinized, Mengzi). He was born in a small state called Zou, which was actually located very close to Kong Qiu's home state of Lu. Allegedly, Mencius was said to have studied under Kong Qiu's grandson, Zisi. Mencius studied the various teachings of Confucius in the Analects and was a firm believer in what Confucius was trying to accomplish. Like Confucius, he spent many years in futility trying to find a political office to be able to speak with leaders of cities. He had a little success in his early years but that was it. Mencius devoted his life studying the teachings of Confucius. This is not to take away from him his unique and personal contribution to the development of Confucianism. Like Confucius, Mencius thought of himself as a transmitter of information and that most of his beliefs were mere interpretations of the past. The biggest contribution he made to Confucianism was renxing, a theory about human nature. He believed that by "developing one's mind to the fullest, one knows one's nature, and by knowing one's nature, one knows Tian." Mencius believed that the journeys of morality starts when born since you are brought in on ren (co-human). He thought that the ancestors and the teachings were able to guide one to maturity. A person who always does the right thing can become a sage. Mencius's moral model that he developed includes the belief that human nature is good naturally and can be even better. Mencius's transmitter concepts could be viewed as radical to Confucius's thinking. He believed in the integrity of people and stressed that leaders should lead a certain manner and to show concern about the rights of the individual rather than the society as taught by Confucius.

The third leading figure was Xunzi, who also contributed to Confucianism in no small manner. Xunzi's philosophy critiqued Mencius's ideas and concepts. While they were philosophical rivals the two never met because Xunzi was born in the state of Zhao in the year 313 BCE, but both of them held political office in their respective states briefly. The main difference between the two was their understanding of the predisposition of human beings at birth. Whereas Xunzi believed that humans are born with a tendency to be selfish and disorderly, which he believed could be corrected with the power of culture, Mencius stressed the good nature of a person. Even though the two differed in styles and beliefs, they both taught that human beings are capable of moral perfection by ritual and textual learning. The high optimism in humans is the most significant view shared by Confucius and these two leading disciples.

BELIEFS AND PRACTICES

Confucianism is seen as more of a way of life than a religion by many because it does not focus on any deity or teach about it. While this is true, there is proof that Confucius did not refute the existence of an ultimate reality or theistic belief nor was he a cynic or a doubter. Confucius regarded *Tian* as a force beyond nature that is in the universe. He also concluded that *Tian* is a reference to heaven. Confucius believed that humans and *Tian* were necessary in the natural cosmos and introduced a concept of self-divination or self-knowledge. In addition to this are the beliefs in *ren* (humaneness), *zhong* (loyalty to one's true nature), *shu* (reciprocity), *li* (traditional rituals), and *xiao* (filial piety). These beliefs join together to create *de* (virtue).

The interesting concept of Confucianism does not lie in its aspect of life and death, but on the principle that sought to make life better here on earth for everyone in the Chinese society. The ultimate goal of the individual and society was to find a better way of governing itself during times of depression, famine, and war. Confucius said, "To govern by virtue, let us compare it to the North Star: it stays in its place, while the myriad stars wait upon it" (*Analects* II, 1). The way one governed them was the cornerstone of reaching the precipice of achievement. The central creed of Confucianism is on governance where rulers serve as exemplars and models of a virtuous society. Confucius said, "in order for one to govern others they must first be able to govern themselves."

Next, Confucius took seriously how people interact with one another—their *relationships and humaneness*. It is important to remember that Confucianism was born during a time of war. Confucius knew that if the country would have any chance of surviving it would have to rebuild its past relationships with the other rulers of the land and with each other. The best summation of Confucius theosophy would be the common universal maxim, "Do onto others as you would have them do onto you." It is a basic principal that implies to treat others with kindness and respect and they in turn will do the same to you, other things being equal. On the matter of relationships, Confucianism teaches about filial (family) devotion or piety. Filial devotion is the most valued virtue that is accorded to both the living and the dead (ancestors). They are classified in pairs which are:

1. ruler and subject
2. father and son
3. husband and wife
4. elder and younger brother
5. friend and friend

Each of these relationships carries with it its respective duties that must be followed devotedly. He believed that human beings can better themselves by showing kindness to everyone they meet and by paying homage to those that they have lost through various ceremonies and rites. In the Analects, Confucius said,

> At home, a young man should be a good son, when outside he should treat others like his brothers, his behavior should be one of trustworthy and proper, and should love the multitude at large and keep himself close to people of benevolence and morality. If after all these activities, he has any energy to spare, he should read widely to stay cultivated. (Analects I, 6)

Another important doctrine of Confucianism is on *education* and *knowledge,* and it is profound. Education was undoubtedly Confucius's main focus since he always spoke about it and also because he saw it as a ceaseless process of self-realization. He taught,

> Only when things are investigated is knowledge extended; only when knowledge is extended are thoughts sincere; only when thoughts are sincere are minds rectified; only when minds are rectified are the characters of persons cultivated; only when character is cultivated are our families regulated; only when families are regulated are states well governed; only when states are well governed is there peace in the world (ibid).

Furthermore, Confucius taught his students that one should live by believing in a code of *benevolence* and that human beings ultimately are the controllers of their own fate. Confucians believe that all human beings are inherently good, but become corrupt and evil through abnormal means, such as ignorance. He charged his scholars to seek a life of virtue so that they could become a "Superior being." Confucius himself had humane and loving relationship and conversation with people. Conversation helps foster strong relationships, and Confucius was very fond of relationships based on the context of the sayings included in the *Analects*. Many of the sayings involved an interaction between Confucius and his students, and the overall text reads like a long conversation between the reader and the writer.

Ritual of *ancestral worship* is a well-known practice in Confucianism. It is the most prominent sacred ritual. This ritual consists of a commemoration of one's ancestors and a sacrifice to them. Over the centuries this practice has become so commonplace in China that it still practiced widely by most Chinese people not just Confucians. The rite is deeply seeded in Confucian tradition and has played a significant role in many of the ancient Chinese dynasties, which has helped carry the practice from generation to generation.

Divination and sacrifice was introduced into Confucianism by the neo-Confucian, Zhu Xi in the twelfth and thirteenth centuries CE. The dyad ritual of divination-sacrifice manifested in different forms as a way of connecting with the ancestors, divinities, and the spirit world had been practiced from primordial time. In Chinese culture, according to Joseph A. Adler, it was more prevalent under the Shang dynasty,

> When divination and sacrifice constituted the central linkage between the heavenly and earthly realms in the religious life of the Shang aristocracy, and the king was the pivotal figure ensuring their harmonious co-existence. Through sacrifice the king acknowledged the higher status of the ancestors and gods and provided for their needs; through oracle-bone divination he received confirmation that their needs were being met and that they were willing to act in favor of the king, his family, and the state he represented. The ultimate goal was to ensure the harmony and welfare of the heavenly, earthly, and social realms (2008, 6).

Within the rites of ancestral worship, rites of passage such as transition into adulthood, marriage, birth and mourning rituals are also performed. In sacrifice food and drinks are offered to the ancestors and oracle consultation done. These traditional rites endorsed by Confucians speak not only of the spirituality of the faith but also of its status as religion.

Zhu Xi's task was to synthesize earlier Confucianism of the Zhou dynasty with that of the Song era by "standardizing the major social rites of passage" in line with "the orthodox Confucian forms and principles" through "a comprehensive system of education and personal moral cultivation by which individuals could approach as closely as possible the ultimate Confucian goal of Sagehood" (6–7). To attain this one has to get rid of all mind–heart imperfection, which is an arduous task. However, with self-cultivation (moral and investigative education, sacrifice and divination) this state of "spiritual clarity" or spiritual self-awareness would be achieved (7). Divination involves an alignment of ones' mind with the absolute, or Heaven (tian). Adler made reference to Mencius, who said,

> To fully develop one's mind is to know one's nature. To know one's nature is to know Heaven. Preserving one's mind and nourishing one's nature is how one serves Heaven. (Mencius 7A.1, in Alan 2008, 9)

Actualizing ones' innate relation with the Absolute requires a realization of the moral existence of the world. It is only when humans who are endowed with this capacity come to realize the inherent morality of the cosmos that one attains self-divination—an awareness of one's own harmonious existence with Heaven (*tian*).

As mentioned above, viewed from the concepts of ren and self-divination, many Confucian scholars believe that people should reach for their potential and become "perfect persons," because the purpose of existence is to reach our fullest potential as humans. For a person to become a "perfect person," it would take a considerable amount of time, patience, and moral fortitude. However, not everybody can attain this perfect personhood for, in Confucius's view, two types of people exist in the world: the *junzi* and the *xiaoren*. In the *Analects*, it states, "The profound person understands what is moral. The small person understands what profitable is (IV, 16). The *word junzi* means "lord's son," which is the description for a "great person," whereas *xiaoren,* meaning "small person," represents the one who has not participated in developing *ren* in his or her action.

SACRED TEXTS

After the death of Confucius, his work was continued through the actions of his students. Scholars are not very certain as to the extent of the teachings he wrote down by himself. Most of Confucius's teachings were done orally. These students traveled all around spreading the word of their teacher and ultimately compiled all of his lessons into one universal manuscript through which the very soul and spirit of Confucius flowed, the iconic book known around the world as the *Analects* or the *Lunyu*. The *Analects* is a complete interpretation of the teaching of Confucius by his disciples and has been the premises of Confucianism since then. His students or *ru* also contributed to the texts of Confucianism in their own way, which form a greater portion of Confucian texts. The texts of Confucianism are grouped into two: the *Four Books* and the *Five Classics*.

The Four Books
- The Great Learning
- The Doctrine of the Mean
- The Analects of Confucius
- The Mencius

The *Analects*, one of the *Four Books*, is held as a sacred text and consists of *Five Classics*, which transmute into the main doctrines of a social philosophy known as Confucianism.

The Five Classics
- The Classic of Poetry
- The Classic of History
- The Classic of Rites
- The Classic of Changes
- The Spring and Autumn Annals

The *Five Classics* describe and relate to the history of China with a concentration on Confucius home state of Lu, on divination, and on the practice of rituals and festivities. A sixth book, the Classic of Music is referred to but was lost by the time of the Han Dynasty.

HOLIDAYS AND FESTIVALS

In Confucianism symbols are very rare and usually relate to learning. There have been images of Master Kung fu tzu (Confucius) that were seen, and the pictures of his educational disciplines are displayed in paintings or statues. The images of Confucius and his saints were spread widely due to the discovery of the first Confucian temples during the Han dynasty in China. Through the images you can see the major pillars of Confucius's teachings, in royal attire to show their rank, or in a meditative garb. While specific pictures are uncommon, one famous picture shows the meeting of Confucius with Laozi the famous Taoist sage who was said to be an expert in the Zhou dynasty.

Taoist believers utilized a symbol, the consummation of the *yin* and *yang,* also known as the *Taiji* (Great Ultimate), which is recognized all over the world. Scholars say it is not known when the image for the *yin* and *yang* was first created or who created it. The image for the *yin* and *yang* is one of the most consistent images of the Eastern Asia religions. Many scholars of Confucianism believe the symbol is connected to the cosmos and how *qi* became stronger through rituals, specifically those who practice self-cultivation. Images consist of male practicing rituals: archery, music, chariot driving, mathematics, and calligraphy are consistently found in Confucianism art. These aspects are known as the "six arts" that

Two stone sculptures discussing and sitting at a table, one is Confucius and one is Lao Tse, the spiritual leader of Daoism outside in a temple park in Laoshan, China.

were required to be learned by all Chinese men, and they were consistently an educational foundation in the ancient culture and, roots of Confucian philosophy. Out of the six arts ritual, music, and calligraphy, are very strong symbols of self-cultivation in Confucianism.

All time is regarded as sacred in Confucianism. Confucius believed that an opportunity to bring a person into harmony through worship of their ancestors was important. He also deemed some times of the year more sacred and celebratory than others. There are two major festivals that are celebrated in Confucianism. They are *Qingminjie* (the Clear and Bright Festival in the spring) and *Guijie* (The Ghost Festival).

The Ghost Festival occurs on the thirteenth of the seventh lunar month. Ghost Month is similar to the Day of the Dead in Mexico; it is the time when the spirits of the dead wander the earth. It is appropriate to make offerings, which consist of paper houses, clothing, and elaborate meals to ancestors during the festival. Families clean the burial places of their ancestors and conduct worship services during the spring festival. This is why the day of the festival is commonly known as "Tomb-Sweeping Day." There is a common description and explanation for both festivals: the living reach out to the dead during Qingminjie, and the dead visit the living during Guijie.

Confucians pay homage to Master Kong Qiu's birthday on September 28 just as Buddhists do for the Buddha's birthday. It is a tradition for Confucian temples to have vast pageantry involving ancient dance and music of the Record of Ritual. The performance is based off of a ritual manual that was written during the Han dynasty. Even though it is not observed greatly today, it is a tradition for students who are preparing for tests to visit a temple and pray for blessing of the sage Kong Qiu.

EFFECTS ON SOCIETY

Confucius's teachings served as a guide to the rulers of many dynasties. In fact, a thousand years ago, the first prime minister of the Song Dynasty, Zhao Pu, boasted that he could rule the known world with just half the book of the *Analects*. In traditional Asian societies, the nobility fell on Confucius's philosophical ideas to rule the states. Confucianism was first adopted by the Han Dynasty and went on to be utilized by all of the other East Asian governments over the last one thousand years. China has always been extremely influential in East Asian civilization because it is the oldest of them all. This is primarily what helped Confucianism to spread and prosper.

From his sayings it was clear that Confucius was deeply concerned with the more challenging questions in life, like what justifies a person as good or bad, or compassion (morality, humaneness), how rulers should rule (rulership, leadership, governance), self-knowledge, and the teaching and learning process (mentorship) by which virtue is impacted and maturity attained.

Morality and humaneness. Here, the principles to follow include: (1) to live one's life as the best person one can be, (2) to constantly strive to cultivate one's character, (3) to be compassionate and kind, and (4) to act according to one's proper role within the human community (filial piety). These were perhaps his most important social teachings that have influenced his followers and societies such as China, Japan, Korea, and Vietnam where Confucianism is widely practiced.

Rulership and governance. The concepts of renxing (humaneness) and Tian (Heaven-endowed spirit) command obligation and accountability and should motivate rulers to seek after the good and well-being of their people. Thus, both deontological and teleological basis of ethics become motivation for rulers to seek justice, denounce corruption, and pursue the common good.

Self-knowledge. Confucianism challenges people to dig deep and work tirelessly in order to truly know oneself. Proper understanding of *Tian* (Heaven, or Absolute) inspires our inner search in order to be acquainted with the Absolute within so as to attain one's "Heaven-endowed" moral nature. However, this inner search should be done within the family or community and does not encourage isolation from the family.

Teaching methodology and content. Confucius's teaching method in the form of debate, dialogue, and conversation, which undergirds the Confucian tradition, allows for proper interaction between learners and teachers and also helps to expand and opens up ideas. It is believed that it was his methodology that created the scholarly system or philosophical tradition for which Confucianism is noted. His debates were not confined to those who agreed with him but also with his arch critics on issue of morality, human nature, governance, and citizenship. These issues were not abstracts but that which confronted the people and society on daily basis. That's why Confucianism is said to be one of the most ethical religious traditions in earlier years as well as the modern world.

Confucianism is also criticized as a tool that encourages nepotism, corruption, and trouncing of the rights of the individual specifically, young people because of its teachings of filial piety and loyalty.

Confucianism, like all other traditions, has impacted the global community and through its "Confucius Institutes" is spreading throughout the continent of Africa and other parts of the world. A new wave of influence called neo-Confucianism is sweeping the globe and engaging people about the great philosophical and theosophical teachings and power that the tradition embodies.

KEY CONCEPTS

Ren (Renxing)	Yinyang	Li	Taiji (Great Ultimate)
Kong Qiu (Kung fu tzu)	Mencius	Xunzi	*The Four Books*
Self-divination	Analects	Tian	*The Five Classics*
Ghost Festival	Self-cultivation	Junzi	Neo-Confucianism

Name: _____

QUESTIONS FOR FURTHER STUDY

1. Explain the concept of "outer–inner" opposite and balance.

2. Discuss the concept of yin and yang in Confucianism.

3. How does Confucianism treat the concept of transcendence?

4. Discuss Mencius's doctrine of human nature.

5. What is the role of education and knowledge in Confucianism

6. Discuss the five relationships in Confucius's notion of filial piety.

7. Discuss the legacy of Zhou dynasty in relation to Confucianism.

Judaism

Menorah Jewish traditional candle holder for seven candles

Star of David

HISTORICAL BACKGROUND

Whereas withdrawal and concentrated focus on meditation, yoga, or the idea of asking for alms or food are the strongest expressions of religious practice in Hinduism and Buddhism, this is not the case for Judaism, Christianity, or Islam. Rather for Islam, Judaism, and Christianity, divinity is first of all a personal being. This means two things. One is that he is personal and a "he." All three accept this notion. The other thing is that there is some kind of an immediate, personal relationship that the believer can have with a divine being who is personal.

In the monotheistic religions, history is the venue in which the divine person reveals Himself to humans. This is even more the case for Judaism and Christianity. In fact, Judaism involves a revelation through history which spans approximately 2,500 years, beginning with the time of Abraham. Through history many of the practices and a lot of the understanding of the human/divine relationship enter into the faith. It is with the life of Abraham that the emergence of Judaism begins, and so it is at that point in the biblical account that the study of Judaism begins.

* * *

12 Now the LORD said to Abram, "Go from your country and your kindred and your father's house to the land that I will show you. ²I will make of you a great nation, and I will bless you, and make your name great, so that you will be a blessing. ³I will bless those who bless you, and the one who curses you I will curse; and in you all the families of the earth shall be blessed."

4 So Abram went, as the LORD had told him; and Lot went with him. Abram was seventy-five years old when he departed from Haran.

* * *

7 Then he said to him, "I am the LORD who brought you from Ur of the Chaldeans, to give you this land to possess." ⁸But he said, "O LORD GOD, how am I to know that I shall possess it?" ⁹He said to him, "Bring me a heifer three years old, a female goat three years old, a ram three years old, a turtledove, and a young pigeon." ¹⁰He brought him all these and cut them in two, laying each half over against the other; but he did not cut the birds in two. ¹¹And when birds of prey came down on the carcasses, Abram drove them away.

12 As the sun was going down, a deep sleep fell upon Abram, and a deep and terrifying darkness descended upon him. ¹³Then the LORD said to Abram, "Know this for certain, that your offspring shall be aliens in a land that is not theirs, and shall be slaves there, and they shall be oppressed for four hundred years; ¹⁴but I will bring judgment on the nation that they serve, and afterward they shall come out with great possessions. ¹⁵As for yourself, you shall go to your ancestors in peace; you shall be buried in a good old age. ¹⁶And they shall come back here in the fourth generation; for the iniquity of the Amorites is not yet complete."

17 When the sun had gone down and it was dark, a smoking fire pot and a flaming torch passed between these pieces. ¹⁸On that day the LORD made a covenant with Abram, saying, "To your descendants I give this land, from the river of Egypt to the great river, the river Euphrates, ¹⁹the land of the Kenites, the Kenizzites, the Kadmonites, ²⁰the Hittites, the Perizzites, the Rephaim, ²¹the Amorites, the Canaanites, the Girgashites, and the Jebusites."

* * *

16 Now Sarai, Abram's wife, bore him no children. She had an Egyptian slave-girl whose name was Hagar, ²and Sarai said to Abram, "You see that the LORD has prevented me from bearing children; go in to my slave-girl; it may be that I shall obtain children by her." And Abram listened to the voice of Sarai. ³So, after Abram had lived ten years in the land of Canaan, Sarai, Abram's wife, took Hagar the Egyptian, her slave-girl, and gave her to her husband Abram as a wife. ⁴He went in to Hagar, and she conceived; and when she saw that she had conceived, she looked with contempt on her mistress. ⁵Then Sarai said to Abram, "May the wrong done to me be on you! I gave my slave-girl to your embrace, and when she saw that she had conceived, she looked on me with contempt. May the LORD judge between you and me!" ⁶But Abram said to Sarai, "Your slave-girl is in your power; do to her as you please." Then Sarai dealt harshly with her, and she ran away from her.

7 The angel of the LORD found her by a spring of water in the wilderness, the spring on the way to Shur. 8And he said, "Hagar, slave-girl of Sarai, where have you come from and where are you going?" She said, "I am running away from my mistress Sarai." 9The angel of the LORD said to her, "Return to your mistress, and submit to her." 10The angel of the LORD also said to her, "I will so greatly multiply your offspring that they cannot be counted for multitude." 11And the angel of the LORD said to her,

"Now you have conceived and shall bear
a son; you shall call him Ishmael
for the LORD has given heed to
your affliction.

12 He shall be a wild ass of a man,
with his hand against everyone, and
everyone's hand against him;
and he shall live at odds with all his kin."

13 "So she named the LORD who spoke to her, "You are El-roi"; for she said, "Have I really seen GOD and remained alive after seeing him?" 14Therefore the well was called Beerlahai-roi; it lies between Kadesh and Bered.

15 Hagar bore Abram a son; and Abram named his son, whom Hagar bore, Ishmael.

* * *

In Islam, a significantly different account of the life and experiences of Abraham is found than that which is contained in the Bible. For the study of Judaism, however, the biblical account forms the basis for understanding the Judaic religion and makes the most sense. Actually, in Old Testament scholarship, there is an enormous amount of discussion, sometimes extremely heated discussion, about the historicity of the biblical account. Alternative theories will be mentioned at some points. But it makes the most sense to present the biblical account because that is the basis upon which Judaism, and derivatively speaking, Christianity, focuses the beginning of its own self-understanding. So many of the examples, so many of the ideas, so many of the theological concepts come out of the biblical account, that even though there are challenges to the historicity, one must begin by understanding what the religion says about itself, in its own self-understanding.

Abraham, as the account goes, had two sons: Ishmael and Isaac. Ishmael, as we have seen, is the father of the Arabs. Actually Abraham eventually had a number of other sons from marriage after the death of his great wife, Sarah. Isaac was the son who, according to the Hebrew Bible, was to have been sacrificed, not Ishmael of Islamic tradition. As the oldest son of the great wife, Isaac, according to the custom of the day, was also the ONLY heir of Abraham, his wealth, and the promises made to him by his God. From Isaac there are additionally two sons mentioned in the Bible. Esau, to whom the Bible refers as the father of the Edomites, and his descendants, intermarried with the descendants of Ishmael and so figures into the ancestry of the Arabs as well. The other son of Isaac was Jacob, who had twelve sons. Of these sons, we will identify only a few principle ones, though all are important and referred to over and over in the biblical accounts. The fourth son was Judah. Another son was Levi. The eleventh son was named Joseph. And the twelfth son was Benjamin, a full brother to Joseph.

Jacob had two wives and two concubines that the Bible tells about. One of the important events that occurred in the life of Jacob and his sons comes as a result of the obvious favoritism which Jacob showed to his son Joseph—who was eleventh in line, but the first born to Jacob's favorite wife Rachel. At an opportune moment, Joseph was sold by his ten older brothers (born to the other wife and the concubine) to a caravan. These brothers conspired together because Joseph was obviously the son of the beloved wife—the son to whom it appeared as though Jacob was going to give everything. The passing caravan took Joseph to Egypt where they sold him as a slave to the captain of the bodyguard of the Egyptian king or pharaoh.

In Egypt, Joseph has a number of experiences. The story is fairly contemporary—something like a soap opera. He was in the family of the captain of the bodyguard and rises to the position of chief steward. Joseph is then accused of sexual harassment by his master's wife. So he is put in jail (an indication that the husband of his accuser did not really believe the accusation, but had to do something to save face). Through a series of events, the pharaoh has several dreams that Joseph is able to interpret. The essential meanings of the dreams were that there would be a seven-year famine to occur in Egypt after seven years. Famines were very unusual in Egypt. The Nile flooded every year which provided all the water that the people and crops needed. Not only was there going to be one year without a significant flood, there would be seven years without a significant flood—a major famine. So Joseph recommended that the king save up the surplus during those seven good years, which would occur before the famine, so that there will be food available during the famine years. And the king agreed with the idea, and expressed his confidence in the wisdom of Joseph by making him the vizier over Egypt. The vizier is something like a prime minister, and Joseph was considered as great as Pharaoh, except when Pharaoh was seated on his throne. Joseph oversaw the details of the grain collection in all of Egypt in preparation for the coming famine.

So with that, Joseph rose to essentially the number two place in the leadership of Egypt. When the famine came, it hit not only Egypt but the Levant as well. The Levant is a geographical term referring to the area in which the modern-day states of Syria, Lebanon, Jordan, and Israel, including the West Bank and Gaza Strip, are located. Eventually Jacob and his sons ran out of food and they all had to purchase some food from somewhere or starve. They were pretty wealthy in animals and land but they didn't have sufficient food or grain. So the ten sons went to Egypt to buy food from the vizier, not knowing it was their youngest brother with whom they were negotiating a purchase.

Joseph immediately recognized his brothers but did not immediately reveal his identity to them. Eventually, when all eleven of them come to Egypt, he convinces them of who he really is, and he tells his brothers that they must confess to their father Jacob that they had lied and sold Joseph into slavery and that their brother was really still alive. So then, all of the family moved from the area of modern-day Israel to Egypt. The family had been living in the land that God promised to give to Abraham and to his descendants forever. When moving to Egypt, they gave up that land. In fact, they would live in Egypt for about 400 years according to the Bible.

During the first part of that time period in Egypt, everything is great and wonderful. They enjoy the patronage of the pharaohs, they enjoy the goodwill of the people, and they are settled in the northeastern delta region, which was perfect for farming and pastoral vocations. But eventually a new dynasty, the eighteenth dynasty, arose to power in Egypt. The eighteenth dynasty in Egypt was a native Egyptian dynasty from a long distance south of the delta area. They did not trust the sons of Jacob who now had become very numerous and potentially powerful. As a result, the new dynastic leaders eventually decided that the way to handle the situation of the Israelites was to prevent them from being able to participate in all of the good, the advantages, and the fruitfulness of Egypt. Essentially, in other words, to enslave them, although the nature of their slavery is something one must be careful to understand, because they were *not* slaves in the sense of the old American South. They were slaves more in the sense that they were builders, employees, and household servants, but they were also restricted in what they could do and did not enjoy the opportunities, for instance, to participate in wars alongside the Egyptians, and in the wealth that successful wars meant for the fighters as they looted the cities of the defeated.

If Israelites participated in war, the eighteenth dynasty was afraid they would join with Egypt's enemies and turn and attack and kill the Egyptians, and take what they had. So the Israelites couldn't go out to war, which meant that they couldn't enjoy themselves and participate the spoils of warfare—meaning that they essentially became second- and then third- and then fourth-class citizens in Egypt. Thus, compared with the Egyptians, the Israelites found themselves further and further down the economic and social scale. They felt themselves constantly going backward. The Israelites became so depressed by their situation that they began complaining. If one looks at the Bible, it just simply says that they called out (complained) and their cry rose up to God (i.e., the God of their ancestor Abraham). It does not say that they called out to God. They just cried out, and God took the initiative and began the process of rescuing them from this particular situation, because, according to the Bible, they were children of Abraham. And this initiative to rescue them was done through one of the children of Levite—a person by the name of Moses.

MOSES, EXODUS, AND THE FIRST FORMATIVE STATE

Moses spends the first forty years of his life, through a particular incident that occurs shortly after his birth, being raised in the household of pharaoh. He is raised to be one of the commanding generals of pharaoh's army—one of the leaders of Egypt; only he seems to have been kept aware of his Israelite roots through the work of his mother, who had been his wet nurse and eventually his nanny. At the age of forty, according to the Bible, Moses was out inspecting a building project when he saw an Egyptian overseer at the building site disciplining a couple of Israelites for something that they had done. The overseer was disciplining them extra harshly and Moses took the overseer aside and killed him. The next day Moses was out, and he saw some Israelites arguing. As he sought to intervene, they asked him if he would kill them like he did the overseer. Realizing his deed had become common knowledge, Moses fled from Egypt knowing that for having killed the overseer he himself would be killed.

The next forty years of Moses' life were spent as a shepherd in the Sinai wilderness. There he married and fathered some children. After forty years, he has a particular spiritual experience where, according to the Bible, he encountered God in a burning bush. Sent back to Egypt to rescue the Israelites from their oppression, through a series of ten different events, God demonstrated his power over the Egyptian gods until finally pharaoh decided to release the Israelites—their cattle, their children, their wives, their belongings—and, in fact, allow them to take anything from the Egyptians and leave Egypt. The final event that convinced pharaoh to release the Israelites is the event known as the Passover. According to the Bible, on the night of Passover, an angel of death went through all the land of Egypt and every house that had not been prepared—the preparation was to take the blood of a lamb and to place it on the door post and the lintel of the house—the firstborn was killed by this angel of death.

Only the Israelites were instructed what to do and so were spared from this catastrophe. Once released, they left Egypt. There was the normal route used by traders which would go back to the land that God had, according to the Bible, promised Abraham and his descendants. Unfortunately, this was also the way that the Egyptians would go if they changed their minds and followed the Israelites. So instead, they turned south to where there is a body of water separating Egypt from the Sinai Peninsula. In a miraculous event, the water divided and the Israelites passed through on a land bridge of sorts to the other side of the body of water. Then once the Israelites passed through as the Egyptian army pursued them to the other side, the water began to close across the land bridge. The Egyptians fled back, but most of them drowned in the sea dividing Egypt from the Sinai Peninsula.

* * *

5 When the king of Egypt was told that the people had fled, the minds of Pharaoh and his officials were changed toward the people, and they said, "What have we done, letting Israel leave our service?" [6]So he had his chariot made ready, and took his army with him; [7]he took six hundred picked chariots and all the other chariots of Egypt with officers over all of them. [8]The LORD hardened the heart of Pharaoh King of Egypt and he pursued the Israelites, who were going out boldly. [9]The Egyptians pursued them, all Pharaoh's horses and chariots, his chariot drivers and his army; they overtook them camped by the sea, by Pi-hahiroth, in front of Baal-zephon.

10 As Pharaoh drew near, the Israelites looked back, and there were the Egyptians advancing on them. In great fear the Israelites cried out to the LORD.

15 Then the LORD said to Moses, "Why do you cry out to me? Tell the Israelites to go forward. [16]But you lift up your staff, and stretch out your hand over the sea and divide it, that the Israelites may go into the sea on dry ground. [17]Then I will harden the hearts of the Egyptians so that they will go in after them; and so I will gain glory for myself over Pharaoh and all his army, his chariots, and his chariot drivers. [18]And the Egyptians shall know that I am the LORD when I have gained glory for myself over Pharaoh, his chariots, and his chariot drivers."

19 The angel of GOD who was going before the Israelite army moved and went behind them, and the pillar of cloud moved from in front of them and took its place behind them. [20]It came between the army of Egypt and the army of Israel. And so the cloud was there with the darkness, and it lit up the night; one did not come near the other all night.

21 Then Moses stretched out his hand over the sea. The LORD drove the sea back by a strong east wind all night, and turned the sea into dry land; and the waters were divided. [22]The Israelites went into the sea on dry ground, the waters forming a wall for them on their right and on their left. [23]The Egyptians pursued, and went into the sea after them, all of Pharaoh's horses, chariots, and chariot drivers. [24]At the morning watch the LORD in the pillar of fire and cloud looked down upon the Egyptian army, and threw the Egyptian army into panic. [25]He clogged their chariot wheels so that they turned with difficulty. The Egyptians said, "Let us flee from the Israelites, for the LORD is fighting for them against Egypt."

26 Then the LORD said to Moses, "Stretch out your hand over the sea, so that the water may come back upon the Egyptians, upon their chariots and chariot drivers." [27]So Moses stretched out his hand over the sea, and at dawn the sea returned to its normal depth. As the Egyptians fled before it, the LORD tossed the Egyptians into the sea. [28]The waters returned and covered the chariots and the chariot drivers, the entire army of Pharaoh that had followed them into the sea; not one of them remained. [29]But the Israelites walked on dry ground through the sea, the waters forming a wall for them on their right and on their left.

* * *

The Bible says nothing about what happens to Egypt afterward, but focuses on the experiences of the Israelites in the Sinai desert. There the Israelites took a circuitous path for a year until coming to the place where Moses had his experience at the burning bush. This place was the beginning of the first formative stage in the development of Judaism as, through Moses, they are given a law. A part of this law is what is generally called the Ten Commandments. However, the law that they are given is much more than just the Ten Commandments. The law that they are given is also a whole structure of legal and civil and criminal code by which the people are to live.

According to the Bible, it was not just Israelites that left Egypt; what is called a "mixed multitude" left Egypt. It is known from Egyptian historical sources that there were Ethiopians, Libyans, Philistines, Israelites, and probably others all of whom were living with Egyptians in Egypt. Likely some from these other groups had seen what was happening in Egypt and gone to live with the Israelites, who were not experiencing the calamities that were affecting the rest of Egypt. It is logical to assume that some members of these different groups also joined in the departure from Egypt. However, because of their diversity, they would have had radically different traditions, cultures, and backgrounds than did the Israelites. What the law provided was a religious, civil, moral, and criminal structure for all the people who were together under the leadership of Moses. Thus, when the Israelites went out of Egypt into the Sinai Peninsula, these other people were also among them, and eventually intermarried with them. What this law did was to unite them together into a single united group of people, which were known thereafter as Israelites. At the same time, the law became the foundation of their common civil and religious life and practice.

* * *

20 Then GOD spoke all these words: ²I am the LORD your GOD, who brought you out of the land of Egypt, out of the house of slavery; ³you shall have no other gods before me.

4 You shall not make for yourself an idol, whether in the form of anything that is in heaven above, or that is on the earth beneath, or that is in the water under the earth. ⁵You shall not bow down to them or worship them; for I the LORD your GOD am a jealous GOD, punishing children for the iniquity of parents, to the third and the fourth generation of those who reject me, ⁶but showing steadfast love to the thousandth generation of those who love me and keep my commandments. ⁷You shall not make wrongful use of the name of the LORD your GOD, for the LORD will not acquit anyone who misuses his name.

8 Remember the Sabbath day, and keep it holy. ⁹Six days you shall labor and do all your work. ¹⁰But the seventh day is a Sabbath to the LORD your GOD; you shall not do any work—you, your son or your daughter, your male or female slave, your livestock, or the alien resident in your towns. ¹¹For in six days the LORD made heaven and earth, the sea, and all that is in them, but rested the seventh day; therefore the LORD blessed the Sabbath day and consecrated it.

12 Honor your father and your mother, so that your days may be long in the land that the LORD your GOD is giving you.

13 You shall not murder.

14 You shall not commit adultery. ¹⁵You shall not steal.

16 You shall not bear false witness against your neighbor.

17 You shall not covet your neighbor's house; you shall not covet your neighbor's wife, or male or female slave, or ox, or donkey, or anything that belongs to your neighbor.

18 When all the people witnessed the thunder and lightning, the sound of the trumpet, and the mountain smoking, they were afraid and trembled and stood at a distance, 19and said to Moses, "You speak to us, and we will listen; but do not let GOD speak to us, or we will die." 20Moses said to the people, "Do not be afraid; for GOD has come only to test you and to put the fear of him upon you so that you do not sin." ²¹Then the people stood at a distance, while Moses drew near to the thick darkness where GOD was.

* * *

There were actually three things that developed in the early religious tradition while at Mt. Sinai. The first was the law mentioned above. Then, a priesthood was established, drawn from the family of Levi and Aaron. The Levites were identified as those who would be responsible for the general maintenance and care of the items used in religious rituals. The family of Aaron, brother of Moses and descendant of Levi, was designated the family out of which priests would come. The role of the priests was to actually perform the religious rituals established under the law. The third thing that developed at Mt. Sinai was the creation and erection of a portable center for religious rituals called a Tabernacle. Based on a design said to have been revealed by their God, it became the focal point for religious rituals for the Israelite people. Later, it would be replaced by a permanent structure, a Temple, which would be erected at the city of Jerusalem.

Prior to the Sinai experience a very important ritual of the Jewish faith, Passover, had been instituted. To this day, Passover is the most important religious ceremony in the Jewish religious calendar. It is a time when all pause to remember the departure from Egypt as a result of their God's intervention and to celebrate their being set apart by that God as His people. The law is likewise important as the basis upon which Jewish religious practice is understood. At this point in the life of Israel, the law was barely developed, but during the ensuing centuries, it would occupy a larger and larger role in their civil and religious life.

After a year spent at Mt. Sinai, the people began to travel toward the "Promised Land" and had the opportunity to enter it in a quick conquest and to take over all the land they would eventually occupy and which would then be called Israel. However, the fear that their God might not be with them prevented them from being willing to do so, and as a result, they spent the next thirty-eight years wandering around in the desert wilderness of Sinai until finally they made their way east of the Jordan River and, under a new leader, Joshua, who had been Moses's chief of staff. Joshua led the people to enter the land—now as a new generation since most of the old generation that left Egypt died during that thirty-eight years. They crossed the Jordan River and began a conquest of the territory, which scholars estimate probably took about seven years.

SETTLEMENT, KINGSHIP, AND THE SPLIT

Having more or less subdued the land, they had to establish and maintain a claim to it. To do this, the land was subdivided into twelve territories: one region for each tribe, based on the size of each tribe. Each was then to go to its assigned area and establish full control in their area. They did not do a very good job of establishing their control, however, and for the next approximately 300 years, they went through major periods of time when they would lose control of the cities and be forced to live in the surrounding area only. The people to whom control was lost were those who previously ruled the land, and whom they were to displace. This period is known as the period of the Judges.

At the conclusion of the Judges period, after about 300 years, the Israelites began to compare themselves with other nations. They realized that they had developed an unhealthy pattern in which they would gain land under a strong Judge, then lose the same land again. They would gain strength under a good Judge, and then lose that strength. However, all the nations around them had kings, and the Israelites thought that the strength of their enemies was because they had kings. As a result, the last of their Judges, Samuel, was induced by their insistence to appoint for the people a king. The first king was a descendant of Benjamin, named Saul. Saul's appointment was something of a compromise because he had his good points and his bad points. He allowed himself to get diverted in his attention to ruling by pursuing a strong rival to his throne so that after somewhere between seven and twenty years of his reign, he was killed in battle against the Philistines. The Philistines were part of the people who had attacked Troy in 1250 BCE and later moved to a new home in the Eastern Mediterranean because of a dispute about military prowess back in their home territory of the Greek isles. In Saul's place, his rival, David, eventually became king over all of Israel. David was quite popular with the people, especially with his own tribe—the descendants of Judah—and was also identified as the one of divine choice.

David reigned for forty years. However, during this entire period, the Israelite kingdom was only united in the person of the king and was really two separate, smaller kingdoms: Israel (all the northern tribes) and Judah. As long as both smaller kingdoms were satisfied with the person who was king, they would remain loyal to him. Since, during this time, the king was from Judah, it was natural that Judah would support the king. But if the northern tribes grew dissatisfied, they were able to rebel against the king's leadership and choose their own king. Near the end of his life, David appointed his son, Solomon, to succeed him and made him co-regent. It was David's desire to build a permanent Temple to their God, but he was restricted from doing so, and it was Solomon who would actually build the Temple. He would also expand the control of his kingdom to include all of the land of Jordan, Syria, and Lebanon, as well as all the land of Israel including the region today called the West Bank and the Gaza Strip. Solomon did not appoint his son and successor as co-regent, so after Solomon's death the kingdom split; the northern tribes preferred someone else as their ruler. The exact extent of Solomon's kingdom is not agreed among scholars, some saying it extended to encompass all the area identified above. However, others say maybe only up to Damascus.

After the kingdom was split, the dividing border ran just north of Jerusalem; the northern kingdom continued to be called Israel, while the southern kingdom was called by the name of its largest tribe, Judah. The descendants of David continued to sit on the throne of Judah until the Babylonians destroyed it in 587/6 BCE. However, the northern kingdom had a very different and much less stable experience. They went through something like twelve or fourteen different dynasties (ruling houses) between 925 BCE and 721 BCE. The kingdom was eventually destroyed by the Assyrians in 721 BCE. When this kingdom was destroyed, most of these people were transported by the Assyrians to other locations across the Middle Eastern world. These are sometimes known as the Ten Lost Tribes. They more or less tend to be lost to history. Nevertheless, there was a group of them that moved south and established residences around Jerusalem and more or less assimilated into Judah except for retaining their tribal heritage. Those Israelites living in the north who were not carried away by the Assyrians intermarried with people who were transported by the Assyrians into the area that had been the northern kingdom. Out of those marriages comes a group of people known as the Samaritans. The Samaritans thought of themselves as Jews, but the Jews would never accept them as such, and during the ensuing centuries there would be a lot of strife between these two peoples. There is still a sect of Samaritans living in the region of Nablus in Israel (the West Bank).

When the Babylonians destroyed Jerusalem in 576 BCE, they destroyed the Temple and the city of Jerusalem along with the villages in its surrounding environment.

* * *

The leading people—the descendants of the royal and noble families, the priests, the wealthy people, and the skilled tradesman (in other words all the people except the dirt poor farmers)—were all taken into exile in Babylon where they had to start a new existence. However some Israelites, mostly the poor and people from Judah who lived in the outlying regions, continued to live in the southern kingdom under

Babylonian governorship. This event begins what is known as the Babylonian Exile. The experience at Sinai was the first formative stage in the development of Judaism. The Babylonian Exile would be the second formative event in the development of their religion. It is important, at this point to again emphasize that the account of the Israelites being in and leaving Egypt and going into the land of Israel and establishing their national existence by a conquest of Canaan under Joshua, the rise of the house of David, all of these are questioned by some scholars, and there are alternative theories. However, it is important, before one considers alternative theories, to consider what the religion, itself, believes. After the reign of King David, and to some extent even during his reign, there exists strong historic and physical evidence for the historical accounts found in the Bible. But for the events prior to that time, there are divergences of opinions. For example, among many Jewish scholars who are historians today, the most popular theory seems to be that there were perhaps two exoduses that took place or perhaps it was a group of Israelite slaves that escaped from Egypt. They got together in the Sinai region, and there they made a political alliance with political dissidents in the area. Following this agreement, all of these together overthrew the city-states in the region of Israel, established their own dominance, and then formed a coalition held together by a religious tradition they created. While there are a lot of others theories, as well, it is not really necessary to go into them rather only be aware that they exist.

Before continuing with the changes occurred in the Israelite religion during the Babylonian Captivity, which was the next formative stage in the development of Judaism, it is important to consider a particular promise that Israel's God is said to have made to King David. According to the Bible, God promised to David that one of his sons would be the one to create a permanent religious center/Temple, and that he would always have a descendant sit on the throne in Jerusalem, so long as the kingdom existed—something like an eternal dynasty. In the Jewish perspective, these two ideas are considered distinct, the former being fulfilled by the historical actions of Solomon. The latter is more problematic since the physical kingdom did not persist. However, during the Babylonian Captivity, the prophets and the people envisioned a revived kingdom in the future, during which time a descendant of David would again sit on the throne. This descendant would be called the Messiah, and the hopes of many Israelites/Jews began to turn toward that future day when the Messiah would arise and rule the Jewish/Israelite kingdom from Jerusalem and enjoy the prominence and prosperity Israel popularly remembered under the rule of David. Christianity also has developed an understanding of these same ideas, but Christians see these two concepts—the one to build the Temple and the one to rule—merged together into a single person, and that eternal occupant is also the son of David, Jesus. This Messianic expectation, though understood differently by Jews and Christians, plays an important role in the development of both faiths during the first century CE.

THE BABYLONIAN EXILE AND THE SECOND FORMATIVE STAGE

The Babylonian Exile marks a major transition in Israelite/Jewish religious and self-understanding. A segment of Old Testament scholarship asserts that it was not until the Babylonian Exile that much of the Hebrew Bible was fully compiled and written down. That idea is less and less popular today as new discoveries and reassessment of former scholarship continues to challenge this previous idea concerning authorship of the Hebrew Bible. Many scholars today accept that at least during the time of David, if not before, major segments of the Hebrew Bible had been written down. Conservative scholars say it was written down a long time before that, almost contemporary with the event. But many, perhaps most, scholars today recognize at least large segments of the Hebrew Bible as having been written down at least during the time of David and Solomon rather than during the Babylonian Exile. In any event, the Babylonian Exile represents a monumental transformation for the development of Judaism, which may for the first time properly be called Judaism. This is because of the ethnic shifts which occurred after the fall of the northern kingdom, which left the only remaining kingdom of the Israelites as the kingdom of Judah. The people of that kingdom were Judahites, which was apparently shortened to Jew (i.e., Judah), and their faith was then that of the earlier Israelite period. With the transformations during the exile, the faith of the "Jews" becomes "Judaism."

Prior to the exile, there were several important features to the faith of the people: the land, the Temple, the city of Jerusalem, and their ethnic and religiocultural identity as the people of their God. However the loss of the land meant they were physically separated from the place where they believed their God was Lord (an idea common in the ancient world that a divinity was lord over only certain territory, and if separated from that territory, the people would also be separated from their divinity). The loss did not end there, however. With no Temple meant no sacrifices, and with no sacrifices, there was no relationship with their God. In fact, the loss of Jerusalem, and all of these aspects of their identity meant both estrangement from their God and that their whole Jewish identity was in question.

In response to the situation, and perhaps because their exile did not actually happen in a single event but in stages over a period of fifteen or more years, leaders among the people and the priests began to reform the notion of Jewishness and the practice of their religious faith. Through the prophets, it was revealed that their God was with them, even in Babylon, meaning that a relationship was still possible, and that retaining their own identity was a meaningful act. The new approach did not substitute for the Temple, etc., as such, but offered an alternative approach for those not physically located in the land they believed their God had promised to them. The primary components of the new approach included the Jewish law and education therein to keep pure and alive the heritage and traditions; prayer, which was perceived as a substitute for sacrifice; and the local meeting center, the synagogue (actually this word is a later Greek word for their meeting houses), which most scholars believe began to develop at this time. It is possible that the synagogues might have had some precursors back in the land of Israel, but the exile is the first known emergence of the synagogue. The synagogue, in fact, became the center of their ethnic and religious life. Temple rituals were not carried out at the synagogue but rather this was the place where the people, especially the children, were taught and where the people prayed together. It was also the community center and meeting place for the community. Finally, it was also a hostel, or lodging place, where Jews traveling through the area might find lodging rather than in secular locations less suited to their traditional religious practices.

One of the principle aspects of Law involved the laws regarding keeping of the Sabbath. Not only would this become an extremely important element of developing Judaism, but the laws of the Sabbath would also be important in the beginning of the Christian period. The Sabbath was a day of rest and spiritual activity and reflection on the seventh day of the week. For the Jewish tradition, that day of rest takes place on Friday night through Saturday at sundown. In the Israelite/Jewish tradition, their days are measured from sundown of one day until sundown the following day. The Sabbath became representative of the enormous importance that is now assigned to obedience to the Jewish law. By the end of the Babylonian Exile, then, some of the most fundamental elements of Judaism as it exists to this day emerged in not only Jewish practice but Jewish self-understanding. In fact, a second, portable approach to the Jewish religion was established. This portable approach would allow the Jewish people to spread far across the ancient world and yet feel they were maintaining an essential connectedness to their God, their religious traditions, and one another.

In 539 BCE, the Persians defeated the Babylonians and took the city and kingdom of Babylon. Three years later in 536 BCE, the Persians issued what is known as the Law of Return. What it meant for the Jews and other displaced peoples dating to the Assyrian conquests was that they were allowed, with Persian patronage (the Persians would actually pay the expenses and provide the supplies), to return to their ancient traditional homelands, rebuild their Temples, rebuild their cities, and restore their ethnic identities and ways of life. Politically, they would still be provinces of Persia, but they could restore their national and ethnic life. Over the next hundred years, about 50,000 Jews went back. The remainder continued to live in Babylon or wherever they had been scattered. In Jerusalem, the people eventually rebuilt the Temple and the city, and with great effort tried to reestablish their lives and Jewish identities along the line of Jewish faith and practice that had existed before the exile. So the result was two centers of Jewish communities: Jerusalem and Babylon. Correspondingly, there were two approaches to Jewish faith and practice that would begin to exist side by side: the older, preexilic tradition centered around the land and the Temple with its services, and the newer, portable tradition, which developed during the exile.

In addition to the two principle communities, the effect of the Assyrian invasions, the Babylonian invasions, and the Babylonian Exile had the impact of dispersing Jews all around the ancient world generally, and specifically around the Mediterranean world. There was a large community in Alexandria, Egypt. There were Jews who would eventually be found in Greek city-states. By the time of the New Testament period, there was a substantial community of Jews in Rome as well as throughout ancient Turkey (called Asia Minor at the time). Eventually, there were also Jews all across North Africa. This is really a third group of Jews, the Diaspora, which was made possible through the development of the portable form of Judaism, which developed during the exile.

Together, these three groups form the focus of what occurs in Judaism during the time that is sometimes called the intertestamental period—between the Old Testament and the New Testament. In Babylon, by and large, life continued for the Jews there just as it always had. In terms of conquest, military action, and things like that, the Jews in Babylon were more or less shielded. There was only one major period of conquest that they endured, which involved the Greeks and their Persian enemies. The Jews of Babylon maintained contact with Jerusalem. But in matters of religious interpretation and practice, they more or less gave deference to Jerusalem. These Babylonian Jews can't be written out of Jewish history, but they have an entirely different history. However, because of the more shielded nature of their world, it is the experience of the Jews in the West that is the primary source out of which modern Judaism developed.

POSTEXILIC LIFE UNDER GREEKS AND ROMANS

In the Diaspora as, well as in the Eastern Mediterranean region and in Jerusalem, there came one conquest after another. From 536–332 BCE, the Jews in the West were under Persian control, which was ended with the conquests of Alexander the Great. From 333 until 201 BCE, the Jews living in the ancient land of Israel as well as across North Africa were under the control of the one Greek ruler, Ptolemy, and his descendants. Those living north of the Mediterranean and north of Ancient Israel were under a different Greek ruler, Seleucus, and his descendants (either named Seleucus or Antiochus). Four wars were fought in the land of ancient Israel between the Ptolemys and the Seleucids for control of that territory (it was central to control over trade traffic between East and West and therefore a prized piece of real estate).

Conversion to Judaism: One of the interesting changes that this period of Greek introduction to Jews stimulated was the issue of conversion. Under the preexilic pattern, a person who was not born Jewish might become a Jew simply by choosing to become so and begin living with the Jewish people, following their lifestyle and observing their religious traditions, including circumcision if the person was male. The Greek were actually impressed with the Jews during the first decades of encounter, perceiving them as philosophers, and the only ones who really tried to live their philosophy. As a result, some Greek eventually sought to become Jewish. However, the Jewish practice for receiving converts was not particularly satisfying to the Greek mind. In their mystery religions, conversion included certain rituals, including baptism (with water, milk, or oil, or perhaps even blood, depending on the mystery) and instruction in the religion, and the Jewish leaders apparently began to use a similar procedure to receive converts. The person would be circumcised if male, begin instruction in Jewish traditions and practices, undergo a ritual baptism (at which time the person was said to be "born again"), and at the conclusion of the process, if appropriate, present an offering at the Temple in Jerusalem. The interest among non-Jews in becoming Jewish eventuated in a very strong evangelical momentum among some Jewish sects until after 135 CE. While conversion is deemphasized in Judaism today, there is still a distinct procedure, drawn from earlier patterns, which is used. Perhaps the most significant aspect in modern times is the requirement that the prospective convert be officially discouraged at least three times over a period of two years. If after that the person still desires to convert, then the process is begun.

After 201 BCE, the land of ancient Israel, the center for Jews in the West, came under control of the Seleucid rulers. In 167 BCE, Antiochus IV Epiphanes became so enraged with the difficulties in handling the Jews that to completely extinguish it he essentially outlawed Judaism altogether. He went so far as to go to the rebuilt temple in Jerusalem and sacrifice a female pig on the altar to Israel's God in the Temple area. Then he sent soldiers to every town and every village and, at the point of a sword, required that they burn incense to one of the Greek gods in violation of their Jewishness. In 167 BCE, a family of priestly descent refused to do the sacrifice demanded by Antiochus's soldiers. They not only refused to do it but they took a sword away from one of the Greek guards and began killing all of the Greek soldiers in their village of Modiin. They also killed those in the community that were willing to make the sacrifices that the Greek soldiers demanded. They then fled to the nearby hills where they made a united effort to drive the Seleucids out of the land and free it and make it independent. This revolt is known as the Maccabean Revolt.

The Maccabean Revolt: The intense phase of the Maccabean Revolt goes from 167 to 164 BCE. In December 164 BCE, the land was, for all intents and purposes, independent of Greek control. At that time, the Temple in Jerusalem was cleansed and the worship of the Jewish God was again instituted there. The independence became official in 142 BCE, beginning the period known as the Hasmonean period. The Maccabean Revolt continues to be celebrated in Jewish tradition during the festival of *Chanukah*, which looks back to the successful revolt in 164 BCE, after which the temple was cleansed and the Jewish worship services were restored. This independent Jewish kingdom remained independent until 63 BCE. In 63 BCE, Rome appeared at Jerusalem as a patron ruler of the traditional Israelite territory, but they do not incorporate the region formally into the Roman Republic. Instead, the Roman general Pompey installs Antipater, the father of Herod the Great as a kind of prime minister for the Jewish people in the region around Jerusalem. In 37 BCE, Rome made Herod the Great king of the Jews, giving him the traditional area of Israel as his kingdom. He was actually appointed king in 40 BCE but would only succeed in capturing Jerusalem, with Roman help, in 37 BCE, at which time he actually began to reign.

The Rise of Interest Groups: During the years of domination by the Persian and Greek empires, a complex web of political and religious loyalties developed among the Jews, particularly those living in the traditional land of ancient Israel. Some supported the old Persian rulers, while others were glad for the new freedoms they felt they had under the Ptolemies of Egypt. Later, there were those who were glad to be rid of the Ptolemies and under the Seleucid rulers of Syria. Others just wanted to be left alone by everyone, and then there were those whose main focus was on the observance of the religious traditions—either the preexilic or postexilic. The events leading up to the Maccabean Revolt and during the revolt itself combined to produce a number of different, defined political parties among the Jews living in their ancient land, who at the same time had a strong religious component to their politics. Those who solely sought to focus on religious observance, the Hassidim, continued throughout the period.

The rise of the Hasmonean family to control the political and to some extent religious fortunes of the Jews living in their traditional homeland seems to have resulted in a major schism among the priests. Since the time of King David, one family had been the source of all the high priests who served at the Temple in Jerusalem. This was the family of Zadok. Under the reign of Antiochus IV Epiphanes, this hold by the family of Zadok was broken due to the Seleucid king's interference. However, the Hasmonean family was descended from Aaron as well, and therefore also qualified to serve as, and provide sons to serve as, high priest. Thus, with the cleansing of the Temple in 164 BCE, the Hasmonean family began to serve in the role of high priest. And with the successful conclusion of the Revolt in 142 BCE, a kind of theocracy was established in which the de facto ruler of the people was also the high priest. In the opinion of scholars, the priesthood experienced a severe difference of opinion over this matter, some remaining in Jerusalem and its surrounding region, but supporting the Zadokite high priesthood, others giving up and withdrawing to a remote area near the Dead Sea to seek a purification of their Jewishness, and their traditions, which could not be had with the current high priesthood, and others remained supportive of the Hasmonean family's role in control of the high priesthood.

It is believed that those who supported the Zadokite family became the persons later known as Sadducees. Those who withdrew are thought to have been the Essenes. The Essenes seem to have established some sort of religious center at the northwestern corner of the Dead Sea, at a site today called Qumran. This may have served as some kind of a retreat center for their adherents since there were also Essenes to be found in most of the cities and towns throughout the region. Part of their activities seems to have included copying of religious texts, some of which were discovered in 1947 and the years following, known as the Dead Sea Scrolls. These date from 200 BCE to about 70 CE, and include copies of all of the books of the Hebrew Bible except the book of Esther. These texts predate all previously known texts by approximately 1,000 years, and demonstrate the accuracy of the later texts. In response to assertions sometimes made that the texts were changed during the period between 100 and 800 AD (as the Christian Church developed and spread, and as Islam arose and spread), these demonstrate that, in fact, virtually no changes (and none of any significance) occurred during this entire time period.

One other important political/religious party developed during this period, which was called the Pharisees. These may have come out of the *Hassidim* (a sect of orthodox Jews who follow the Mosaic Law strictly), since their religious focus was on the faithfulness of Jewish Law and practice, and the correct observance of these traditions. Alongside the traditional scriptures, there developed an Oral scripture which, they claimed, dated back to Moses and which helped to explain and support the observance of the Jewish Law and traditions according to the understanding of the Pharisees. By 135 BCE, all of these different sects were clearly defined and referred to in writings from the time. While the Essenes had withdrawn, the other two parties sought to influence the political process and so competed with one another for the support and influence of the Hasmonean high priestly rulers. Initially, the Sadducees were the ones with the upper hand in this competition, but by 77 BCE, that was changing due to violence between the two parties. The upper hand then went to the Pharisees, but the violence between them continued.

Despite all of the political drama, the kingdom of the Hasmoneans spread rapidly, first to the south where the Idumeans (ancient Edomites) had moved into the Negev and Philistine coastal area after the Babylonian captivity, then north to subdue the Samaritans, and eventually the region of Galilee and then the Golan Heights. The Idumeans were forcibly converted to Judaism, but the Samaritans were left alone as a subject people under Jewish control. By 64 BCE, the Hasmonean kingdom had enlarged to encompass virtually all the territory west of the Jordan River, which had been part of the kingdom under King David. But inwardly the government had become religiously and morally corrupted, and the political/religious parties with it. By 64 BCE, the two heirs to the Hasmonean throne were fighting between themselves for control. When Rome defeated the last remnant of the Seleucid kingdom, both brothers sent delegations to the Roman General Pompey to ask his assistance in accrediting the new ruler. After some time of thought, Pompey decided that one should be the high priest and the other the king, all as a puppet kingdom under Roman authority. The brother designated to be the high priest was not satisfied and so returned to Jerusalem to try and take everything for himself, causing Rome to lay siege to Jerusalem in 63 BCE, and exile that brother, leaving the other brother in charge of everything.

Though the Hasmonean family retained the throne and high priesthood for the time, true authority was placed in Roman hands, and the real power was invested in a man named Antipater, who was of Idumean descent (rather than traditional Jewish lineage). Antipater understood the Roman ways, and successfully courted political friendship with Rome. In 49 BCE, when Julius Caesar was pursing Pompey toward Egypt, Antipater offered help to Caesar's forces and Judaism was granted official Roman recognition as a legitimate religion ("*Religio Licta*") under Roman Law. This meant that even if the Romans did not understand nor follow Judaism, they had no legal basis to afflict, persecute, or disrupt Jewish services and activities, and they were safe in their communal enclaves. Antipater also installed his two sons as governors over Jewish provinces in the Hasmonean kingdom, one of whom was Herod, who governed Galilee.

Another important development during this period of time was the rise of a revolutionary underground within the Hasmonean kingdom. Some saw what was happening with Rome and Antipater as leading to a violation of Jewish independence, which had existed for the previous century or so. These people resisted the rulership established by Rome and Antipater, sometimes quite openly. In Galilee, one of Herod's successful campaigns at the beginning of his political career was to flush out and eliminate some of these revolutionaries. He did not eliminate the revolutionary spirit from Galilee, which would arise again and again until finally crushed by Rome in 68 CE. The situation also caused many common people, and perhaps even some of the Pharisees, to begin looking at what was happening as somehow preparing the situation for the coming of the Messiah they were hoping would arise since the days in Babylon. In fact, the book of Daniel even seemed to suggest that the right timing had come for this event. As a result, during the reign of Herod, an expectation of imminent appearance of their Messiah was widespread among the common people who were religiously observant.

King Herod: The death of Julius Caesar occurred in 44 BCE, and Antipater was assassinated the following year, leading to an attempt to overthrow the Hasmonean kingdom sanctioned by Rome. After six years of uncertainty, Antipater's son, Herod, named as king of the Jews by the Roman Senate, succeeded in capturing the city of Jerusalem and the territory of the former Hasmonean kingdom.

Though ruling with tyrannical methods, he brought peace, stability, and prosperity to the region, and his close association with Mark Antony, and later with Augustus Caesar, brought favor upon himself and the kingdom over which he ruled. Nevertheless, the Messianic hope flourished, perhaps helped by the continuing presence of Rome and the fact that Herod was neither from Jewish lineage, nor a true Hasmonean (he had married a Hasmonean princess). Also, the other religious parties now experienced a severe shock. Previously, one or the other party would provide the legitimacy for the ruler. But for Herod, his sole claim to legitimacy was Rome, and he had no reason to regard with the Pharisees or the Sadducees as political partners with him. And the Essenes, who were still estranged, offered no contest to him (and may even have collaborated with him). The Sadducees and Pharisees, then, became solely religious parties in character. The Sadducees were mostly of the priestly families, concerned with the Temple and its services, and because it was the preexilic tradition, which more strongly focused on the Temple, this was the tradition with which they can be most closely identified. The Pharisees seem to have been associated with the exilic and postexilic tradition centered around the synagogue. Their teachers, Rabbis, would dominate the weekly services, and their interpretation of the Jewish Law, widely taught by them, seems to have dominated the understanding and daily practice of Judaism—both in the traditional land of Israel, and throughout the Jewish world, even across the Roman empire and into the East. Finally, a new party, of revolutionaries, was beginning to emerge during this period, which a century later would lead to war with Rome and total collapse of the Jewish political presence in the region until last century.

It was near the end of the reign of Herod the Great that Jesus of Nazareth was born. At the time that Jesus was born, Herod the Great was harboring an enormous paranoia of anyone that might try to take his place, especially before he died. This is the reason for the otherwise extreme actions recorded of Herod regarding Jesus's birth. Nevertheless, what makes Jesus important as far as the study of Judaism and the Jewish world is concerned, is that Jesus was a Jew. He was raised in a Jewish home. He was educated in the synagogue. He was educated in all of the traditions of Judaism. He was born a Jew, lived a thoroughly Jewish life, and died a Jew. However, what also makes Him unique is the different perspective on Judaism that Jesus presented, which was radically different in emphasis than was current among the religious leaders of his day. The religious leaders of Jesus' day focused primarily on the Law, the Sabbath, and the traditions. Now, if a different emphasis had been all that Jesus did, he probably would have just been written off by the Jewish world as somebody who just had a different perspective. Jesus's distant cousin, John (called "the Baptist") had a different perspective as well. And Jesus might have just been written off like John. But, unlike John, Jesus also claimed to be God. We will discuss more concerning Jesus and the concepts of Christianity separately, but it is necessary to see how completely Christianity emerges out of Judaism rather than viewing its beginning as somehow a radically separate and distinct religious tradition.

LITERARY WORKS, REVOLTS, AND SECTS

Revolts and the Destruction of the Temple: After Herod's death, his kingdom was divided into thirds. His son Archelaus received from Rome the areas of Judea, including Jerusalem and Samaria. Another son, Herod Phillip, received the area in what is today called the Golan Heights. Then, a third son, Antipas, received Galilee and a region east of the Jordan River known then as Perea. Archelaus was a lousy administrator, and so in 7 AD he was deposed, and Rome began sending their own representatives, whom they called *Praetors*, to rule over Judea and Samaria. The preferred site of residence for these Praetors was a city called Caesarea. This city was a Roman-style city that Herod the Great had built to provide a port for import and export. In typical Herodian fashion, it was the second largest port in the ancient Roman world. The significance of Caesarea, however, for the Jews was that under the Praetors the political center shifted, and a special ruling council, the **Sanhedrin**, controlled the Jewish affairs under Roman oversight. The Sanhedrin was composed

Ultra-Orthodox man praying

©Chris Parypa Photography/Shutterstock.com

mostly of **Sadducees**, with a few **Pharisees**, meaning that to some moderate degree, the Sadducees and the Pharisees regained a measure of political importance, especially the Sadducees, because of their domination of affairs in Jerusalem. At the time Archelaus was deposed, a Roman taxation census was taken, provoking a revolt led by a man named Judah from Galilee. This revolt, though suppressed, only went underground to be revived later in the century in a war that would prove devastating for the Jews of the region. Rome's response to Judah's revolt was to crucify him and one thousand of the insurrectionists, hanging on crosses throughout Judea and Galilee, effectually proclaiming to the people: "Cross Rome, and this is what you get."

After several uncomfortable decades of direct Roman authority over the traditional Jewish homeland, during which time the Roman administration became quite corrupt, another Jewish revolt erupted—this time against Rome—in 66–70 CE. Historically, the revolt was neither extreme, nor lengthy. Rome crushed the revolt in four years, and concluded the entire event by 74 CE. However, for Judaism, the revolt would be more devastating. The most significant consequence was the destruction of the Temple and the city of Jerusalem in 70 CE. This brought to a crushing end any hopes for a renewed, independent kingdom. It also created the context for survival of only the postexilic practice of Judaism as long as the rebuilt Temple existed, but could coexist, even if uncomfortably. But without the Temple, the preexilic traditions and approach to Judaism were again impossible. In addition, for a time, Rome even forbade the Jewish people access to the city of Jerusalem or the area where the Temple had stood. The destruction of the Temple and the city of Jerusalem also undermined all religious and political roles for the Sadducees, and they disappear from the historical record. There is some indication that the surviving Sadducees may have sought refuge around the Sea of Galilee area, have been converted to Christianity, and thereby disappear from the Jewish record.

Prior to this revolt, it seems that Christianity was more or less regarded as a sect of Judaism, even if uncomfortably, perhaps even heretically so. The biggest issue between the Jews and the Christians, actually, was the Christian inclusion of Gentiles among their number, which Judaism strongly resisted. However, beginning with this revolt in 66 CE, in which Christians were substantially absent and nonsupportive, there would begin a decades-long period of growing separation and increasing competition between followers of the two traditions. In the aftermath of the revolt, Rabbis met together in a town called Jamnia, close to the modern city of Tel Aviv, where the process of preserving Judaism yet again began. This constitutes the third major transition in the development of Judaism and initiates the period sometimes referred to as Rabbinic Judaism.

Rabbinic Judaism and the Hebrew Canon: The Rabbis began the process of recording all of the oral tradition of Judaism into what is called the *Mishnah*. They also began preserving other writings and religious legal rulings. Also, traditions to counter assertions by Christians regarding the nature of Jesus's birth and His resurrection began to be circulated widely. Thus, after this first Jewish revolt against Rome, a body of literature that is considered definitive in the Jewish world begins to be developed, and the Jewish and the Christian worlds seemingly "bounce off" each other in their efforts to define themselves.

By 90 CE, the Jews formally identify their canon and scriptures. This was not really a big deal since most of these writings had been in circulation for hundreds of years or more. The oldest may have dated back over a thousand years. However, this point was when what appeared to be the most decisive books out of all the Jewish writing, the ones most important in clarifying and understanding their faith, were established. Those are what are today referred to as the *Taanach* and consist of exactly the same texts as are found in the Protestant versions of the Old Testament. However, in the *Taanach*, the texts are arranged differently, with the result that there are three volumes: the *Torah*, the *Neeviim* (prophets and historical books), and the *Ktaviim* (writings and poetry such as Psalms and Proverbs). The Mishnah preserved the traditions not included in the books of scripture, and additional writings preserved the legal opinions.

Between 70 and 132 CE, there was sporadic persecution by Roman authorities of Jews and Christians for various reasons, though it was not completely clear to the Romans that Judaism and Christianity were developing into separate religious traditions. Then in 132 CE the Bar Kochba (or Bar Kosiba) Revolt, a second revolt against Rome, broke out.

The Bar Kochba Revolt (132–135 CE): This was a major revolt against the Romans by the Jews. It lasted until 135 CE and proved to be even more devastating for the Jews than the first revolt had been. It was also costly to the Romans; some Roman historians even date the beginning fall of Rome to this revolt. Again, during the Bar Kochba Revolt, the Christians did not come to the aid of the Jewish insurgents, even though, still a hundred years after the beginning of the Christian Church, it is estimated that perhaps half of all Christians were from a Jewish tradition. Thus, it seems to be at this time that Judaism and Christianity decisively separated. Following the revolt, the Roman emperor, Hadrian, attempted to suppress the practice of Judaism totally within the Roman Empire. Not only were the Jews banned from Jerusalem, but from all of Judea (the revolt had been mostly fought in the outlying regions of Judea). Across the empire, he had all Jewish scrolls and writings which could be found confiscated and burned. The Jews were forbidden to practice circumcision or celebrate any of their festivals, and they were prevented from assembling together in their synagogues on the Sabbath. Consequently, it was also at this time that Judaism ceased to be evangelical in its practice and began to follow a path focused more on preservation and maintenance of the traditions among those who were Jewish.

©Pavel Bernshtam/Shutterstock.com

Masada fortress and King Herod's palace in Israel Judean desert

JUDAISM IN THE CHRISTIAN, ISLAMIC, AND SECULAR WORLDS

Talmudic Judaism: The following 1,500 years were difficult for Jews in the Western world. In the Mesopotamian Valley region, the Babylonian Jews continue to pursue their vocations, practice their religious traditions, and live their lives more or less undisturbed by the things that took place in the West. Even with the Persian invasions, the rise of Islam, and the Turkic invasions of the area, the Jewish people seem to remain apart from all of these events and be barely affected by them. In the West, however, the immediate persecution under Hadrian was short-lived since he died in 138 CE. The new emperor did not retain the severe policies, and the Jewish people began to live their lives and practice their religion openly and with little interference again. Near the end of the century, the Jewish leaders in Galilee began the process of compiling all of the Jewish writings together into a more succinct form for instruction. This process was completed about 210 CE by Judah ha-Nasi, a leading scholar of the religion at the time. The product of his efforts was the *Talmud*. This is a multi-volume source in which, for every verse on the *Taanach*, all teaching and ruling about that verse are given, all the scholarly arguments and legal opinions involving that verse are recorded. The Talmud became the basis for the understanding and practice of Judaism thereafter (a similar effort was undertaken by the Babylonian Jews, so there are actually two Talmuds, mostly including the same or similar material but drawn from two different geographical regions, so that the one from the West is known as the Palestinian Talmud and the one from the East as the Babylonian Talmud). Into the so-called Middle Ages, there were additions to it as exceptional teachers added material of their own, and theoretically there still could be, though this has not been the case for a long time now.

Judaism under Christian Rome: In the century after the Talmud appeared, Christianity became the popular religion of the Roman Empire, and eventually the official religion of the Empire. By 400 CE, Judaism was the only religion tolerated in the Roman Empire other than Christianity. The result was for Jews to move into communities at the fringes of the Roman Empire where they had a greater measure of freedom. This movement results in substantial communities of Jews forming in the regions now called Spain, Central/Eastern Germany, and Southern Russia, as well as into the Southern Jordanian region as far as into Northern Arabia.

With the rise of Islam, Jews in North Africa and Spain, as well as Southern Jordan and Arabia found themselves cut off from the Jewish communities in the remnants of the Roman world. During peaceful periods, there was communication between these different communities of Jews, but they shared different cultural and political conditions.

Generally speaking, the Islamic regions were more or less tolerant of the Jewish communities, but opportunities for greater cultural involvement in these regions were nonexistent. In the remnants of the Roman world, the Jews found themselves severely restricted in many ways. They were not permitted to own land, and therefore they could not pursue agricultural occupations. Though some pursued skilled trades, eventually these trades became dominated by guilds with very Christian domination. The one place where the Jews were able to prosper was lending money, and the pawn broker occupation became the most common occupation among the Jews. In a culture which was not money-based, the Jews actually provided an extremely important service as the source from which European nobility could borrow money to finance their wars and other activities. The actual reason why the system developed this way was that the Christian Church had ruled that lending money at interest was usury, and was therefore forbidden for Christians. However, the Jews were permitted to make loans at interest since they were not Christians and therefore not governed by a religious law applicable only to Christians. It was from this basis that European banks developed, though eventually the Jews were also crowded out of that role by others.

The experience of persecution and anti-Semitism in Western Europe also seems to stem from the financial role the Jews held in society. Since they made loans and charged interest (often very heavy interest), payment was also expected. When people did not have the money to repay the loan, the easiest way to deal with that was to raid the residence or office of the source of the loan and burn the attesting document. If problems developed, the next best thing was to eliminate the originator of the loan. Sometimes, as occurred during the beginning of the first crusade, whole cities seized the opportunity to settle accounts in this way. As a result, local lords built protected enclaves in many European cities for the Jews since the local lords needed the Jews for their own monetary purposes. These enclaves were known as ghettos. It would not be until the time of the Renaissance and the later Age of Enlightenment during the 1700s that the Jewish people in the West would have free access to the social and cultural world in which they lived. When this access was available, it had profound effects on the faith and practice of Judaism, perhaps provoking a partial fourth transformation.

Judaism Response: As a result of the Renaissance, and especially during the Age of Enlightenment, notions of equality and new ideas of education and science began to circulate. The Jewish people had always preserved a measure of education in their own society because of the role and importance of being able to read the scripture. It was also important to be able to do this because of the financial vocation in which so many were employed. As new universities based on enlightened thinking began to be established, the Jewish people were far more advanced in their educational preparedness for this kind of study than were most Europeans. Thus, Jews were represented in the educational world, and later the vocations that depended on education, in far greater numbers than their actual presence in European society. They were, at an early point, bankers, doctors, lawyers, scientists, engineers, etc. And since many of these occupations provided lucrative incomes, these also rose to dominate social and political roles, all of which also created a significant measure of discomfort among many Europeans about how the Jews were seemingly dominating virtually every aspect of European life. This was especially the case in those European countries in which history had brought many communities of Jews to live.

Education also had a second impact on the Jewish communities of Europe. As a result of the thinking that swept certain social circles in Europe, many Jews found a ready acceptance of many new things. This resulted in a liberalization of thinking on the part of those so affected. In time, a new approach to traditional Judaism emerged in Europe called the **Reform Movement**. This movement sought to reevaluate traditional Jewish practices in light of the new understandings and philosophical ideas of the Enlightenment. Laws concerning food, practices on the Sabbath, and even, eventually the most basic understandings of life and how the scriptures should be viewed changed among those who pursued the Reformed approach to understanding Judaism. Their practice was truly a reformed practice of their Jewishness. Those who did not adopt the Reformed approach were considered **Orthodox**, and some who were extremely observant were known as **Ultra-Orthodox** or even **Hassidim**. In a moderating position between these extremes, yet a third approach to Judaism also developed during the nineteenth century, known as *Conservative*. The theosophical understanding of Judaism among Conservatives was closer to that of Reformed Jewish tradition, but the actual practice of Judaism preserved many of the Orthodox practices.

With the unfolding of anti-Semitic persecution across Europe and Russia during the later nineteenth century, additional forces within Judaism began. Some migrated to the United States seeking a greater measure of freedom in yet another developing land. Others began both hoping and actively working for restoration of a Jewish homeland in the territory of their ancient, traditional homeland in the Middle East. These latter individuals began the movement known as **Zionism**. Under the banner of Zionism, Jews began to return to their traditional homeland. The action was given a boost by World War I, as Britain officially supported the creation of a Jewish homeland in exactly the place where the Jews had originally lived. World War II further stimulated the migration of Jews to that area, and the Holocaust brought support for the Jewish effort, which resulted in the establishment of the state of Israel in 1948. Initially, the migrations into the territory, which again became Israel, was from Jews known as **Ashkenazim**. Whether Reformed, Conservative, or Orthodox, these Jews are from the European and Russian worlds and have been influenced culturally by those worlds. After the formation of the state of Israel, Jews known as **Sephardim** also began moving into Israel. Generally speaking, these are Jews who lived under Muslim rulers. The Sephardim, religiously, share a great degree of common Jewish understanding with the Orthodox among the Ashkenazim. But their cultural practices are closer to those of Muslim traditions than any of the European cultures, and even among Sephardim there are differences whether one came from Africa, Turkey, or the Mesopotamian region.

In Israel, all of these have been brought together creating these difficulties because of the different interpretations of Judaism and because of their customs drawn from widely diverse geographical areas. Additionally, in Israel a new "sect" has emerged, sometimes referred to as **secular Jews**. In actuality, this is not a religious distinction, but an ethnic and cultural distinction. The *secular Jew* is one who is ethnically Jewish, but who rarely, if ever, practices any part of the Jewish traditions, ceremonies, or observances. Nevertheless, there are certain basic aspects of Judaism that all practice to some extent (except perhaps the secular Jews) regardless of their particular emphasis, and of which all these traditions share in common.

FEASTS OR FESTIVALS

The practices and ceremonies of Judaism today can be divided into several categories. On a daily basis, perhaps the most overarching practice is known as kashrut or kosher. This refers to the dietary laws associated with Judaism. While the laws are reasonably extensive, they relate both to the type of foods permissible and to the way in which the foods are prepared. Thus, Judaism forbids the eating of anything from the pig (pork, bacon, ham, etc.) and shellfish (shrimp, clams, scallops, lobster, etc.), but meat from the cow, chicken, deer, sheep, goat, etc., is perfectly permissible. Nevertheless, the cow, sheep, etc., must be slaughtered in a particular way before it can be considered acceptable. In addition, for the observant Jews, including the Conservative sect, it can only be served with certain other foods (nothing dairy), and for the very orthodox, even separate plates and utensils must be used.

Every week, the celebration of the Sabbath is the most visible symbol of Jewish tradition. As in ancient times, there remain many legal constraints regarding the Sabbath, though the observance of these laws depends on the level of orthodoxy one pursues. The Jewish calendar is a lunar one, in which the day begins with sundown and ends with sundown the following day. Most commonly, the observant will attend synagogue services in the evening on Friday, and perhaps again on Saturday morning. The remainder of the day is dedicated to family time and quiet. Saturday evening frequently becomes a time of partying and celebration before the beginning of the week. In the ancient period, synagogue services consisted of prayer and teaching, but in some branches of Judaism, which have been influenced by Western Christian tradition, the synagogue services or something of a modified worship service. Still, the primary purpose is for prayer and teaching, while the entire Sabbath experience also includes significant family time together.

Matzo for Passover with Seder with wine on plate

The Jewish tradition follows an annual cycle of religious celebrations, mostly focused on the agricultural cycle in Israel, which was the traditional homeland and the place in which these celebrations were established. The beginning of the Jewish religious calendar is in the spring of the year, usually sometime in March, at the new moon. This follows the celebration of *Pesach* (**Passover**), which is a special evening commemorating the departure from Egypt under Moses. The service is centered around a special ceremonial meal known as a Seder, and the service initiates a weeklong celebration known as the Feast of Unleavened Bread.

This is usually a holiday period in Israel, and elsewhere many Jews may take vacation during this time. The main feature is the proscription in consuming or touching anything with leaven, such as bread. This remembers the swift departure from Egypt before the bread had time to leaven, and the length of time necessary before the dough was again leavened and baked bread would rise. Today, the period ends with a second ceremonial meal. This celebration is actually the high point in the Jewish annual cycle, and misunderstanding of the ceremony has also provoked many vicious rumors about the ceremony in earlier centuries.

After a period of fifty days following Pesach, the festival of **Pentecost** takes place. During the time the Temple was standing, farmers would come to the Temple with the first fruits from their harvests which were presented before their God, after which they would return to the fields and harvest all the remainder for themselves (except for required offerings to the Temple and priesthood). Pentecost concluded the spring cycle of festivals. In the early fall, just after the summer and the summer harvest, a second cycle also occurs. This cycle is sometimes referred to as the High Holy Days. It begins in early to mid-September with the celebration of the civil new year, **Rosh HaShana**. This is mostly a secular holiday with parties and merriment similar to the celebration of the New Year in the Western world. A few days later comes the most sacred day of the year in ancient times and still one of the most important in the Jewish calendar: **Yom Kippur**. In ancient times, this was the day when the high priest would enter the Temple with the blood of a sacrifice by which the people understood that all of their sins against their God over the previous year was then forgiven. Today, with no Temple standing, the day is one of introspection and prayer, observed even by many who tend not to participate in the religion at any other time. A week later, the **Feast of Tabernacles (Booths)** takes place. These temporary shelters are intended to relive vicariously the experience of the ancestors of the Jews living in the wilderness for forty years after leaving Egypt. In modern times, a special booth is set up made of thatched palm fronds. Within the booth (which may be set up in a synagogue for the entire congregation, or on an individual's balcony or roof) family and invited guests usually eat dinner, and sometimes the children sleep, pretending to be "camping out."

One final celebration in the annual cycle is that of **Chanukah**. This is celebrated in December and was a late addition to the annual cycle, celebrating the successful revolt under the Maccabees. It is not a religious holiday, strictly speaking, but something of a nationalistic holiday, expressing the longing for a restoration of an independent Jewish kingdom.

There are also a couple of celebrations which take place once in a person's life. Every Jewish boy, at the age of eight days, is circumcised according to an ancient ritual, symbolizing his inclusion among the people of Israel. Even among the secular Jews, this ceremony is practiced. At the age of thirteen, the young men experience the ceremony of **Bar Mitzvah**. This is a coming-of-age ceremony, which recognizes the young man, thereafter, as a mature member of the religious community. It is frequently a very extensive and elaborate ceremony in which thousands of dollars may be showered upon the young man as a gift to help him begin his journey of manhood. There is no clear indication of when the ceremony began to be celebrated, but it appears to date back perhaps nearly two thousand years, and the rituals associated with it will vary depending on where the family or community lives. At a very late date, a companion ceremony for young women was begun, perhaps slightly over a century ago. The **Bas/Bat Mitzvah** ceremony is much more sedate and is common only in certain Western countries, or in Jewish communities which have had extensive contact with Western culture and tradition.

There are many other ceremonies that different branches of Judaism celebrate. Perhaps most significant is the role of these ceremonies and celebration within Judaism. For the last two thousand years, it has been that the ceremonies and celebrations were the distinguishing characteristics of the Jewish religious experience. From the Jewish standpoint, it is both the ceremony and the ideas that they represent that are significant religiously. As the people of their God, the Jews perceive themselves already to have a certain relationship with Him. But through the ceremonies they learn, maintain, grow, and benefit in that relationship. By keeping these ceremonies and laws, they also provide something of a witness to the rest of the world concerning their religion and their God.

KEY CONCEPTS

Covenant	Pesach or Passover	Council of Jamnia	Hassidim
Succoth/Feast of Booths	Sabbath	Orthodox Judaism	Sephardim
Mishnah	Reform Judaism	Ashkenazim	Synagogue
Conservative Judaism	Ethical Monotheism	The Holocaust	Secular Jews
Zionism	Esther	Essenes Prophet	
Sanhedrin	Pharisee	Messiah	
Rabbinic Judaism	Rabbi	Palestinian Talmud	
Judah ha-Nasi	Babylonian Talmud	Talmud	

QUESTIONS FOR FURTHER STUDY

1. What is a covenant? Name and describe the types of covenant in Judaism.

2. What was the role of Abraham and David in Judaism, Christianity, and Islam?

3. Explain the role of Moses and Aaron in the formation of early Judaism.

4. Name the Twelve Patriarch and explain the role of the Levites.

5. Explain the Jewish concept of God, salvation, and the afterlife.

6. Name the Jewish rites of passage. Describe any three of them.

7. The Maccabean Revolt and the Hasmonean dynasty was a Jewish liberation movement. Discuss the high and low points of Jewish identity under the Hasmonean dynasty.

8. Discuss the event that led to the separation of the North (Israel) from the South (Judea)

9. Explain the significance of the six major festivals of Judaism.

10. Discuss the contribution of Judaism to world civilization.

Christianity

INTRODUCTION

Studies in Judaism, particularly the ancient or traditional form of Judaism provide the backdrop to Christianity—the creation story and the stories of the Patriarchs and Moses as well as the prophets and the sociopolitical events associated with them are all part of the Christian story. That is to say the Jewish Patriarchs—Abraham, Isaac, and Jacob, the Exodus and place of Moses in Jewish history, the Law, the prophets, the personalities such as Kings David and Solomon, etc., are simply assumed as background out of which the Christian interpretation of faith develops. Thus Christianity has its roots in Judaism and was initially considered a sect like other sects within Judaism. This understanding is focused in the person of Jesus of Nazareth, and then in the life and faith of the early Church.

Jesus was a Jew, born to Jewish parents in the Jewish town of Bethlehem, a few miles south of Jerusalem, and raised in the Jewish town of Nazareth in Galilee. His education and religious tradition was that which young Jewish males received during the second Temple period, and the substance of His message was essentially Jewish but with a different emphasis than that which was common among the religious elite and scholars of His day. As with Judaism, there exists a lot of debate among religious scholars about different aspects of the life and ministry of Jesus, as well as the development of the early Church. Our approach here in studying Christianity will begin with the traditional self-understanding of the Church regarding

1. the life and ministry of Jesus of Nazareth,
2. the life, faith, and development of the early Church,
3. the subsequent expansion and development of the Church in the context of the Roman Empire with which Christianity became firmly associated after 312 CE.

Thus, an overview of Christian development reflects the following sequence:

Until 312 CE	The formation of the Church institution under Rome
After 312 CE	The further defining of Christian thinking and practice
314 CE	Edict of Milan that ended all religious persecution
312–395 CE	Structuring of the Church as a religious institution
395–565 CE	Theological refinement within the Christian Church
565–1053 CE	Gradual political and religious separation of the Church, East and West
1053–1054 CE	The Great Schism—Catholic and Orthodox sects separate
1054–1517 CE	Catholicism reaches its zenith (1215 CE) and begins decline
1517–1570 CE	Waves of Protestant Reformation in the West (Catholic Church)
1570–present	Gradual acceptance of co-existence of multiple denominations in the West
1054–present	Emergence of regional identities in Eastern Christianity

History plays an important role in Christianity as it does in Judaism and Islam, and history must be written, read, or seen from a wider lens—social, cultural, political, and economic, a local event and international or world event. Christianity is understood in the context of history.

NEW TESTAMENT

Chronological Tables of Rulers during New Testament Times

Roman Emperors

27 BCE– 14 CE	Augustus
14–37 CE	Tiberius
37–41 CE	Caligula
41–54 CE	Claudius
54–68 CE	Nero
68–69 CE	Galba; Otho; Vitellius
69–79 CE	Vespasian
79–81 CE	Titus
81–96 CE	Domitian

Herodiun Rulers

37–4 BCE	Herod the Great, king of Jews
4 BCE–6 CE	Archelaus, ethnarch of Judea
4 BCE–39 CE	Herod Antipas, tetrarch of Galilee and Perea
4 BCE–34 CE	Philip, tetrarch of Ituraea, Trachonitis, etc.
37–44 CE	Herod Agrippa I, from 37 to 44 king over the former tetrarchy, and from 41 to 44 over Judea, Galilee, and Perea
53–c. 100 CE	Herod Agrippa II, king over the former tetrarchy of Philip and for 56 (or 61) over parts of Galilee and Perea

Procurators of Judea After the Reign of Archelaus to the Reign of Herod Agrippa

6–8 CE	Coponius
9–12 CE	M. Ambivius
12–15 CE	Annius Rufus
15–26 CE	Valerius Gratus
26–36 CE	Pontius Pilate
37 CE	Marullus
37–41 CE	Herennius Capito

CHRISTIANITY: THE PERSON, LIFE, AND MINISTRY OF JESUS OF NAZARETH

Jesus's relationship to David, Israel's Great King: Jesus descended from David through both His mother's and Joseph's family ancestries. According to the Bible, Israel's God gave certain promises to David regarding an offspring of his that would be the one to create a religious house. He would have a son who would build a temple but then Christians perceive a second aspect of that promise—an offspring who would be, you might say, the eternal occupant on the throne or, said another way, David would always eternally have a successor sitting upon the throne of Israel. In Christian thinking, these two merge together into one, and that eternal occupant is a descendant of David—also the son of David—Jesus. So the Jews interpret this passage and promise as referring to Solomon, and then all of the descendants of Solomon through the several generations until Babylonian exile, whereas Christians interpret this reference as Jesus being referred to in the promise that was given to David.

The city of Bethlehem, The Church of the Nativity of Jesus Christ

Birth and Early Childhood: He would grow up in the typical manner of a Jewish child of His time in Galilee.

Late Childhood: That means that from about the age of three until the age of twelve He went to the synagogue every day where He received religious instruction and began memorizing parts of the Torah. By the time He was twelve, He probably was capable of quoting large portions of the Old Testament from memory in Hebrew. It was at about time that He would be received into full adulthood in the Jewish community, though historians are divided as to whether there was a Bar Mitzvah ceremony that the male child would go through in the first century CE to mark this passage to manhood.

Young Adult: However, by the age of 13, He would ordinarily have ceased His formal religious training at the synagogue and begun to apprentice under His father and the work that His father did. This would ordinarily continue over the next six years, as He learned an occupation. Thus, after about the age of twelve or thirteen, Jesus's primary activity was learning the occupation of Joseph, which was that of a skilled tradesman. The word "carpenter" used in many translations of the New Testament really means a skilled tradesman. This is someone who was skilled in all of the various kinds of trades which included carpentry, leather working, metal-smithing, etc. It is likely that Joseph died before Jesus reached the age of thirty, because there is no mention of Joseph during the years of Jesus's ministry, especially at critical points where one would expect mention if Joseph were still alive.

During most of the years of Jesus's younger life, He lived in a difficult world under the occupation of Roman authority. The Praetor sent by Rome lived on the Mediterranean coast at a city known as Caesarea on-the-sea, close to Mount Carmel. It was a Roman-style city that Herod the Great built, and had a seaport which was second only to Corinth in the ancient world of its day. When Archelaus was deposed, a man from Galilee, known as Judas the Galilean, took offense at the Romans, the Roman gods, and the Roman census. He regarded all of these as an ungodly attempt to impose Roman authority and Gentile rule over God's people. He gathered a group together led a rebellion against the Romans. Rome responded in Rome's usual way. Eventually one thousand of the insurrectionists were crucified and left hanging on crosses around Judea to demonstrate to the people, "Challenge Rome, and this is what you get." This occurred in 8 CE and would certainly have conveyed the very strong sense that anyone accused of insurrection, anyone found guilty of even possibly fomenting a rebellion or anything like that, could expect to be crucified because that was the way that Rome handled that sort of thing. The threat, elsewhere, however, was less since Herod's sons continued to rule until after the years of Jesus's life and ministry. Antipas continued to rule the area of Galilee as well as Perea for decades after his brother Archelaus was deposed—until 36 CE, and likewise, Herod Phillip in the area northeast of the Sea of Galilee.

His Ministry: First, the Initiation: Jesus would continue in the vocation of a skilled tradesman until He was about 30 years of age, in 27 CE, when according to the New Testament, He began an itinerant ministry, which became extremely controversial for the Jewish world of his day. This change of "career" began when Jesus went to the area of Jerusalem and Jericho during the winter of His thirtieth year and was baptized by His cousin, John, called by the people "the Baptist." John had apparently earlier that year gone out to the Jericho region, and he had begun baptizing people in the Jordan River. Baptism was not originally a Christian rite. It was not even originally a Jewish rite. Baptism was originally a ceremony that was used by the mystery religious cults among the Greeks, like that of Dionysus. In some cases, a person would be baptized in blood, and sometimes in water or even milk. The original concept of baptism was that the individual was "covered over" by some particular substance, be it water or blood or whatever. It did not necessarily mean immersed. It did not necessarily mean sprinkled, nor any other specific method of administration. It was simply the idea of covering over. The cult of Mithra, popular with the Roman army, used a baptism in blood in which the initiates went into a pit with a grate over them. Then a bull was led standing over the grate. When they cut its throat the initiates were covered in the bull's blood and hence "baptized." Then the bull was dressed out, cooked, and all present celebrated a big meal together.

The Jews, in approximately 250 BCE to maybe 200 BCE, began using baptism as part of the process for when a person converted to Judaism from some other kind of a religion. Prior to that time, essentially to become Jewish, a man simply was circumcised and lived among the Jewish people, followed the Jewish law and traditions, and so on. But after about 250 BCE, the Jews began using baptism in a manner similar to the way the mystery religions were using it. By the time of Jesus, a complex process for becoming Jewish had been developed, including the use of baptism, anointing with oil, making a sacrifice, and several other actions in the process of becoming a full Jew.

John the Baptist was a Jew, in fact a second cousin to Jesus. At the Jordan River he was proclaiming a somewhat different concept of baptism and encouraging the people to adopt a serious approach to their Jewish practice, something beyond simply observance and obedience which he associated with the act of repentance in order to prepare for the coming of the kingdom of God. There was a great expectation among the Jews at that time that they were living in the age when the Messiah was going to come. The Messiah was the one whom they believed was the descendent of David who would come and make the Jewish nation the predominant nation and the ruling nation on earth. But what John was essentially saying was that they needed to prepare for that, not to just anticipate the coming of such a kingdom. His message focused on the need to repent, to realize one's need for God, and by baptism, express personally the need for God in one's life and the desire to be a part of His coming kingdom. Otherwise the person will be judged when the Messiah comes. Jesus, along with many other people, went to be baptized by John, showing agreement with John's message.

This was the initiation of Jesus's public ministry. After a sojourn of forty days in the Judean wilderness, fasting and contemplating about what is going on and what direction His ministry would go, Jesus began an itinerant ministry.

Second, He Selected Twelve Disciples or Assistants: After walking with the disciples for some time, Jesus prayerfully selected twelve among them to be His assistants whom He named "apostles." The number twelve is symbolic of the original twelve Patriarchs who formed the ancient nation of Israel. The twelve is also a symbol of a new community. They were learners/trainees and messengers to carry on his work.

Third, The Uniqueness of His Message: Jesus engaged in a regular preaching at Capernaum; Capernaum is the city that was the base from which Jesus carried out much of his ministry in Galilee. He didn't just stay there but rather from there He would go out on preaching missions around Galilee, and then eventually come back to Capernaum before going out again—an itinerant ministry. His message emphasized God's relationship with those who seek God. Preached the same as John preached about repentance and the coming of the Kingdom, but for Jesus the kingdom is here. He is the inaugurator. He gave the message a new meaning and application accompanied by miracles to demonstrate that the Kingdom of God has indeed come, which endeared Him to the ordinary people. He had a mass following; the estimates are that about one-third of the Jews living in Galilee and Judea, two Jewish territories in that region, probably had believed in him and came to accept Him as the Messiah, or God's anointed servant, when He was crucified in 30 CE.

Jesus's Controversy and Clash with Jewish Authorities: *The* controversy centered on **(a) the Sabbath**—the Sabbath and the observance of the Sabbath was the most important focus in Jewish life at the time. Basically that day of rest stretches from Friday night through Saturday. The Jews measure their days from night until the next day. To take it a little bit further, the Sabbath becomes representative of the enormous importance that is now assigned to obedience in the Jewish law. The Sabbath was also the central issue for observance of Judaism in Jesus's day, and so it played a prominent role in distinguishing His thinking concerning the Sabbath from that of other Jewish teachers. On the one hand, He was more liberal, and, on the other, He was as firm as other teachers were; **(b) ritual cleansing**—washing of hands before meal; **(c) source of authority; (d) association with social outcasts; (e) controversy over His self-understanding**—there are clearly some times when Jesus of Nazareth claimed to be God Himself, which would be blasphemy according to the Jewish understanding of scripture (unless, of course, He really was), for examples, **"Son of God"** and **"Son of Man"**—the former acknowledges His divinity (unique relationship with God; e.g. He links Himself with Abraham—"before Abraham was, I am," John 8:58; a reference to his preeminent to David); "Son of Man" acknowledges His humanity.

His Death: Jesus was crucified in 30 CE when He was thirty-three years old. The sequence of events were as follows: the last procession into Jerusalem (we now call Palm Sunday); eating the Passover with His disciples and instituting a memorial meal that focuses on Himself—His sacrifice. As He gave the bread and the wine to His disciples, He also told them to "do this as often as you will in remembrance of Me."

The Trial: Once Jesus was arrested and put on trial there were two things that the Jewish religious authorities had to do. The first of the two was to determine that He really was a blasphemer (the charge for which they sought to try Him). Various witnesses were called because in the Jewish law two witnesses had to agree on each charge for it to be considered valid evidence. When no two witnesses' stories agreed, finally the high priest asked Jesus, "Tell us whether you are the Son of God or not." This was a specially formulated question in the Jewish legal structure. Jesus answered, "It is as you say," which was the equivalent of answering "yes." It was a clear claim to be God, or "the Son of the living God" according to the question asked by the priests. The majority opinion was that there was then enough evidence to convict Jesus of being a blasphemer. But there is one further problem.

Because of the unrest and the agitation against Rome by the Jews of Judea that had occurred over the previous decades, the Roman praetor always came to Jerusalem at the time of a Seder—the time of Passover—to make sure that peace was kept in Jerusalem.

The Sanhedrin: The Sanhedrin was the Jewish high political authority trying Jesus, but it was unable to simply convict a person, sentence that person to death, and then carry out the sentence. When the praetor was not in Jerusalem, they may have gotten away with it anyway, but if he was in residence in Jerusalem, they couldn't go out and carry out a sentence of death on their own. Instead the Sanhedrin sought to find a charge against Jesus that the Romans would care about, since the Romans could care less about whether Jesus was a Jewish blasphemer. That was a Jewish problem. To the Romans, that was no reason to execute a person.

The final decision was to accuse Jesus of being an insurrectionist. That, after all, fundamentally was what the Messiah would "have to be." So, in a sense, they basically accused Him of being the Messiah because in their minds, a Messiah would be someone who would come to challenge the existing political authority and then create a Jewish kingdom in place of the existing political authority. The Sanhedrin subsequently presented the case to Pilate saying, "We have no king but Caesar, but He says that He is a king and that He is our king."

Pilate: There were a number of things that happened during the trial, but ultimately the praetor, Pilate, found himself in a difficult situation. Pilate had been appointed the head of the Praetorian Guard, Sejanus. This was the security force that protected the emperor personally, and the imperial family. The problem was that Sejanus was actively conspiring to eliminate the imperial family of Tiberius Caesar so Sejanus could become emperor. Shortly before the time that Jesus was tried before Pilate, Sejanus's plot had been discovered, and Sejanus was executed. Pilate, as a friend and political appointee of Sejanus, was potentially implicated. Sometime earlier, Pilate had been awarded the medal, "Friend of Caesar." Seizing upon that, in the Bible the Sanhedrin responded to Pilate's reluctance to sentence Jesus to death according to their scheme, "If you release that man, you are no friend of Caesar." While it sounds like an idle threat, in fact Friend of Caesar was an actual badge people wore around their neck, one of the highest civilian awards a person could have. Hence what was actually being said was, "If you release this man instead of sentencing Him to death, by the time we go to Caesar and make our accusations against you before Caesar, you are going to lose your position, if not your own head." Pilate was under pressure in whatever he did. Under Roman law, he could find nothing on which to convict Jesus, and to do so was a violation of Roman law itself. But with the angry crowd before him, he risked the threat of a riot, for which he might also have to answer to Rome and perhaps also lose his position or his life. So finally Pilate decided to wash his hands of the situation and let the Sanhedrin carry out the sentence they had decided. So Jesus was taken outside the city and crucified.

The Resurrection: The New Testament account is that three days after He died and was

©doom.ko/Shutterstock.com

A portrait of the crucifixion of Jesus Christ

buried, He left the tomb alive. However, His body physically was not simply resuscitated somehow, but transformed, and He appeared to many in what is known as a resurrection body (resuscitation is when a dead person returns to mortal life but will die again; reincarnation is when some aspect of a person migrates from one mortal life to another mortal life and another, etc.). Resurrection is when the physical body undergoes a complete transformation to an immortal body that is never subject to death again. The person can move freely, eat, and drink, etc., but does not require these things. It was claimed by the Christians that this was the event that occurred to Jesus on the third day. Some weeks later, Jesus's followers began to spread this message of the resurrection, asserting that the resurrection itself demonstrated that Jesus was indeed God, just as He had claimed to be. After forty days of appearing off and on to His disciples, and some of the others that had been followers, according to Christian tradition, Jesus ascended physically to heaven, where He remains. However, the disciples were told that they should remain in Jerusalem until they were given a unique empowerment by the Holy Spirit. Then they were to go out and be witnesses about Jesus even to becoming martyrs around the world for the sake of that message. The word "apostle" actually means "one who is sent" and is usually reserved for reference to those who had been disciples of Jesus during his earthly ministry. After the Holy Spirit empowered them, they believed themselves sent out by the Holy Spirit with the message of His death, resurrection, and God's offer of grace and acceptance to those who would believe their message through faith in Jesus, wherever they might be around the world.

* * *

MATTHEW

*28 After the Sabbath, as the first day of the week was dawning, Mary Magdalene and the other Mary went to see the tomb. [2]And suddenly there was a great earthquake; for an angel of the LORD, descending from heaven, came and rolled back the stone and sat on it. [3]His appearance was like lightning and his clothing white as snow. [4]For fear of him the guards shook and became like dead men. [5]But the angel said to the women, "Do not be afraid; I know that you are looking for Jesus who was crucified. [6]He is not here; for he has been raised, as he said. Come, see the place where he1 lay, [7]Then go quickly and tell his disciples, [8]He has been raised from the dead, mand indeed he was going ahead of you to Galilee; there you will see him.1 This is my message for you." 8So they left the tomb quickly with fear and great joy, and ran to tell his disciples. [9]Suddenly Jesus met them and said, "Greetings!" And they came to him, took hold of his feet, and worshiped him. [10]Then Jesus said to them, "Do not be afraid; go and tell my brothers to go to Galilee; there they will see me."

11 While they were going, some of the guard went into the city and told the chief priests everything that had happened. [12]After the priestsn had assembled with the elders, they devised a plan to give a large sum of money to the soldiers, [13]telling them, "You must say, 'His disciples came by night and stole him away while we were asleep.' [14]If this comes to the governor's ears, we will satisfy him and keep you out of trouble." [15]So they took the money and did as they were directed. And this story is still told among the Jews to this day.

16 Now the eleven disciples went to Galilee, to the mountain to which Jesus had directed them. [17]When they saw him, they worshiped him; but some doubted. [18]And Jesus came and said to them, "All authority in heaven and on earth has been given to me. [19]Go therefore and make disciples of all nations,

baptizing them in the name of the Father and of the Son and of the Holy Spirit, [20]and teaching them to obey everything that I have commanded you. And remember, I am with you always, to the end of the age."[o]

[[l]Other ancient authorities read *the* LORD; [m]Other ancient authorities lack *from the dead;* [n]Gk *they;* [o]Other ancient authorities add *amen*]

Pentecost: The event of empowerment took place fifty days after the resurrection and was coincident with the Jewish Pentecost that year. We will not talk too much about who or what the Holy Spirit is because that is a whole big area of controversy and discussion in New Testament scholarship. However, in Christianity, there is the belief that the Holy Spirit is also God, which leads to the notion of Trinity. The idea, according to Christian understanding, is that God is one, but He presents Himself as three persons to humans. He is the Father, the Son, and the Holy Spirit. The Father refers to a unique type of relationship being offered to those who believe in Jesus with the God who is, was, and always has been in heaven, the God of Abraham, Isaac, and Jacob, the one referred to by the Jews in their prayers and services. The Son is Jesus. The Holy Spirit is understood as that presence of Jesus in the world today among humans, and especially among those who are His followers.

THE LIFE, FAITH, AND DEVELOPMENT OF THE EARLY CHURCH

As a result of the events which occurred, probably on Pentecost of 30 CE, the Christian church was born. It is first established in Judea, then in Samaria (directly north of Judea), and then to various locations around the Roman world as well as elsewhere. Over the next approximately ten years, the early believers, beginning from Jerusalem, went out at least around the Roman world with the message of a relationship with God made available through Jesus's death and resurrection. To those who believed, the Holy Spirit was also given. It was not just a one-time thing that happened on Pentecost of 30 CE but was repeatable, being passed on from Christian to Christian to Christian as they believed and followed Jesus Christ. And these, too, were energized to also take the message they had believed and to tell others about the relationship available through Jesus's death and resurrection. Peter had been the spokesman of the disciples, which were Jesus's closest associates during His time of itinerant ministry. Peter might not necessarily have been the most spiritual person, but the spokesman of a group of disciples of a Rabbi was the person believed "most likely to succeed" in following the teachings of his Master. Whether or not Peter was the one who was regarded by the group as the most outstanding example, it was, therefore, only natural that Peter would also be the spokesman and early leader of the Christian church in Jerusalem after Jesus's death. Soon, those claiming to experience this personal relationship with God sought to unite with others forming little communities of Christian believers, or congregations ("assemblies" was the original word). The small, organized assemblies are what today

Christian world mission concept: The wooden cross on top of the world globe on wooden background

are called churches. In the first century CE, they were more on the order of home cell groups than formal churches and had no formal structures.

The Jewish leaders became incensed at the believers, most of whom were born Jewish, now telling about Jesus and inviting other Jews, and sometimes even Gentiles, to believe in Him. The Sanhedrin had Jesus crucified because of the message that He was proclaiming, including that He was, indeed, God. Now, all of a sudden, after the day of Pentecost, the people who had been His followers and who had continued to live in Jerusalem, began to act boldly. They were telling basically the same message Jesus had preached, and they even started doing some of the same miracles. People were being healed. The lame were walking and the deaf were hearing. Eventually even the dead were being resuscitated. So, whereas they got rid of one Jesus, now it was as if they had more than one of Him running around Jerusalem. The situation seemed to be multiplying and getting out of hand, which created a backlash on the part of the Jewish leadership.

One of the leading proponents among the Jewish leadership of Jewish resistance to the Christians was a young man named Saul. Saul was a native of a town called Tarsus, probably in what is now Turkey though no one knows for sure which Tarsus he was from. In the Jewish structure of education at that time, if a young man showed exceptional promise in his scholarship, then he would be encouraged to study under even greater Rabbis and learn their knowledge. If he still continued to show promise, he would study under still more prominent Rabbis and ultimately work his way to the Rabbis at Jerusalem who were regarded as the greatest of the Rabbis. Saul was in Jerusalem as one of the young men who had shown such exceptional promise. He had already worked his way through all the lesser Rabbis, and he was sitting at the feet of the man who was regarded as the greatest Rabbi of that time, Gamaliel II. Saul was also a Pharisee and was particularly incensed that the followers of Jesus—they were not called Christians yet—were going around teaching about Jesus and doing miracles like He did.

Saul began working to bring the followers of Jesus before the Sanhedrin, to imprison them, or to otherwise persecute them. This situation caused the Christians in the region to go underground, and Christians not native to Jerusalem left the area to return to their homes and villages. Then, when Saul seemingly ran out of Christians in Jerusalem (by that time Christianity had spread to the city of Damascus, Syria), Saul went up to the city of Damascus with the intention of taking as many Jews that were followers of Jesus there as could be found and imprisoning them. However, on the way to Damascus, he had some sort of conversion experience in which he believed he encountered Jesus alive, resurrected, and who appeared to him and spoke to him. This experience led to a complete turnaround in Saul's life. By the time he entered Damascus, he had become a believer in Jesus. Within a few days, he began to preach the same message that he had gone to Damascus to persecute.

This same Saul would ultimately become the man also named Paul, who is the author of much of the New Testament. He would eventually travel on three missionary journeys and around the Mediterranean—three that are known—present the gospel perhaps even before Nero Caesar, who was the emperor in Rome, and maybe even travel as far as Spain presenting the story and the offer of a relationship with Israel's God through belief in Jesus. Paul is regarded as one of the greatest of the apostles and was unique in the sense that, though he was an apostle, he had not been one of the original followers of Jesus. But he was extremely influential in the development of Christian theology because he took the traditions of Judaism and the things that he saw and experienced as a follower of Jesus, and put them together into a system of theology that is largely contained in letters, which comprise a significant portion of the New Testament. There are far more letters from Paul in the New Testament than from any other single person. He became a leading spokesman in defining what Christianity is all about.

Even during the first decades after the beginning of the Church age, while the message concerning Jesus was being rejected by many other Jewish leaders, it was also accepted by many Jews, as well as people of non-Jewish backgrounds. In the period between 30 and 60 CE, Christianity developed across the Roman Empire, partly as the result of Paul's efforts, and all the while was perceived to be primarily a sect of Judaism. The nonbelieving Jews didn't actually say the Jewish Christians were no longer Jews, but just Jews who were misguided or who had become heretics, especially because they associated with non-Jews. And indeed, gradually during this period, many Gentiles also became interested in the Christian message and became believers in Jesus. As a result, while the community of followers of Jesus was still largely Jewish in character, there was an increasing number of Gentiles who were becoming included as part of the Christian community. The presence of these believing Gentiles in the Christian communities added to the determination by the nonbelieving Jewish world to reject the followers of Jesus as in any way being a legitimate expression of Jewish faith. Sometime between 60 and 70 CE, formal rejection of Christians by the nonbelieving Jewish world seems to have become common place, regardless of the Christians' previous religious and ethnic background. Jewish Christians still saw themselves as Jews, however, but as Jews in a different way and with a different perspective on their faith and traditions. But Gentiles did not think of themselves as being Jewish in any way, shape, or form, though they believed they possessed the same religious benefits as Christian Jews.

Eventually, the use of the term "Christian" arose in the city of Antioch, which was in Syria but near the coast of the Mediterranean Sea. There the Christians met very openly. Some were Jews, some were Gentiles, but they were meeting together very openly. Of course, just as was the case for those who had been born Jewish, these Gentile believers didn't worship any other gods. They didn't go to a temple. And, as a term of derision, they were called by the people at Antioch *Christians*. It was a term of derision against the followers of Jesus to start with, not a term used by the Christians to refer to themselves. The Christians had generally called themselves "Followers of the Way."

It is obvious, then, that Christianity has strong roots in Judaism, even though, since the second century CE, the two have gone in vastly differently directions and developed very different traditions. During the first at least thirty-six years, up until 66 CE, Christianity was regarded by the Jews as well as by the Romans as a sect of Judaism. The Jewish leaders considered it a blasphemous and irregular sect. The Romans simply regarded the whole group as Jews. With the exception of sporadic persecution by certain Jewish leadership here and there, Christianity grew freely in the Roman Empire during its first thirty-six years. It would be the Jewish revolt against Rome in 66–70 CE, which would introduce some serious changes into this scenario. By and large, the Christians didn't have anything to do with that revolt against Rome. In fact, there is a body of opinion that suggests that the New Testament Book of Hebrews was written by a Jewish Christian closely associated with Paul, urging the Christians who were in Jerusalem to leave and go across the Sea of Galilee, across the Jordan River to where the rest of the Christians in that area were located. There they would be outside the area in revolt against Rome, and which Rome was going to turn into a war zone as a result of revolt. Clearly, there is no record of any significant involvement by Christians in the Jewish revolt against Rome from 66 to 70 CE. This fact is well-supported in the writings of a careful and now well-recognized historian of that revolt named Josephus. The absence of Christian support for the revolt, especially on the part of "Jewish Christians," created further cleavage between the Jewish and the Christian traditions. Additionally, it seems that somewhere between 62 and 66 CE, the Roman emperor (Nero) became aware of the fact that the Jewish leaders didn't consider Christians to be true Jews. Thereafter, gradually perhaps, Christians came to be viewed by the Romans as a separate religion from Judaism. However, this change of perspective by the Romans also meant that Christianity was considered an illegal religion in the Roman Empire.

CHRISTIAN WRITINGS AND CANON

In the aftermath of the Jewish revolt, as the Rabbis began to record all of the oral tradition of Judaism into what is known as the Mishnah, in the Christian world, the letters of Paul and the letters from other Christian leaders, such as James or John, were being written, circulated, copied, and collected. In the 70s and 80s CE, the gospels of Luke and Matthew were written. Perhaps the gospel of Mark was written earlier (NT scholars believe Mark was the first gospel to be written and was used by Luke and Matthew). Thus, Christian literature was being written and collected at the same time as the Jewish Rabbis were setting forth the Mishnah. By 90 CE, the Jews had decided what they considered their canon, or scriptures to be. The writings had, in most cases, been around for hundreds of years. But now they settled on what would be regarded as the most important books out of all the Jewish writings—those most decisive, critical, and significant in identifying and outlining their Jewish faith and most basic of traditions. These are what are today referred to as the Ta'anach (the Hebrew Bible), or for Christians, the Old Testament. A similar process was also developing among the Christians that would lead to identification of their "additions" to the Ta'anach which would offer the distinctively Christian perspective concerning Israel's God and the role of Jesus and of believers in Jesus in that faith.

In 140–44 CE, there was a Christian deviant by the name of Marcion (sometimes spelt Martian) who published a list of the Christian writings that he regarded as definitive for Christian faith. The church rejected Marcion and his teachings as exemplified by the following statement: "To any church leader, Marcion's heresy was the most shocking deviation from Apostolic truth. He had denied the Old Testament's inspiration and the continuity of the God and Creator with Christ. Bishop Polycarp had known how to deal with him. When Polycarp met Marcion, Polycarp's pupil Irenaeus said he had greeted him as 'the first born child of satan'" (Fox, www.christianorigins.com/marcion.html, 492).

Marcion's 12 Books Canon of the Bible around 144 CE

Gospel according to Luke and Acts
Galatians
I Corinthians
II Corinthians
Romans
I Thessalonians
II Thessalonians
Ephesians (which Marcion called Laodiceans)
Colossians
Philemon
Philippians

The other 15 books

Mathew
Mark
John
Romans
1 Timothy
2 Timothy
Titus
Hebrews
1 Peter
2 Peter
1 John
2 John
3 John
Jude
Revelation

Marcion rejected all the Old Testament and the gospel of Matthew, Mark, John, and the Book of Revelation.

Marcion was a Gnostic. Gnosticism was a theosophical approach to religion similar to Eastern Zoroastrianism, which suggested that there was a certain secret knowledge that someone must possess in order to please the divine realm. The initiated, or baptized, were provided with this knowledge as part of their initiation, and only they could achieve religious success. The books he identified were those, among many others circulating in the Christian communities, which supported his own theosophical approach. In response, various Christian leaders from around the Mediterranean world also began assembling lists of what they regarded as definitive for Christian faith and practice. It took about 200 more years before there was unanimous agreement among Christian leaders on the entire list. But from the very first, there were only a few books that were different among the different lists. Some decades after differences among the lists had disappeared, about 400 CE, Christian leaders identified the books on the list as those of the New Testament, which remains the same today.

INCREASED PERSECUTIONS AND GROWTH

Between 70 and 132 CE, there was sporadic persecution by Romans of Jews and Christians for various reasons. But also, through 132 CE, Judaism remained a very evangelical religion, as was Christianity, trying to make converts to Judaism. However, in 132 CE, when a second Jewish revolt against Rome broke out, the Bar Kochba Revolt, the relationship between Christians and Jews reached the separation point. This second Jewish revolt against Rome, from 132 to 135 CE, was a major revolt, better organized and better planned than the one in 66 CE. Again, the Christians did not help the Jews in their revolt at all. Prior to 132 CE, some scholars estimate that half or more of all Christians had originally been of Jewish heritage and were converts from Judaism. But after 135 CE, the two went their own separate ways. A lot of the Jewish traditions, the background of the New Testament, became lost to Christianity as there was less and less remembrance or focus on the old Jewish ways.

This separation was helped along initially because, at its very beginning in 135 CE, the Roman emperor, Hadrian, forbade the Jews to circumcise their children, to possess copies of the Torah scrolls, to meet on the Sabbath, to carry out any of their rituals, to celebrate the Passover, etc. Meanwhile, the Christians were being unofficially tolerated by the Roman world of the time. In 117 CE, a question about Christians had been raised to Hadrian's predecessor, and [unofficial] toleration was permitted as long as Christians kept a low profile and did nothing criminal. Christians, therefore, felt no obligation to identify with the Jewish population or to endure the restrictions placed upon the Jewish people. So the Christians were able to follow their own traditions and practices in their own way without coming into open conflict with the Roman law.

Christianity had developed through becoming established in urban centers of the Roman Empire. During this period there was a large concentration of the church in North Africa. Many of the leaders (known as Church Fathers) at this time were from North Africa, who would influence the theological or doctrinal position of the church for centuries, even to this present age. Gradually, these urban churches began to establish "satellite congregations" in neighboring villages. In this manner a formal leadership structure developed among Christians, in which the senior leaders in the cities were the bishops. Their assistants were known by various titles (e.g., Deacon) and frequently served in the satellite congregations under the authority of the urban bishops.

Almost two centuries after Hadrian, in 312 CE, following two decades of empire-wide persecution of Christianity (which had only served to expand the numbers of Christians to be found in the Roman Empire), the Roman emperor Constantine converted to Christianity. On the night before his final battle (the Milvian bridge) in which he took control of the Western Roman world, he had a vision of a particular Christian symbol (chi rho) while hearing the words *in hoc signo vinces* ("in that sign you will conquer"). When he awoke the next morning, one tradition says that he had that symbol painted on all helmets and shields of his army before went into battle. And, sure enough, they won the battle. While there is probably more to the story that has not been retained through history, as a result of the experience he had in connection with the battle of the Milvian Bridge, Constantine converted to Christianity. Within two years he, together with Licinius, issued the Edict of Milan, which made Christianity a legitimate religion in the Roman Empire.

* * *

THE "EDICT OF MILAN" (313 AD)

When I, Constantine Augustus, as well as I Licinius Augustus, fortunately met near Mediolanurn (Milan), and were considering everything that pertained to the public welfare and security, we thought -, among other things which we saw would be for the good of many, those regulations pertaining to the reverence of the Divinity ought certainly to be made first, so that we might grant to the Christians and others full authority to observe that religion which each preferred; whence any Divinity whatsoever in the seat of the heavens may be propitious and kindly disposed to us and all who are placed under our rule And thus by this wholesome counsel and most upright provision we thought to arrange that no one whatsoever should be denied the opportunity to give his heart to the observance of the Christian religion, of that religion which he should think best for himself, so that the Supreme Deity, to whose worship we freely yield our hearts) may show in all things His usual favor and benevolence. Therefore, your Worship should know that it has pleased us to remove all conditions whatsoever, which were in the rescripts formerly given to you officially, concerning the Christians and now any one of these who wishes to observe Christian religion may do so freely and openly, without molestation. We thought it fit to commend these things most fully to your care that you may know that we have given to those Christians free and unrestricted opportunity of religious worship. When you see that this has been granted to them by us, your Worship will know that we have also conceded to other religions the right of open and free observance of their worship for the sake of the peace of our times, that each one may have the free opportunity to worship as he pleases; this regulation is made we that we may not seem to detract from any dignity or any religion.[1]

The edict further restored to the Christians every property taken away from them. Constantine and Licinius did this for (1) public order, (2) security, and (3) Divine favor toward personal and state preservation and prosperity.

* * *

CHRISTIANITY DURING AND AFTER CONSTANTINE'S REIGN

Of course, a decision of that magnitude by an emperor had far-reaching effects both politically and socially. Many political associates made it their own religion. He also ordered that the Roman army should be converted to Christianity, and so on. Hence, all of the Roman army had suddenly become Christians, whether they could even pronounce the word or not. All of the changes following legitimization of Christianity tremendously changed the whole internal structure of the Christian church. The church was now faced with a lot of former nonbelievers (idol worshippers, mystery religion practitioners, etc.) suddenly now calling themselves Christians. Many people had no idea what the Old or New Testaments taught, or about the real message of Christianity. Previously, if a person claimed a personal relationship with Jesus Christ and was willing to suffer, even experience martyrdom for that faith, the person becomes a Christian; there was relatively less focus on whether the person believed exactly the "right" things. But with an increasing number of people who had little, if any formal understanding of the Christian message before becoming part of Christianity, the development of a formal statement of accepted Christian theology and faith became important, in order to spell out what were the basic elements of Christian belief. To this end, several major Church Councils met, the first one being at the city of Nicaea in 325 CE. Out of these councils came a number of statements concerning "correct" Christian belief, including, eventually, the Nicene Creed and the Apostles' Creed. Those claiming to be Christian but not agreeing with these basic creeds were treated, legally, as unbelievers. As a result, they often moved to the periphery of the Roman Empire to avoid persecution for their different ideas.

Many practices were adopted by Christian leaders as object lessons to try to help these new converts to understand more about Christianity. One example is the celebration of Christmas. In the pre-Constantinian Roman world, Christmas did not exist. However, there was something called the winter solstice, which was a popular celebration in traditional Roman religion, celebrated with parties and the giving and receiving of gifts similar to the Christmas celebrations today. At the same time, Romans did not commonly celebrate an

[1]"Edict of Milan" (from Lactantius, De Mort. Pers., ch. 48. opera, ed. 0. F. Fritzsche, II, p 288 sq. (Bibl Patr. Ecc. Lat. XI). The text translated in University of Pennsylvania. Dept. of History: Translations and Reprints from the Original Sources of European history, (Philadelphia, University of Pennsylvania Press [1897?–1907?]), Vol 4: 1, pp. 28–30. This text is part of the Internet Medieval Source Book, at http://legacy.fordham.edu/halsall/source/edict-milan.asp

individual's birthday, though they did normally celebrate the birthday of an emperor. After Constantine's Edict of Milan, one of the assertions of the Church was to proclaim that Jesus was the King of kings, and the Lord of lords, greater even than the emperor himself, yet they didn't celebrate His birthday nor even remember for sure when He was born. Furthermore, for the people who were Christians, it was forbidden to participate in such a traditional Roman holiday as the winter solstice. So the Church brought all of this together by making December 25 a day for the celebration of the birth of Jesus—not that it was the actual birth day of Jesus (He was probably born in September). But what became important was the celebration of Jesus's birthday. In a similar way, Christian leaders used a variety of object lessons associated with Roman tradition and Christian beliefs to try to help the new converts, who had come out of various backgrounds into Christianity, to understand more clearly the Christian message and life.

Easter is another ceremony that was developed into a popular celebration during this period. Easter was originally simply a celebration of Jesus's resurrection. There are some who assert that Sunday worship services began as a celebration of Jesus's resurrection, and the Church just celebrated it every Sunday. However appealing the theory, it probably is not accurate because most of the early Christians had been Jewish and they worshiped on their day of worship, which was Saturday. It is pretty well established that up until about 132 CE, some Christians, at least, celebrated their day for worship, even as Christians, on Saturday. But Easter was different. It was a unique event in Christian tradition and after 314 CE, the Church added to it things like *Lent*, which established a period of preparation for the celebration of Easter during which one gave up certain things. The idea was that by giving these things up, the believer better identified with the sacrifice that Jesus made in His crucifixion.

After the legitimation of Christianity in 313/4 CE, Church leaders, especially in the West became increasingly important as civil authorities in the cities, began receiving secular authority, such as judge-ships. Constantine also gave the Churches and their leaders, tax exemptions and other benefits. After some time, the church in the West began to merge with the state in many respects. This resulted in an increasing secularization of the formal Church structures. Consequently, some among the common people (the laity) who sought a deeper personal experience of Christianity began to withdraw to remote areas and establish the beginnings of what would grow into the monastic movement. For many centuries, these monasteries would become alternatives to the urban churches for those seeking deeper experiences of Christianity. When the Western and Eastern Christian Churches started drifting apart, the monasteries would continue to exist for personal spiritual retreats, education, and continued spiritual experience of Christianity alongside the urban churches. In an effort to enable Christians in the Roman Empire to have access to the Bible in their own language (Latin), in about 400 CE, a monk by the name of Jerome translated the entire Old and New Testaments into Latin, producing what was known as the *Vulgate*. The Vulgate remains one of the important early sources of New Testament understanding and the basis for Roman Catholic translations today, alongside manuscripts in Greek and Hebrew. One other theologian who would influence the theo-logical direction of the church and the church's relationship with the state or society was Saint Augustine, Bishop of Hippo in North Africa.

Over ensuing decades and centuries, the Church leadership developed and evolved as it added more and more structure appropriate to the prevailing social and political situation and as the Church itself changed. By 395 CE, under the direction of the Roman emperor Theodosius, all religions were destroyed in the empire except Christianity, which became the official and only legitimate religion of the empire. Judaism was tolerated because of its association with Jesus and the beginnings of Christianity. But all other religious traditions in the Roman Empire were aggressively extinguished under his reign. Gradually, the church in the East became more theological as it hosted various doctrinal councils. And the Church leadership in the east developed a collegial relationship among equals, except that the bishop of Constantinople, the capital city of the eastern empire, was acknowledged as the senior leader among equals and referred to as the *Patriarch*. Later, as the Eastern Church would develop in new regions such as Russia and Armenia, the senior leader in those regions would also come to be known either as Patriarch or sometimes as *Metropolitan* (e.g., the Patriarch of Alexandria, the Patriarch of Antioch, the Metropolitan of Moscow, etc.).

THE SCHISM AND THE DEVELOPMENT OF THE EASTERN AND WESTERN CHURCHES

The church in the West was generally cut off from the Eastern branch of Christianity by the Germanic invasions beginning about 400 CE. As a result, it became more involved in the day-to-day political and practical matters of life, focusing on authority and survival rather than theological matters. This resulted in the formation of a very different structure within the Western Christian world than developed in the East. This difference was primarily due to the historical unfolding of the political and social situation. As the bishops had become more involved as secular leaders in the urban world, not only did the people look to monasteries for the spiritual experience of Christianity, but the leaders of the monasteries became an alternative religious leadership to that in the urban churches. In the time of Pope Gregory I, approximately 600 CE, the Western Church was reorganized into a hierarchical structure among the urban bishops, with the bishop of Rome (the Pope) at the top, and various levels of bishops and archbishops under him depending on the relative importance of the churches these individuals served. Other practices also developed under Gregory's leadership, such as the worship service, which came to be known as the Mass. The Mass is the "complex of prayers and ceremonies that make up the service of the Eucharist in the Latin rites" (*Catholic Encyclopedia*). Gregory initiated a mission to Southern England to convert the people there to Christianity, and emphasized the benevolent role of the Church in assisting people who were suffering under the oppression of Germanic domination in some former areas of the Roman Empire.

The increasing doctrinal interest in the East, and the authoritarian interest in the West, alongside linguistic and political and economic differences signaled a gradual drifting apart of the eastern and western Christian Church traditions and practices over the next several centuries, even though the beliefs were basically the same. By 1054 CE, there were really two churches in existence. The one in the West was more practical and authoritarian, and the one in the East was more theological and fraternal. In 1054, a disagreement arose over the right of the Byzantine (Roman emperor in the east) to involve himself in Church affairs. The Pope's representative felt he did not receive respect appropriate for a representative of the Pope and excommunicated the emperor and the Patriarch of Constantinople. In response, the Patriarch of Constantinople summarily anathematized (excommunicated) the Bishop of Rome (the Pope). The result was that every Christian everywhere was, therefore, excommunicated by one side or the other, in essence, splitting the Christian world between East and West. Thereafter, two different growth patterns and historical developments occurred in the Christian Church.

The Church in the East came to be referred to as *Orthodox*, which emphasized their claim of retaining and maintaining the true Christian doctrines and beliefs. From the Orthodox Church, today there is the Greek Orthodox, Russian Orthodox, Armenian Orthodox, Eastern Orthodox, Coptic Orthodox, etc. These are not different sects that have somehow broken from the mainstream Orthodox tradition. Rather, as the Orthodox Church moved into other areas like Russia, the church that was established there just began calling itself by the regional or ethnic terminology. They are all basically one, looking to the Patriarch of Constantinople as ultimately the head of the Orthodox Church and experiencing fraternal relations between their different "branches." Unlike the numerous divisions and sects that developed in the Western Church, the Orthodox Church remains, yet today, relatively close to the structure and beliefs that characterized it from early times.

After 1054 CE, the Church in the West came to be referred to as *Catholic*. The word Catholic means universal, and the idea conveyed was that they were part of the "universal Church" headed by the Bishop of Rome, also known as the *Pope*. Between 1054 and 1215 CE, the Pope increasingly arrogated to himself authority over the secular as well as the religious affairs of the West. Eventually, he was powerful enough that without an army, he could establish and depose kings and princes in the Western European world. It was under the authority of the Pope that the *Crusades* began in 1095 CE, the Pope promising all who would agree to participate that he would assure them of complete forgiveness of all their sins (and hence if they died on crusade a certainty of immediate entry into heaven), and that the Church would look after all their property in trust for them. At the very height of Papal power, the Catholic Church established what it regarded as the *sacraments*—the specific rituals of the Church in which the presence and power of God were most specifically experienced. These seven sacraments were: baptism, confirmation, Eucharist, ordination, penance, extreme unction, and marriage. These seven sacraments would play an increasing role in the power the Catholic Church would have over its people for many centuries.

After 1215 CE, the authority of the Popes began to decline as the European monarchs began to devise ways to assert a greater measure of authority over their kingdoms. Indeed, kingdoms began to be associated with geographical borders only at this period, rather than based on sworn political loyalties. With the benefit of territorial integrity, kings began to challenge the role of the church for legal and social control over the people in their kingdoms. The outbreak of the Renaissance and internal strife between various factions within the senior leadership of the Catholic Church served to further weaken the hold of the church over the affections of the people. In the early 1300s CE, two, and then later three Popes would establish themselves, each claiming to be the true representative of Jesus Christ in the world. To further establish their claim to authority, these various Popes sought the support of the European kings, which came at a price—and the whole situation became part of the national struggles waged across medieval Europe for political control. Gradually, the role of the Popes devolved into raising funds and seeking just to retain their positions against a European intelligentsia who believed the Catholic Church had become too big for just one person to supervise. In the midst of all of this, the emphasis on spiritual things too often got lost in form, function, and pursuit of power.

PROTESTANT REFORMATION AND AFTERWARD

In 1517, the beginning of what is known as the Protestant Reformation erupted as *Martin Luther* tacked his *95 Theses* on the wall of a church in Wittenberg, Germany. These statements challenged the Catholic Church to debate certain issues concerning the sacrament of Penance which at the time

Martin Luther at University of Wittenberg

©Brad Scot Lark/Shutterstock.com

Out of love for the truth and the desire to bring it to light, the following 95 propositions will ꞈed at

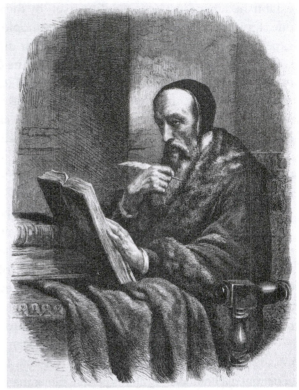

©Marzolino/Shutterstock.com

John Calvin of Geneva

©Nicku/Shutterstock.com

were being promoted by the Church. This situation was not the first time the Catholic Church had been challenged by reform-minded individuals among the clergy (Church leaders) or the laity. Indeed, a century earlier, England had been influenced by *John Wyclif*, who also taught ideas very similar to those Luther expressed in his Theses. And in 1417 CE, after a student of Wyclif named *John Hus* had been burned at the stake by the Council of Constance, the entire region of Bohemia developed a reformed kingdom separated from the Catholic Church which would last for two centuries. Elsewhere across Europe, reform-minded groups such as the *Anabaptists* were also questioning various ideas and practices of the Catholic Church, and advocating personal spiritual disciplines and practices that seemed to offer a more deeply spiritual experience than that found within the Catholic Church of the time. But it was Luther, supported by the nationalistic interests of the German nobility and the electioneering associated with the choosing of a new Roman Emperor that became the historical focal point for reform.

Unable to silence Luther, and with the support of German nobility against the Pope, the Protestant church began to develop—in Germany under Luther; in Zurich, Switzerland, under Zwingli; later in Geneva under John Calvin; and in England under the sponsorship of King Henry VIII. These were not coordinated efforts, though some contact occurred between different Protestant Reformers. As a result, the Protestant church splintered into different sects, or denominations, precursors to such as exist today. Eventually, the Catholic Church came to be called the Roman Catholic Church to emphasize its association with the Pope at Rome, and its distinction from the other Western churches. The reform under Luther and Zwingli erupted at about the same time and shared very similar ideas. Calvin's reform was a bit later than the others and provided the ideological basis for the Reformation across much of Europe. This was because, in Geneva, Calvin established a seminary to train preachers to go out and teach the reform ideas, used a printing press to disseminate the ideas, published a major work of systematic theology, which attempted to clearly explain the reform ideas about Christianity, and offered refuge to reform Christians from elsewhere across Europe who might be experiencing persecution for their ideas. In England, the reform began because of a dispute between the king and the Pope over a marriage annulment the king sought. When the Pope hesitated, the king took matters into his own hands and established what became the Church of England, which quickly became heavily influenced by the reformation then occurring on the continent.

CHRISTIAN MESSAGE, WORSHIP, AND FESTIVITIES

The essential message originally preached by the early church was that God has opened up a new way for humans to enter into a relationship with Himself. The old way was through sacrifices, law, and so forth. The new way was through faith in Jesus Christ—faith and trust that through His death and resurrection, He who was God had acted as the ultimate sacrifice. According to this message, Jesus had been raised from the dead and because He lives, and because one believes and trusts in Him, God's Holy Spirit is sent into the life of the believer. This person then experiences a dynamic, immediate, intimate personal relationship with God, not through a priest, sacrifice, mediator, etc. This was the essential message that was reflected in Paul's writings to the people of his day, and which was recorded in the New Testament to be carried on through the centuries. With the Renaissance and the rise of greater freedoms and education in Europe, educated people in and out of Church leadership positions regained the ability to read the Bible for themselves, in the original Greek and Hebrew. There they had found a very different Church and a very different experience of Christian faith than they saw around them in the Catholic Church. The message of the Reformation was not a new or reformulated Christianity. Substantially, it was a return to the approach to Christianity that was reflected during the New Testament period, and despite the numerous divisions and denominations which emerged from the Reformation, among all Protestant Churches, this understanding of Christianity remains essentially the message that is offered today. In response to the Reformation, Roman Catholicism, at first, retrenched, but then in ensuing centuries also underwent a reform of its own, in some ways, so that the message of the Roman Catholic Church today is much closer to that advocated by the early reformers of the Protestant Reformation.

The primary rituals, or sacraments, agreed upon by all parts of the Christian Church are two, though the Roman Catholic Church still acknowledges the seven identified in 1215, and the Orthodox Church informally recognizes more than just two. But all Christian churches agree on two primary sacraments. One is baptism, which is a symbol of one's becoming a Christian and entering into this dynamic relationship with Jesus Christ just described. The second is Eucharist, or Communion, or Lord's Supper. Depending upon what a particular church or denomination understands it to mean, essentially all agree that it is a look backward toward the sacrifice that Jesus made which thereby offers to all humans this means of relating to God, and also is a celebration of the entire believing Christian community, past, present, and future. Communion is something that is practiced on a repeated basis, while baptism is generally thought of as a one-time experience. In the Roman Catholic Church, there is usually a worship service (mass) that concludes with Communion. This is performed every day of the year. So it is possible to take Communion as frequently as every day of the year or, in many churches, it is something that is celebrated once a month or three or four times a year.

For most Christian congregations, Communion or Eucharist forms a central part of their worship experience. It is based on the events that occurred during the Passover Seder that Jesus celebrated with His disciples shortly before He was handed over to the authorities by His disciple Judas, and eventually crucified. The *Seder* includes *matzah*, saltwater, boiled egg, mixed plates (mixed fruits), shank of a special lamb, bitter herbs, lettuce (stick), and five cups of wine (originally, four cups) or grape juice. The fifth cup is referred to as "The Silent Cup" or "The Cup of Elijah."

The Four Cups represent "Four Expressions of Redemption" in God's promise to Moses in Exodus 6:2–8: "I will take you out," "I will deliver you," "I will redeem you," and "I will acquire you." Each represents a distinct stage and level of Redemption:

Cup #1: "I will take you out" refers to physical exit from the land of Egypt;
Cup #2: "I will deliver you from their bondage" means delivery from servitude;
Cup #3: "I will redeem you" is the divine guarantee that they remain a free people;
Cup #4: "I will acquire you as My nation" to be your God's chosen, which is the goal of the Exodus.

Jesus gave additional meaning to certain parts of the meal. He took the bread reserved to be eaten after the meal, which today is a special piece of Matzah eaten after the meal, and broke bread and gave it to them to eat, saying, "Take and eat, this is my body which is (about to be) given for you." He soon thereafter took one of the cups—today, there are four different times a cup of wine is drunk—probably the one shortly after the meal, and He gave that among his disciples and said, "Take, drink, this is my blood of the new covenant." Christian understanding is that this represents a sacrifice similar to the old Jewish system, by which they could experience a new (personal) relationship with their God. In the Jewish understanding, a relationship with God came through forgiveness and living as people of Israel's God. Only later did the role of the law become the almost exclusive way to such a relationship. What Jesus was saying was that through what would soon occur, the relationship He had with the Father would now be available to them as well, and to all who would believe in Him. In the Christian world, then, the death of Jesus is considered a sacrifice. In the New Testament book of Hebrews, it is specifically identified as a sacrifice for humanity similar to the sacrifices of the bulls and goats made on behalf of the Jewish people under the Jewish law.

As He gave the bread and the wine to His disciples, He also told them to "do this as often as you will in remembrance of Me." What initially was the practice of the early Church was actually to eat a whole meal, and at the very end of which they would take wine and bread and distribute it among themselves to celebrate the crucifixion and resurrection of Jesus. However, in some places, some people would come to this meal with plenty to eat and some with little. The ones who had a lot to eat sat and gorged themselves while the ones that didn't have much to eat did with their meager resources or starved. Then they were supposed to come together and share this fellowship ritual with one another, symbolizing their unity, their oneness, and their caring for each other. Perhaps by about 70 CE, it was no longer common to eat an entire meal whenever they would remember Jesus's death in this way. Rather what they would do was to eat at home, partaking only of the bread and the wine together. Everybody received an equal amount and no one was left out. This practice is what later on came to be known as Communion or Eucharist. The idea is that it is a replication of this last meal—the Passover Seder—and a remembrance of the importance of Jesus's death as a sacrifice for all who are willing to believe.

There are many other services to be found in the Church as well: healing services, prayer services, deliverance services, etc., but Baptism and Communion or Eucharist are the two that virtually all of Christianity agrees upon as being primary ceremonies of the Church. There are also two main festivals celebrated in Christianity today. One is the celebration of Christmas. Even though Christmas Day is not the day on which

The multicultural and global identity of Christianity

©Dawn Hudson/Shutterstock.com

Jesus was actually born (and the Orthodox Church uses a different calendar than does the West, so that Christmas day falls on January 7 each year), it is the celebration of Christmas which is universal throughout Christianity. It is celebrated throughout all of Christianity as one of the major festivals of the Church year. The other major festival is Easter. Like Christmas, it is usually at a different time each year, and between the Western and the Orthodox Churches, different calendars are used so the dates also usually do not correspond exactly in any given year. Nevertheless, Easter is always in the spring of the year. It is usually around the time of the Jewish celebration of Passover. Of relatively less note in the Christian world, but a third festival celebrated particularly in Roman Catholic and Orthodox traditions, is the day of Pentecost. This festival date is always determined as fifty days after the day on which Easter is celebrated during the year.

Probable Calendar of the Life and Ministry of Jesus Christ

- Birth—4 or 5 BCE
- Flight to Egypt— 4 or 5 BCE
- Return from Egypt— 3 or 4 BCE
- Visit to the Temple— 8 CE
- John the Baptist's Ministry Beginning—26 CE
- Jesus Baptized by John—26 CE
- Year of Inauguration—26 CE
- Year of Popularity–27 CE
- Year of Opposition—28 CE
- Year of Crucifixion/Death—29 or 30 CE
- Pentecost (Induction of the Church)—29 or 30 CE

Important Changes that Occurred in the Western Church

- Imperial bishops as imperial state officials
- Emperor Theodosius II declared Christianity as official religion of the Empire
- Charlemagne instituted "Christian kingship"
- Church merges with the state
- Bishop Siricius was the first to apply the term "pope" to himself
- Pope Leo I (Leo the Great) took the title *pontifex maximus*, "chief priest," formerly used by the Roman Emperors in reference to the state cult
- Gelasius was the first pope to be called the "Vicar of Christ

KEY WORDS

Christ	The Kingdom of God	Pentecost	Resurrection
Pilate	Herod the Great	The New Testament	Peter Paul
Caiaphas	Edict of Milan	Apostle	Ecumenical Councils
Calvinism	Anabaptists	The Reformation	The Great Schism
Constantine	Pentecostalism	Patristic	Constantine the Great
Papacy/Pope	Augustine of Hippo	Sacraments	Baptism
Gnosticism	Marcionism	Monasticism	Lord's Supper/Eucharist
Martin Luther	Patriarch of Orthodoxy		

QUESTIONS FOR FURTHER STUDY

1. Who is Jesus Christ of Nazareth?

2. How does one become a Christian according to the New Testament?

3. Identify and discuss the areas of Jesus's controversy with the religious leaders.

4. According to the gospel, why did Jesus die? What is the meaning of the resurrection of Jesus?

5. What is a sacrament? List the sacraments in Catholicism, Eastern Orthodoxy, and Protestantism.

6. What is canonization of Christian scriptures? Discuss the pros and cons of the process.

7. What is Christianity's contributions to world civilization?

8. Outline some major challenges that the modern church are confronted with.

9. Has the Christian church become too much political? Why or why not?

Islam

OVERVIEW

Islam enjoys a certain amount of background that is shared with Judaism and Christianity including some historical elements. Also, as with Judaism and Christianity, Islam is monotheistic, meaning not only a belief in one god but only one God exists. There are no other gods. There may be other spirits, but those spirits are not powerful in the same sense that the one god is powerful. In Islam, Judaism, and Christianity, the role of history is more profound than in Eastern religions because it is through the human/divine interaction that the elements of the faith are revealed. Like Judaism and Christianity, there is a certain legal dimension associated with the religion, as well as moral dimension. As with Judaism and Christianity, the primary way in which the religion is practiced

©Naghiyev/Shutterstock.com

is daily living. In other words, monasticism, meditation, yoga, and things like this are not the primary way in which adherents to Islam, Judaism, and Christianity express their religious activities. There are a few who withdraw to monasteries in Christianity, but they are by no means considered the holy people, the highest way, the leading teachers, or the leading spokespersons. There was a time in Western Christianity when that was the case, but monasticism has long ceased to be the main center of spirituality in any part of mainstream Christianity.

As mentioned earlier in the study of Judaism, for Islam, Judaism, and Christianity, divinity is first of all a personal being, meaning that God is personal and a "he" and that He has some kind of direct, personal relationship that the believer can have with Him. In Islam, the divine being is Allah, whose role is to rule. It is important to understand that the term "God" is a title, not a personal name. It represents, one might say, "the office." For instance, if you talk about someone being president, that is the title of the role that person fulfills. In a similar way the term "God" is referring to a role, a title, that the being that lies behind that title fulfills. For Islam, the principle role that Allah fulfills then is to rule. What does he rule? He rules not just this world, but the universe—the entire cosmos—the stars, galaxies, this more limited world, everything. Allah's role is to rule the whole thing according to Islam. Allah is believed to rule directly; there are no intermediaries.

The role of humankind is to submit. In Islam, the most fundamental thing is the issue of submission to what is believed to be the will of Allah. The most fundamental thing in Hinduism is maintaining order in the universe. The most fundamental thing in Buddhism is to eliminate suffering through selflessness. The most fundamental thing in Islam is the issue of obedience. Islam believes that Allah created humanity as a unique creation rather than in the sense of evolution. Humans were created as distinct from the animals and all other life forms. For Islam, when Allah created man, he gave him the responsibility to be the tenant controller of the world, and man's responsibility is, therefore, to be a good steward of what Allah has entrusted to him. He is the tenant controller of the world, a responsibility fulfilled by obedience to Allah. By so doing, humans demonstrate the "good sense" of Allah in entrusting to humans this stewardship of the world. Thus, in order to demonstrate that sensibility, humans are to keep Allah's laws.

Islam believes that humans are born innocent. There is no concept of original sin in Islam nor is there a concept of a fall from grace into sin of which humans need redemption. Since humans are born innocent they are born fit to go to heaven. So if an infant dies, in the Muslim understanding, they believe that the newborn is transported immediately to paradise. Also, there is no need for a savior or Messiah. There is no need for a redeemer or intermediary with Allah. Islam actually means to submit. The one who submits is a Muslim. What humans do need is to prove themselves individually and personally worthy of this stewardship that Allah has entrusted to them. They do that in two basic ways. One is worship of Allah according to the prescribed laws and directions that have been handed down. The other one is through good deeds, again according to the prescribed laws that have been handed down by the religion. Both point to the responsibility of the faithful in Islam.

Life after death for Muslims is either reward or punishment, based on what one did in this life. There is no purgatory in Islam. This means either reward (paradise), or punishment (hell), based on an individual's deeds. Said another way, if Muslims prove themselves worthy through their worship and good deeds, then with that innocence into which they were born, they will enter paradise. If they were innocent, but failed to properly worship, to properly live up to their stewardship, to do the good deeds that Allah has set forth, then at death will come punishment rather than paradise. There the person remains forever. Only if Allah chooses to do otherwise will this not be the case. Paradise is described differently by different sources. Some express it in a metaphysical sense. Others express it as an actual location or spiritual existence. Some perceive that only Muslims will be there. Some perceive that others may be there, but in a secondary status. One of the interesting things about Islam is that all people who are "people of the book" (the Bible, that is to say Jews or Christians) also have a place in the afterlife. They just don't have the preferred places. Preference is given, according to Muslim understanding, to Muslims, which of course is considerably different from the understanding of either Judaism or Christianity.

Actually, except for Muslim martyrs, Muslims believe when a person dies this leads to a state of dreamless sleep. There, one awaits Jesus's return in what Christians call the Second Coming (the technical term is *Parousia*). "*And (Jesus) shall be a sign (for the coming of) the Hour (of Judgement): Therefore have no doubt about the (Hour) but follow ye Me: this is a Straight Way*" (Surah 43.61). Muslim scholars, like Jusuf Ali (Quran translator), have interpreted this text to mean the second coming of Jesus: "This is understood to refer to the second coming of Jesus in the Last Days just before the Resurrection when he will destroy the false doctrines that pass under his name, and prepare the way for the universal acceptance of Islam, the Gospel of Unity and Peace, the Straight way of the Quran" (The Holy Quran, 1337 cited in message4muslims.org).

According to Message for Muslims Trust, Abu Huraira, a companion and disciple of Muhammed and narrator of the Hadiths had also said, "By Him in whose hands my soul is, the son of Mary (Jesus) will shortly descend amongst you people (Muslims) as a just ruler and will break the cross and kill the pig and abolish the Jazzy (a tax taken from the non-Muslims, who are in the protection, of the Muslim government). Then there will be abundance of money and no-body will accept charitable gifts" (Bukhari Volume 3, Book 34, Number 425 cited in message4muslims.org)

At the time of the Parousia, Islam believes that all will at that time awaken from the dreamless sleep and judgment will take place. It is at that time that Muslims will actually be judged according to the deeds done in this life. They will then pass from judgment into a paradise which is actually a paradisiacal earthly existence (not a new heaven and new earth of the book of Revelation in the New Testament). They believe that at the Parousia, Christians and Jews will also be reawakened and judged at that same time and receive the rewards that they have earned in this life.

Jesus, for Islam, was a prophet who stands in a long line of prophets beginning from Abraham passing through Moses and David and even John the Baptist. They accept all of the Old Testament personalities as prophets including the Jewish King David. However, for Islam, Muhammad was the final prophet whose word is superior to any of the previous "prophets" and is authoritative in the event of any contradictions with any former "prophets." This is one reason why Jews and Christians, at least in theory, have a role in the afterlife.

HISTORY

Islam develops against the events occurring in two different realms. One is the development of the Arab people because Islam began as a religion primarily centered in the Arab world. Some historians of Islam suggest, in fact, that Muhammad sought to give the Arab people a religion of a "book" similar to what the Jews or the Christians had. It is not truly clear either from the *Quran* or any of the other things that occur during Muhammad's own lifetime, or shortly thereafter, that he ever envisioned Islam as a religion that would be meaningful for more than the Arab people. Today it is commonly believed among Muslims, however, that the early vision for Islam was for more than just the Arab peoples. But not all Muslim scholars are convinced beyond all doubt that Muhammad perceived Islam as spreading beyond the Arab world. It was fundamentally a religion for the Arab people. The fact that it spread beyond Arabia is secondary. Thus, it is necessary to look at the emergence of the Arab people before looking at the development of Islam.

The Emergence of Arabs: The emergence of the Arab people begins with the stories in the Old Testament book of Genesis related to Abraham. According to the Old Testament book of Genesis, Abraham was first of all a Semite. In other words, he was of a particular ethnic extraction. He was living close to the Persian Gulf in a city known as Ur. While he was at Ur, according to the Old Testament, he began to have a spiritual stirring. The people that lived at Ur worshipped a number of idols as gods. Abraham somehow began to doubt the efficacy of these idols and the gods they represented. The Jewish rabbis have an interesting story about Abraham that, when he was going through this quest, he tried worshipping the sun but the sun went down at night so it wasn't universal. He tried worshipping the moon but the moon disappeared during the day, so it wasn't universal. He tried worshipping various stars but they disappeared during the day, so they were not universal. Water comes and goes, so it is not universal. Storms also come and go. It was during this process that God spoke to Abraham and said that he should worship Him and be faithful to Him. According to the story, Abraham's father was an idol-maker. One day when his father was out collecting orders for idols, Abraham went into the "garage" and took a sledgehammer with which he destroyed all of the idols in the storehouse, except for the biggest one. He put the sledgehammer in the hand of the biggest one. When his father returned home, he marched out into the garage and was aghast. He yelled, "Abraham." "Yes, father?", Abraham replied. "What happened?", his father asked. Abraham responded, "Isn't it obvious? The idol with the sledgehammer got mad at all the other idols and went on a rampage and broke them all up." His father replied, "That's impossible. I made the things." Abraham responded, "That's just it. Don't you see? How can you worship something you made with your own hands?" So, they were run out of town. There are, of course, various other reasons besides this story for why Abraham and his family left Ur. Whatever the reason, for a period of time they lived at a place called *Haran*. Then Abraham and some of his family (his father had then died), journeyed into the land that God had said that He would show them, and that land is the land that today is known as Israel when you include the West Bank and the Gaza Strip into the territory.

Abraham was married to his half-sister, Sarah, but he had no children. This was vexing because he had no one to whom to leave his wealth, and he was a fairly wealthy individual in terms of livestock. What Abraham needed was an heir. Initially he anticipated that the heir was going to be his servant, who was from Damascus. But during a famine, Abraham went to Egypt where he got himself into trouble with the pharaoh and received all kinds of riches as gifts from the king, lest the God of Abraham be dishonored. Returning into the land that God had promised to him with all of these riches, he also brought an Egyptian girl, Hagar, as a servant girl for his wife. Since Sarah was by this time over eighty years old and had no children, Sarah suggested Abraham impregnate Hagar as a surrogate, and that any child born from that union would be Sarah's (this was a cultural tradition among the people of the Middle East of that time). Abraham agreed, and soon Hagar became pregnant. Her son was called Ishmael. For thirteen years Ishmael was the only son and apparent heir of Abraham. However, when Ishmael was twelve years of age, Sarah became pregnant. The following year Sarah had a son named Isaac. As long as Ishmael was the only son of Abraham, regardless of who the mother was, Ishmael was the heir of everything that Abraham had. But when Sarah, Abraham's true wife (Hagar was a concubine), gave birth to Isaac, then her son suddenly displaced and dispossessed Ishmael of everything. Ishmael and his mother eventually were forced from the family home and they moved toward Arabia where Ishmael became the ancestor of the Arab people. Even the Arabs sometimes refer to themselves as Ishmaelites, children of Ishmael. With the young Ishmael and his mother driven out of town, Isaac is the son of Abraham who would ultimately inherit everything from Abraham, which according to Jewish understanding includes the promise of God to Abraham of the land, which is today the land of Israel and all of the spiritual benefits that go along with that promise. Isaac eventually marries his cousin, who has two children who are twins. One is Esau and the other is Jacob. Through a ruse, because Esau is older, Jacob actually winds up being the one who gains the birthright, hence the inheritance, whereas Esau is left with very little. Esau will ultimately go across the Dead Sea and the Jordan River to dwell in the area of what is today the Kingdom of Jordan. His descendants eventually intermarry with the Ishmaelites so that today, Ishmael and Esau, according to the Bible, are the common ancestors of the Arab people. Jacob fathers twelve children who are ultimately the ancestors of the Jews. It must be noted also that Abraham had other children with other women when Sarah died.

One of the differences between Muslims and Jews (and Christians) arises over this story. Muslims do not believe that the Old and New Testaments as they exist today are the original accounts. They maintain that there was a different, original account that was changed by the Jews and the Christians once Islam arose and spread during the 600s CE. Muslims maintain that Jews and Christians changed the Old and New Testaments so as to eliminate the legitimacy of Ishmael's inheritance to Abraham as a first son. It is important to realize that copies of the Old Testament made about 100 to 200 years BCE (approximately 900 years before the rise of Islam) have now been discovered in the Dead Sea Scrolls, and these contain virtually the same text as is found in all modern day Bibles. Nevertheless, on the basis of supposed changes, Muslims maintain that Ishmael all along was the one who was to inherit that which Abraham had because he was the firstborn regardless of Isaac's birth. In association with this issue, Muslims have a different account of the Biblical story of the sacrifice of Isaac on Mount Moriah. According to Genesis, God said to Abraham, "Take your son, your only son" which refers to Isaac, who was the son of the true wife, according to the Old Testament. Abraham was instructed to offer Isaac as a sacrifice to God on Mount Moriah. Abraham was stopped by God from completing the sacrifice just at the last moment, offering a substitute instead. Jews and Christians agree that the site where the Jewish Temple later stood is on this site, on which the Muslim Dome of the Rock is located today. However, Muslims say that the Bible is inaccurate at this point because of changes made by Christians and Jews, and that it was Ishmael, not Isaac, who was to worship with Abraham. And today, it is maintained by Muslims that it was the site of the Kaaba in Mecca, not Mount Moriah, where Abraham and Ishmael had worshipped. There is no archaeological basis to choose between the historicity of one story or the other, so faith is usually what determines which story is considered historical.

For many centuries, the descendants of Ishmael and Esau were desert dwellers in Arabia. There were, in the region, a few oases, such as Mecca and Medina, and a few towns located around the coast. But the vast territory of Arabia was mostly uninhabited except by nomadic Arab tribes. These tribes maintained herds and flocks of animals, moving from place to place, usually on a semi-yearly cycle. All of Arabia was broken up into territories under the control of one or another of the tribes. In the immediate time period before Muhammad was born, there were political changes both in Arabia and in the world around it. At this time, there was one tribe that, through intermarriage and through political and economic negotiations, was becoming the largest and strongest tribe in all of Arabia. That tribe was the *Quraysh* tribe, with its family headquarters at Mecca. By 570 CE, the people of Arabia had returned to the polytheism from which Abraham had fled. Mecca was the site of a religious shrine as well as an important economic and political center because of the Quraysh tribe. It was the economic crossroads for most caravans that moved through Arabia, because there was one main trade route to Damascus, meaning all of the trade traffic between the West and the East across Arabia had to go through the city of Mecca. The black stone of Mecca, where the *Kaaba* is located, had become a site of religious pilgrimage connected with the polytheism of Arabia, but before Muhammad's time there existed no clear evidence that the black stone was necessarily related to a tradition involving Abraham and Ishmael. It is commonly believed that it was probably a meteorite stone which fell to earth at a very early time, though maybe after the Ishmaelites were already in Arabia (perhaps in the polytheism of the people they saw the rock as a special sign from some god or gods). In a building around it, shrines had been created to honor virtually all of the Arabian gods. In this way, a traveler from any region in Arabia, taking a caravan across the desert, could stop at Mecca and pay homage to his particular god at the *Kaaba*.

As a result of various wars and struggles that were going on elsewhere, there were a number of communities of Jews that had migrated southward into Arabia. There is a mountain ridge along the western edge of Arabia known as the Hijaz Mountains. At the base of these mountains are the oases of Mecca and Medina. The Jews established themselves along the base of these mountains as far south as Medina, where there were three Jewish communities to be found. There were also Arabs around Arabia who had grown disenchanted with idol worship and wanted something more. For various reasons, they were unable to find satisfaction in the religion of the Jews in Arabia, nor in the Christian traditions of the Byzantine Empire. These could be called monotheistic Arabs. They worshiped one god but, in a sense, they were seekers rather than adherents to any particular religion. Some lived in the caves of the Hijaz, following the pattern of Christian monks who lived as hermits in desert caves, some even being regarded as prophets. Another monotheistic religious influence around Arabia even before Muhammad was born were the Byzantine Christians, represented not only by cave-dwelling monks, but by urban centers such as Damascus, which were found in the Middle East, and in which Arab merchants pursued trade with the Western world.

LIFE OF MUHAMMAD AND ORIGIN OF ISLAM

His Life: Muhammad was born approximately 570 CE. Some say it was the August 20, 570 CE while other scholars say it may have been as late as 575 CE. He was orphaned by the age of six. According to Arabian tradition at that time, an orphan was a social outcast no better than a slave or foreigner. As an orphan, according to Muslim tradition, he was sensitive to suffering, including the fate of the indigent and the poor. Muhammad's uncle, Abu Talib, took him into his family and raised him as one of his own children. Muhammad was first a shepherd, which was the common occupation of a child. Later, he began to travel with a caravan and learned a trade that was the most common adult occupation of that time—a camel driver. The best camel drivers could become caravan leaders and heads of caravans. According to Muslim tradition, Muhammad was regarded as honest, trustworthy, and upright, and a custodian or trustee of people's belongings, securities and assets.

> It is said that "[h]e never turned anyone away empty-handed from his house and always gave preference to the needy over his own needs. He was so merciful that . . . people living under and around him call him as most humble and merciful . . . and if he had nothing to give, he apologized to the needy person" (ibid). The Quran speak of him as a mercy to humankind: *That we have sent not thee (O Muhammad) but as a mercy to the whole of humankind, as a mercy to all the world*" (Sura [2010], 21:107).

These were qualities that he had demonstrated as a caravan leader. During his trips, he also had contact with Jewish, Christian, and Arab monotheists (or their traditions) as he traveled between Mecca and Damascus. Some of the stories of Jewish tradition, Christian tradition, and some of the ideas of monotheism likely influenced his thinking during this period of time, and in later years as well. In 595, he took an order, as part of a caravan, to Damascus, Syria, for a wealthy widow by the name of Khadijah. When he returned, he married Khadijah. He was twenty-five at the time; she was forty. After he married Khadijah, for the next fifteen years, he continued to take caravans. Of course, since she was wealthy (actually her wealth was his after their marriage), it was not necessary for him to take caravans, but he did so though with decreasing frequency as he became increasingly interested in the religious aspects of life.

By the year 610 or 612 CE, Muhammad had largely retired from being a camel driver and had begun a personal religious quest. According to Muslim tradition, he would go into the caves that were in the mountains near Mecca, sometimes for days or even weeks, meditating and seeking and searching. One day in the year 610 or 612 CE, he claimed an angel, Gabriel, appeared to him and revealed to him that Allah had heard his prayers and wanted him to know that there was but one "God," *Allah*, and that *Allah* was calling him to go back to his people and to proclaim this to them, and if they do not turn from their idols and submit to Allah, he would quickly come and judge them. The way in which ancient peoples understood the notion of polytheism is that there was always a great god as well as various manifestations of that great god. Some of the manifestations were greater, such as the moon, the river, or the storm god, and some were lesser gods. The great god was believed to have set the world in motion and was the creator god. He then "stepped back" as it were, and the manifestations, like the sun and moon, first perceived as simply attributes of the great god, eventually became worshipped as gods themselves. Since they were directly involved with human livelihood and human existence, it was these gods that tended to be eventually worshipped by people. They are what became idol gods. The word *Allah* (Arabic) and the word *Elohim* (Hebrew) come from the same root word: *EL*. In the development of Jewish thought, *Elohim* is the God of Abraham. In Arabic thought, the great god of their polytheistic pantheon was *Allah*. Muslims claim that *Elohim* and *Allah* refer to the same divinity. Muhammad's claim, then, was that an angel from the one and only great God had communicated directly with him.

According to popular Muslim tradition, Muhammad returned to the city of Mecca and began proclaiming exactly this message said to be from Allah to the people of Mecca. Tradition indicates that his wife quickly accepted the message and was converted. A few other people were also converted to the message, but most people in Mecca resisted it. Periodically, for 23 years, Muhammad would receive what he claimed were additional revelations, which he would then take into Mecca and proclaim. It is reported that he often did this in the courtyard of the Kaaba, to the discomfort of visitors and city residents alike. Since he was still under the protection of his uncle, Abu Talib, there was little the residents of the city could do but endure Muhammad's actions. On the other hand, the situation gradually began to take a serious political and economic toll on Mecca. Caravans began to send representatives into the city to purchase supplies while the majority of the caravan awaited their return from outside the city. And the embarrassment of Mecca in being unable to silence or otherwise control Muhammad weakened the city's prestige in Arabia, along with the prestige of the Quraysh tribe.

By the year 619, the number of followers is estimated to have been two to three hundred. Most of them were slaves or from among the lower classes. This means very few people in Mecca, that is, very few members of the Quraysh tribe, had believed the message. Nevertheless, Muhammad was gaining a reputation, claiming to be a prophet of Allah, and this was spreading along the trade route between Mecca and Damascus. The year 619 was a turning point in Muhammad's life. In that year, both his uncle, Abu Talib, and his wife, Khadijah, died. From an emotional standpoint, the death of Khadijah was the most devastating, and one from which he may never have really completely recovered. After her death, he would eventually go on to marry again and again, eventually including ten additional wives (Ayesha, his third and favorite wife, married to him when she was nine years old). From the political standpoint, the death of Abu Talib was the more critical event. The death of Abu Talib removed all political and social protection from Muhammad. During the previous decade, there had been moderate to minor persecution of followers of Muhammad. They might have some rocks thrown at them. On occasion, they might be cornered in the market and beaten by ruffians. Meccans might refuse to sell to them. But Muhammad himself, because he was under the protection of his uncle, continued to experience the kind of civility that any legitimate member of the Meccan community received. With the death of his uncle, he was now simply an orphan again and didn't belong there with the rest of the Meccans, and he began to be persecuted as well. The next two years, from 619 to 621 CE, became increasingly difficult. By 621, it was clear that survival itself was an issue, and the Muslims could no longer continue to live in Mecca.

The Hijrah: To the north of Mecca lay the oasis of Medina, where for some time strife between the Arab communities was endemic. There were nine Arab communities and three Jewish communities coexisting at the site. The Jews had little to do with the Arabs and their problems, except as it related to commercial matters. By 619 and 620, the Arab communities had heard of the claim of Muhammad to be a prophet of Allah, and they traveled to Mecca to investigate the claim. This was done because, if confirmed, he might be able to help unravel the complex matrix of conflict that had developed between the nine Arab communities at Medina. The first group returned with a favorable report, so the next year a second group was sent, also returning with a favorable report. Efforts were then initiated to urge Muhammad to come to Medina to act as a referee (something like a judge in the manner of the Old Testament) between these various Arab communities, to help bring peace and to settle their blood feuds. This situation was exactly the answer Muhammad needed, though it is not clear that the *Medinans* intended that all the Muslims would also migrate with Muhammad to Medina. But if all the Muslims left Mecca all at once, they might be attacked in the desert and killed. So small parties departed at night, when they would be least missed. In such small numbers, nobody would pay a lot of attention to their departure, so in 621 CE the migration of Muslims to Medina began. Eventually, in mid-622 CE, Muhammad and the last few remaining followers in Mecca all departed for Medina. The name of that event is known as the *Hijra* (migration). This is the beginning of the Muslim calendar (years are expressed in Islam as "AH," which means "after the Hijra"), and would usher in a broad transformation for Islam.

While it is not clear that the Medinans had invited all of Muhammad's followers to come to Medina, their presence introduced another community to Medina, which upset the delicate ecosystem of the oasis. Medina was able to support twelve communities, but they didn't have any extra work or flocks, nor extra means of income for this community of Muhammad's followers. The Medinans gave the followers of Muhammad virtually nothing, and so for the next couple of years, from 622 to 624 CE, the way that the Muslim community existed was either by foraging or from Muhammad's personal funds (either the wealth he had from Khadija or what he received as a judge). Second, at Mecca, Islam had been a religious movement, but at Medina, Muhammad's role changed, and with that so did all Islam. He was no longer just a prophet and leader of a religious movement. At Medina, he was also a political, economic, and social leader. Because of this new situation which combined these roles into one person, any of the things that he said eventually had the force of divine law so that at Medina, his judgments were regarded as the commands of Allah himself. The result was a religious tradition in which one cannot separate the political and the religious spheres. The Western world emphasizes separation of the religious sphere from that of the state. But for Islam, it is intellectually impossible to separate the religious and the political world of Islam because the political commands that are embodied within the Muslim system are regarded as the very words and commands of Allah.

By 624, the Muslim community was just barely surviving, and it was clear to Muhammad that something more needed to be done. There was a "law" of the desert that is still common among desert dwellers, that if there is a caravan traveling through the territory and a tribe is in need, the tribe has the right to stop the caravan, take what is needed (not more than that), and then let the caravan proceed on its way (Western countries practice the same thing, but call it by the term "taxes"). Muhammad learned of a Meccan caravan returning from Damascus that was traveling near Medina, and the Muslims carried out a raid on that caravan to take the food and other things they needed. They were outnumbered 900 to approximately 300 (or fewer), but they caught the Meccan caravan off guard. The Muslims from Medina returned with all kinds of goods to provide for their needs while a very embarrassed and angry caravan continued to Mecca. The people of Medina regarded this as a great victory, perhaps because of Allah's favor, and Medinans began to see the Muslims from a different perspective.

The following year, 625 CE, the Meccans came with an army to retaliate against Muhammad and the people at Medina, but they were unable to successfully subdue the oasis of Medina, which was again perceived as a victory for the Muslims.

Many of the people in the Arab communities, and none in the Jewish communities, began to convert to Islam. Also, nomadic Arab tribes in the vicinity of Medina started to make political alliances with Muhammad. The next year, 626, the Meccans tried again to defeat Medina, and again were not successful, whereupon even more people at Medina and other nearby tribes either united politically with Muhammad or committed themselves to Islam as well. Two years later, 628 CE, Muhammad sought to make a pilgrimage to Mecca. He took a large group of followers and together made the several days journey to Mecca. However, when they reached the hill overlooking Mecca, the Meccans thought they came to invade and sent leaders out to meet the Muslims. Instead of a war, it was agreed to defer this first Hajj by a year. In exchange, the leaders of Mecca agreed that the next year the Meccans would vacate the city for three days and let the Muslims perform their pilgrimage, after which the Muslims would leave and the Meccans could return to the city. Within that year, however, most of the people of Mecca perceived this as a concession by their leaders to a victory for Islam (why would the Muslims, once controlling the city of Mecca, be willing to surrender it back to the polytheism of the Meccans, which Islam was rejecting) and converted to Islam. In 629 CE, instead of the Meccans leaving, they joined the pilgrimage. By the following year, all idols had been removed from Mecca, and the city became a religious center for Islam.

During the years Islam was growing stronger at Medina, particularly after 625, the Jewish communities grew fearful of the increasing importance of Muhammad and the Muslims at Medina. Arabs who were resisting Muhammad's increasingly powerful leadership at Medina began to involve the leaders of the Jewish communities in their resistance. There are several traditions about what happened during this time period. Some say that one of the Jewish communities was subsequently permitted to leave because they chose to do so rather than remain any longer under the political control of the Muslims. The other two were reluctant to leave and were massacred, men, women, and children, by the Muslims. Another tradition relates that one community of Jews was massacred, and only a few from the other two communities of Jews managed to make their escape. One tradition is that the massacre erupted because of an attempted poisoning of Muhammad by the wife of one of the Jewish leaders while hosting Muhammad for dinner. From 626 onward, however, a tremendous rift has existed between the Jews and the Muslims. When Muhammad went to Medina, the direction of prayer was toward Jerusalem. It is said by some that when the Jews at Medina rejected Muhammad as their Messiah, which according to their tradition he could never be since he was Arab, then the direction of prayer was changed from Jerusalem toward Mecca. Whether true or not, in doing that, he also integrated into Islam some elements of previous Arab religious practice, such as the shrine of the Kaaba and the pilgrimage to Mecca.

The Jews, every year, celebrated a feast in the spring known as Passover, which involved a week of special observances preceded by fasting. As a celebration for Muslims, distinct from the Jewish celebration, the month-long Ramadan celebration was instituted. This also became the celebration of Muhammad's receiving the first of what he claimed were revelations from Allah in 610 or 612 CE.

The Umma: One of the dramatic changes to occur in Islam was the shift from the tribal character of Arabia. A person's basic loyalty was to their family, their clan, and their tribe. But for Muslims, it was necessary to forsake these loyalties to be part of the one community of Islam, the Umma. And as tribes created political and religious alliances with Muhammad and the Muslims, they also had to give up their individual identities and become part of the Umma. Thus, gradually, the whole sociopolitical structure of Arabia changed. One of the fundamental beliefs in Islam is every Muslim is equal to every other Muslim. But this ideal did not work always. For instance, the people that migrated from Mecca to Medina enjoyed a degree of respect that was higher than those who converted at Medina. Those who converted at Mecca and Medina enjoyed a higher level of status in the very early years of Islam than all other Muslims. Nevertheless, there are certain symbols of equality which are retained to this day. For instance, when a person goes on the Hajj, whether he is a senior diplomat or a dirt farmer, the person wears a special white robe that is strictly for the Hajj, and everyone wears the same type of robe. Most camp out in the same camping facilities. They all do the same acts. And on a daily basis whenever they pray, all Muslims perform the same actions. These are equalizing mechanisms in Islam intended as object lessons to demonstrate that everyone is equal. The transformation from the tribal structure to the *Umma* did something else for Arabia. It did not last for very long, but during the time that it did last, Arabia became a tremendous force—not only in Arabia but throughout the entire central region of the world, stretching all the way across North Africa, and east to India.

Islam conceives of the world as two spheres. There is the Muslim sphere and the sphere of war or struggle/jihad (the non-Muslim sphere). War does not necessarily mean military action but can range from personal efforts to submit to the will of Allah when not living in a Muslim environment, to defensive actions on behalf of the Umma, to actual military action. In this regard, the *Quran*, which is the scripture for Islam, very clearly states a Muslim may make a peace treaty with the infidel (the non-Muslim), but for no more than ten years. At the end of ten years it may be renewed for another period of time not to exceed ten years. But in the Muslim world no peace treaty is valid after ten years if it is with a non-Muslim, unless renewed.

During the remaining three years of Muhammad's life, he focused on the conversion of the rest of Arabia to Islam. Some of it came by political alliance and some by the point of a sword. According to some interpreters, Muhammad perceived himself as in the position of Moses, in that as Moses gave a divine law to the Israelites for them to obey and follow, so he had likewise given a law to the Arabs, to which they should obey and submit, and seek after Allah. His intention was that at least everybody in Arabia would become a Muslim.

Muhammad died in 632 CE after a week's illness (perhaps associated, according to some scholars, with the attempted poisoning six years earlier) and before naming a successor (some maintain he named his son-in-law, Ali, successor, but this was apparently not recognized by the leadership, if indeed it did happen). Since he had no son to succeed him there were two principle concerns that had to be settled. One was who was to be his successor and the second question was the meaning of succession. Muhammad was regarded as a prophet of Allah so when he died, would the person who succeeds him be a prophet as well and receive additional revelations from Allah (an issue that may have actually been settled before Muhammad's death, in the "word" that there would be no prophets to arise in Islam after him)? The decision of the elders of the Umma was that whoever succeeded Muhammad would only be a temporal religious leader. That person would assume the religious as well as the political leadership, but based upon what Muhammad had already communicated as being from Allah, with nothing supplemental. The next question was who should succeed to leadership? Muhammad had a daughter named Fatima, but, of course, as a woman she could not inherit the leadership. She was married to Muhammad's relative by the name of Ali. One group of elders supported Ali, but when the elders of the Muslim community met together to decide, many felt that Ali was too young and they really needed someone older, wiser, and who had been involved in the movement from its earliest days. So they decided among themselves on Abu Bakr.

Caliphs and Caliphate: Abu Bakr had been around since the initial days of Islam. He had been one of the first converts to Islam. The word for "successor" is *Caliph*, so he became the first Caliph, and the ruler of all of Arabia. Abu Bakr was an old man by the time of his election, however, and he wouldn't actually live too long. This may, in fact, have been a factor in the decision to choose him since already some tribes were beginning to leave the Umma and seek Arab monotheist prophets of their own choosing. Without swift, decisive action, the Umma might well have collapsed. It was this issue that Abu Bakr primarily addressed during his brief rule. Sometimes it was at the point of a sword again, and sometimes he succeeded in restoring tribes to the Umma by using economic or other kinds of political pressure. By the time that Abu Bakr died in 634 CE, two things had happened. Arabia was back within the fold of Islam, and he had named his successor. The man that he named to be his successor was Umar.

Umar had been a leading general who had carried out raids in the northern Arabian Desert. As Caliph, Umar expanded his military activities. In 635 CE, he entered Damascus and the region of the Levant (modern day Lebanon, Syria, Israel, and Jordan). The next year, 636 CE, he opened a new front going the opposite direction, toward the east into the Mesopotamian Valley and Iran, the armies of Islam eventually reaching as far as the Indus River. In 639 CE, Egypt began to fall to his control. By the year 700 (several decades after Umar's death), all of coastal North Africa would be under Muslim control, most of the territory having fallen during the ten years that Umar ruled. When he died in 644 CE, he had not named his successor so that two factions again arose among the elders of the Umma—those that wanted to see Ali as the Caliph and those supporting another one of the early converts to Islam named Uthman (Othman).

Uthman was a member of the last clan in Mecca to convert to Islam, the *Umayyads*. Uthman himself was one of the first converts (unlike the rest of his clan), but the year 644 CE was only a little over thirty years from the beginning of Islam. The idea of a tribal society and tribal ties and family relationships did not die easily and had remained very strong in the minds of many people. What the situation between Uthman and his clan meant was that to many people, Uthman might not really be true potential leadership for Islam. Further, Uthman had (or gained) a reputation as a drunk, and a licentious womanizer who grew fat and happy off of the wealth of the raids that the army continued prosecuting. Uthman began collecting the written copies of what Muhammad had claimed were revelations from Allah. Some scholars maintain that during Muhammad's lifetime, as he would have one of these "revelatory" experiences, and then report to the people what he said that Allah had told him, an official scribe wrote those things down, though from the beginning, this may not have been the case. Also, some statements were memorized. Some who could write might have done so on scraps of leather or parchment. Over the two decades of Muhammad's leadership, these amounted to a substantial number of sources, but there had been no systemized collection of these things. Uthman initiated the systematic collection and editing of these sources into a single book, which is called *Quran* (Revelations). This is the book that compiles, according to Muslim understanding, all the commands Muhammad claims he received from Allah. Under Uthman, even this deed also created an enormous amount of controversy. He was accused of having omitted some of the sayings that were particularly unfavorable toward his family. So in his own lifetime, there were people who said that the Quran that he had compiled was not legitimate because it was incomplete. This led to an early division in Islam over whether the Quran was really authoritative. Today it is accepted by all Muslims as the authoritative book of Islam, but initially there was a division over that point.

Uthman appointed his nephew, Mu'awiya, as the governor of the western province of Damascus, which essentially meant Damascus, all of the Levant, and Egypt—which gave a member of his own family an immense amount of political control. By 654 CE there was a major faction from modern-day Iraq that had gradually developed from smaller factions who came together and joined to support Ali. This faction decided that Uthman was an imposter and not a good Muslim. The Quran that he had compiled was incomplete, and he gave political powers to members of his own family. In 654, the faction initiated a systematic attack against Mu'awiya and the kingdom under Uthman's control as civil war erupted within the Umma. In 656 CE, Uthman was assassinated by a group of fanatics from Egypt known as *Kharajites*. These were religious purists who had joined with the supporters of Ali. The same problem of succession occurred again, as the elders of the Muslim world met to decide that the time had come for Ali to be the Caliph.

In 656 CE, Ali was chosen to be the new Caliph. However, Mu'awiya at Damascus refused to recognize Ali as the Caliph. This meant that not only Damascus but the Levant, Egypt, and other areas in North Africa refused to recognize Ali as the Caliph. As a result, from 656 to 661 CE, there is continual strife between the supporters of Mu'awiya and those who supported Ali as Caliph. So Ali never ruled over the entirety of the Muslim world. In 661, in a battle located in Mesopotamia, the forces of Ali were overpowered by the forces of Mu'awiya. Ali was killed; his forces were exterminated, and Mu'awiya gained complete control of the Muslim world. He made Damascus his capital, which shifted it out of Arabia and away from Medina. He established what is known as the Umayyad Dynasty, which for the next one hundred years ruled the Muslim world. The supporters of Ali came together, ideologically speaking, as Shiites. The supporters of Ali more or less merge with the Kharajites, but there are actually Kharajites still to be found—for instance, in North Africa. They became the opposition. Those who support the Caliphs of Mu'awiya and his family are known as the *Sunni*. The Sunni recognized Mu'awiya as the legitimate Caliph in 661, and they recognize the Quran that was prepared by Uthman as the only and complete one.

Division: Shiite and Sunni: Since that time, enormous differences in religious practice as well as social, political, and economic issues have developed between the Sunni and the Shiites. About 90 percent of all Muslims are Sunni, whereas approximately 10 percent are Shiites. Throughout the history of Islam since 661 CE, the Sunni have dominated the political world of Islam. Wherever Islam has spread, almost always it has been Sunni Islam that has been in the forefront. They are the ones who have enjoyed the wealth and the riches of conquest, and who have been primarily involved in international relations, whether for good or bad. Until recent times, Sunni were the ones who were most visible in references to Muslims. The Shiites have a different history. The Shiites have always been in the minority. The Shiites have always been the poor and the oppressed within the Muslim world. Except for Iran after 1500 CE, the Shiites have never enjoyed any significant degree of political power. The successor dynasty to the Umayyads, from 750 to about 1300 CE, was known as the Abbasids. They cleverly made an alliance with the Shiites, promising that after overthrowing the Umayyads, a Shiite dynasty could be established. But after assuming power, within two years they refuted the agreement and again the Shiites remained politically disenfranchised. For that reason, they have also never shared in the riches of conquest, nor of peace, in the Muslim world.

The differences between Sunnis and the Shiites also extend to how they understand their religion and even its practices. The word "Sunni" means "orthodox," which asserts that they have the true, orthodox, genuine Muslim tradition. The estrangement between Sunni and Shiite is so great, that they sometimes don't consider each other true Muslims. So much is this the case that Sunnis sometimes reject Shiites as truly Muslim (Shiites return the rejection toward Sunnis too). Implicit within the Shiite sense of self-existence is the role of struggle, almost to the point of celebrating struggle. Stretching as far back as Ali, any position in the Muslim world, any political favor that Shiites have ever enjoyed they have had to gain through struggle. One of the popular holidays among the Shiites celebrates the martyrdom of a son of Ali.

They take a sword and slash their head. Then they pat it with their hand to encourage bleeding, until they get blood all over. Finally, they parade through the streets of the town. Even children as young as five or six years of age participate in this event.

The Shiites have an entirely different internal dynamic by which their religious practices operate. For the Sunni, each one theoretically is an interpreter of Muslim living in that the Quran is believed to be the express word of Allah and is to be obeyed, followed, and submitted to. Everything else is more or less a matter of personal interpretation (based upon instruction from religious scholars). Sunni religious leaders (*Ulamas*) offer instruction from the Quran, and other sources to help the individual Muslim decide the right course of action. In Shiism, it is completely different. Shiites agree that the Quran is the literal word of Allah. Whether or not it is complete is a moot point today. However, in Shiism, historically, an Imam was a religious leader who had divinely endowed authority to interpret the Quran. There are in Shiism a number of different sects (the *Seveners*, the *Twelvers*, and others) based on the number of Imams a sect believes existed. Shiism believes Ali was the first Imam. After him came additional Imams, the process continuing for at least seven generations. During the Middle Ages, some Shiites believed that the Imamate stopped with the death of the seventh Imam. Those who accept this tradition believe interpretation stopped at that point, and they seek to learn interpretation only through the seven Imams. For most other Shiites, the twelfth Imam disappeared. While he was probably murdered, nobody knows what happened to him. Subsequently, there arose the legend of the *Mahdi*, a belief that the twelfth Imam was taken to heaven as the hidden Imam and would return at the end of time to prepare Muslims for the coming judgment day. In his place, the Ayatollahs and Mullahs became the teachers of Islam for the Shiites.

Traditionally, the Shiites have been the ones with less education so that religious leaders, Mullahs, teach them how to apply the Quran in their daily lives. More than this, each Shiite patterns his life as well as his understanding and interpretation of Islam, after the teaching of one of these Mullahs. The Quran and other sources structure the life of the religious leader, in their words, thoughts, and deeds. All other Shiites follow the example of their chosen religious leader as they live out their lives. The same pattern also exists among the Mullahs. Additionally, some Mullahs are regarded as better interpreters, better at understanding the nuances and the fine distinctions concerning the practice of Islam. This has resulted in a hierarchy of Mullahs. At the top of the hierarchy are the senior-most Mullahs, who over a lifetime of interpretation and serving as religious leaders have come to be universally recognized as the best for their understanding of Islam and interpretation of the Quran. These are the Ayatollahs.

SOURCES OF AUTHORITY

Muslims understand their religious traditions and practices on the basis of several sources. The first is, of course, the Quran, which is considered to be the very words of Allah. This is not open to interpretation or criticism and is the only basis for submission. The Quran contains 114 chapters, called Suras, and is a little bit shorter than the New Testament in length. Muslims often memorize significant sections of the Quran during childhood and strongly observant Muslims may memorize the whole thing. Whereas in Judaism and Christianity very few can even quote more than maybe a handful of scriptures, in Islam there is a greater emphasis on knowing the Quran and integrating that into one's lifestyle. Themes in the Quran include the nature of Allah, the eternity of the human soul, and judgment. There are also directions on day-to-day life in the religion: worship, marriage, divorce, the position of women, fasting, alms, and pilgrimage. Observant Muslims also believe that history is cyclical at best, that it is similar to a circle constantly going around, or else human history has been in decline since the days of Muhammad. Thus, for Islam, the Quran and all of the commands in the Quran and all of the injunctions in the Quran are from a better time when humans were living a better life than they do in the present. Therefore, the morality, the ethics, the criminology, and everything else in the Quran is, for a Muslim, of a higher quality than whatever exists today. The Quran represents for Muslims the loftiest level of human morality, human wisdom, human goals, human ethics, and so forth.

This assumption has also resulted in what is one of the biggest conflicts in Islam today. The Quran is set within an unsophisticated, nontechnological society rooted in a seventh century desert culture. Today, new technologies, new ideas of morality, new ideas of ethics, and so forth, challenge Muslims to seriously integrate the modern world, and especially that of the West, with the notion that the world of Muhammad's day was a superior world to the world of today. This is one of the underlying tensions between the West and radical Islam. Radical Muslims see a conservative Muslim culture as the zenith of all human societies. Another problem has to do with the role of women in Islam, and the role of women in the Western world. For instance, during the Persian Gulf War in 1991, some of the Saudi women found out women in non-Islamic countries such as America could drive. Of course, they knew it before then, but they actually came face-to-face with the reality in 1991. There was a real uproar in Saudi Arabia when some of the wealthier men's wives took a twenty-car caravan of Mercedes through Riyad just after the end of the Persian Gulf War to press the government to give them the right to drive. There are, of course, reasons that the rules in the Quran about the role of women exist. But there are many Muslim women who struggle between the way that the West understands the role of women and the way that the Quran does.

The *Hadiths* are collections of three different traditions: what are reported to be sayings of Muhammad (not included in the Quran), what are reported to be deeds of Muhammad (not in the Quran), and what are reported to be things to which Muhammad gave his silent approval. The way these arose is that from 632 to until after 661 CE, people would have recollections of things that they said happened, including recollections of comments and events that were not written down. These might even have been something someone heard, or heard secondhand or thirdhand. The Sunni have six collections of *Hadiths*. The Shiites have five. The Hadiths contain detailed instructions on prayer and other Muslim practices and beliefs. For instance, in the Quran, Jerusalem is hardly mentioned (and then only in connection with Jews). But in one of the Hadiths, there is a story that one night Muhammad had a dream or vision in which he was transported by a flying horse first to Jerusalem, to the site of the Jewish Temple Mount (where later the Dome of the Rock was constructed to commemorate this story), and from there he was taken to heaven where he met Allah and claimed to have received additional revelations. Before day, he was returned to Jerusalem and from there he was transported back to where he was sleeping. From the Muslim standpoint, this forms one basis for their claim to the sanctity of Jerusalem. The details on prayer, washing, the prayer rugs, the process of kneeling, bowing, touching their forehead to the floor, etc., all are found in the Hadiths. Instruction on alms is in the Hadiths, along with instructions on other forms of giving.

One of the differences between the Hadiths and the Quran is that the Hadiths are not regarded as the very words of Allah. Some Hadiths, however, are considered as more authoritative than others. It is not just an issue of the chain of authority, because some chains of authority are regarded as fairly reliable while others, even a very long chain, are still regarded as weak. Also, the Hadiths, unlike the Quran, are open to scholarly criticism. No Muslim who is observant will offer criticism of the Quran of any sort—literary criticism or theological criticism. The Quran is perfect in the Muslim view. But the Hadiths are open to question, to challenges, and to interpretation. They are the first source of understanding of the Quran by which religious leaders understand to apply the Quran in a given context and a given situation. Thus, they are considered an important source of authority, second after the Quran, but do not possess the absolute authority over the Muslim's life which the Quran holds. The Hadiths mostly indicate a direction that the Muslim should follow in a given situation rather than an authoritative pronouncement on an issue.

The next lower level of authority is *Sharia*, the Muslim religious law. In an idealized Muslim society, the entire society—the government, the civil law, everything—will be

Al-Azhar mosque in Cairo

ordered and structured by Sharia. The closest example that exists today is perhaps in Saudi Arabia. The Sharia is believed to be structured from decisions that have been based in the Quran and the Hadiths by former legal scholars in Islam. These were compiled and systematized into a law code that provides religious structure for Muslims to understand, on a daily basis, how to faithfully live their lives. The formative period of the Sharia is during the first four Caliphates. But as circumstances changed during later centuries, other things were added to the Sharia. With Muhammad's death, no more additions to the Quran were possible since he was the final prophet of Allah, according to Islam. It is doubtful that anyone today would find a new, truly authoritative account of anything drawn from Muhammad's life. Therefore, it is doubtful that anything would be added to the Hadiths today. However, it is possible in any generation for a situation to arise that would require the further development of Sharia, though this would require great caution today. The oldest surviving university in the world, the Al-Azhar Mosque, is located in Cairo, Egypt, to train Sunni scholars in the Quran, the Hadiths, and the Sharia. Today, there are many other training centers as well.

There are no clergy in Islam as such, only religious leaders such as Mullahs and Ulamas and the Ayatollahs. These leaders are laymen with training in the Quran, the Hadiths, and the Sharia who serve as an information reservoir and interpreter of Islam to the Muslim community. Muslims look to these leaders for advice, and they gradually rise above the other lay people as local religious leaders. These are the ones who address the congregation at Friday prayers. They also sometimes go on to become involved in further study and lead religious factions or become senior scholars. Muslim religious leaders and laity live similar to Westerners in many ways. However, in countries such as Saudi Arabia, where Sharia is the basis of civil law, there are significant differences. There men and the women are not permitted to eat together, and there are dietary laws that closely follow those of the Jewish tradition. Under the Sharia if one is guilty of stealing, the penalty is to cut off a hand. In Sharia, the adulterer is stoned. Sharia is a very decisive system with little room for any appeal of judgment. Under Sharia, if a man wants to divorce his wife, he walks to the public square of the city to proclaim, "I divorce you. I divorce you. I divorce you." In some traditions he takes his sandal off and places it in her hand. In others, he takes a piece of paper that says "I divorce you" and that is it.

One of the major spiritual movements within Islam is known as *Sufi*. The Sufi movement attempts to have a more personal religious experience. Some Muslims have sought a deeper experience than the Five Pillars offers them, and the Sufi movement began very early, within the first two centuries of Islam, in which groups called brotherhoods began meeting together to find a deeper spiritual intimacy. They wore undyed wool. They practiced an austerity close to the asceticism of Eastern religions. They believed that love for Allah was expressed first of all in self-control, and then secondly, in denial of the world's pleasures. They would meet together for prayer and for discussions about how to love Allah more, how to withdraw from the world's pleasures, how to maintain selfcontrol, etc. Afterward, they begin a process of chanting, reciting Quranic verses, using the prayer beads that are used as a mnemonic to recall the ninety-nine names of Allah, and they begin individual dancing as a spiritual exercise leading to an ecstatic experience. This ecstatic experience is known as the Whirling Dervish. Sufism is found today among both the Sunnis and the Shiites. It is probably one of the least political aspects of Islam, though at times the brotherhood has provided fertile political associations. Nevertheless, it is primarily an attempt through some sort of ecstatic experience to intimately be a part of the religion.

A splinter religion of Islam is Bahá'í, which comes out of Persian Shiism. It has its beginnings with a person named Ali Muhammad, whose nickname was Bab. He began claiming, in 1844 CE, to be a messenger of Allah to proclaim the coming of the Messiah. In short order, he was executed for claiming to be a prophet and as an enemy of the Persian state. In 1863, in Iran, a person named Babullah, claimed to be the Messiah that Bab was saying would come. He claimed that his appearance heralded a new era for the world. Most significant of his teachings was that all the prophets of all the other religions had received revelations from Allah. This equates all of these religions as equal with Islam, and it doesn't matter which religion one follows because they are all equal. He rejected polygamy, slavery, jihad, and asserted the oneness of all religions as working for same goal. Therefore, instead of fighting among one another and maintaining the individual religious identities, the world's religions ought to come together to create one world community, one world government, one language, and one religion. Eventually, he was exiled from Persia and took refuge in the economic and political backwater of Mount Carmel (today in Northern Israel), where he established a Bahá'í study center on Mount Carmel. Bahá'í has since spread around the world with its call for one religion, one faith, one community, and one government. It urges the study of all religions for their essential truths, but it proposes no particular religious doctrine.

There is also the more evangelical wing called the Ahmadiyyah Movement (the Ahmadis), which originated in India, and now claims over 10 million followers worldwide. The Ahmadis believe that the founder, Hazrat Mirza Ghulam Ahmad of Qadian (a small village in India), had come in the spirit of Christ as a Muslim prophet. His coming was the second coming of Christ, which happened in the spirit for he came in the spirit of Christ as John the Baptist came in the spirit of Elijah. Born in 1835 in the village of Qadian, Ahmad called himself a prophet and messiah not to announce a new law but to renew Islam and the teachings of Prophet Muhammad that contemporary Muslims have wandered away, a claim traditional Islam rejects. After his death, the group split into two branches over leadership. One called itself Qadian, who stresses the prophethood of Ahmad whereas the other party, called Lahore, regards Ahmad as only a reformer. Both have their headquarters in the United Kingdom (BBC News online). The Ahmadis have missionary zeal and provide social services including helping converts to learn Arabic. In many instances they use both the Bible and the Quran in their missionary activities. The movement has branches in thirty-eight cities in the United States.

FIVE PILLARS OF ISLAM

There are five basic elements in Islam. These are known as the Five Pillars of Islam. These are what you might think of as the basic devotional obligations of all the Muslims who worship Allah. There is no real order to these, which include: the witness, prayer, alms, Ramadan/fasting, and the hajj. *The witness* is the statement, "there is no god but Allah, and Muhammad is his prophet," which serves as a statement of belief shared by all Muslims regardless of the different sects within Islam. To convert to Islam, in fact, one needs only to repeat this statement sincerely in the presence of two or three Muslims. Muhammad, of course, is the founder of the religion. (This witness is both a basic belief within Islam, and a source of religious difficulty between Islam and the other Abrahamic religions, Judaism and Christianity. Muhammad lived about 580–600 years after Jesus's earthly life and ministry and is not recognized by Christians as a prophet at all. Jews also perceive Muhammad as just a founder of the Arab religion known as Islam.)

The prayer is practiced five times a day (morning, noon, mid-afternoon, evening, and bedtime) and is regarded by the Muslims as an act of submission to Allah. The aim of prayer is not so much to obtain anything for oneself but to strengthen one's ties with Allah. It is a part of submitting to Allah and strengthening the ties to Allah. It is also regarded as an act of love. Prayer in Islam is not an especially spontaneous interaction between the individual and the divine realm but involves an important series of specific acts, some performed numerous times, to express submission. At the appointed time, one must wash certain portions of the body, remove the shoes, and turn in the direction of Mecca, prepared to kneel on a rug or prayer rug spread for the purpose of prayer. In a specific sequence, one stands, bows, kneels, and bows the head pressing the forehead to the floor before Allah. All the while, verses from the Quran are either chanted or recited. Depending on the time of day, the sequence is repeated three to five times. Only at the very end does one perhaps make some personal request. Muslims believe Christians are too personal when they use the term "Father" in prayer. Although the Muslims have ninety-nine names for Allah (creator, sustainer, merciful, beneficent, etc.), not one of those names is "Father."

Alms (the technical term for this is Zakat) is actually a tax imposed by the Muslim religion on all Muslims. It amounts to 2 1/2 percent of certain kinds of income (for example wages, but not gifts). Land, houses, personal possessions may all be given. Technically, payment is voluntary, and related to the intensity of a Muslim's devotion. It is normally received by a trustee organization established for the purpose, called the Wakf, and once payment has been made, it becomes the possession of the Wakf irrevocably. The Wakf then holds those gifts on behalf of the entire Muslim community, known as the Umma. The Wakf can dispense its holdings; the Wakf can sell them and give the money to some particular purpose, or whatever the trustees determine. Often the Wakf dispenses part of the alms to Muslims who are in need. While supposedly a voluntary offering, Zakat has at times been required by Muslim rulers and has sometimes been collected by the state for state uses.

Ramadan is the ninth month of the Muslim year and involves a month of fasting. The Muslims use a lunar calendar just like the Jewish religious calendar. As a result, the month of fasting moves around from year to year. Sometimes it will be as early as March or even January, and sometimes it will be as late as May or July. The celebration began while Muhammad was in Medina, possibly as a Muslim alternative to the Jewish Passover to provide a feast for Muslims that, if anything, would be an even greater celebration. Ramadan is considered to be an act of commemoration marking the first revelation that Muhammad claimed to have received from Allah (just as Passover marks an early event in Jewish history), and celebrating the community of Islam. It is also an act of submission or obedience to Allah, and frequently a time when prisoners are released and judicial sentences commuted. For approximately twenty-eight days, during the daylight hours, Muslims neither eat nor drink anything, not even water. After nightfall, Ramadan becomes a month-long feast. As such, celebrating Ramadan can be a real sacrifice in a Middle Eastern country when one must go without food or water or any kind of drink all day for a month when it

is hot and dry. It is normal during this month for families and friends to gather together and at one another's houses or at a mosque for dinner and fellowship. For some, it is not unusual to eat three or four major meals in the course of the evening. Just before daylight, after which fasting resumes, a person circulates throughout the community with a gong calling people to awaken and eat breakfast before the fast begins again. One result of this schedule is that the people often develop a semi-stupor and may be hardly awake during much of the daytime from all of the feasting and the late hours of the night.

The *Hajj* is a pilgrimage to Mecca that every Muslim who can afford to do so is required to perform at least once. There are special clothes and special practices associated with the journey. The Hajj emphasizes the oneness and equality of all Muslims. The person who has made the pilgrimage to Mecca then receives the title "Haj" or "Haji/Haja" in front of the person's name (Al-Haji for men; Haja for women).

TEMPLES, WORSHIP, AND DEVOTION

Probably the most central physical element of the Muslim religion is the mosque. In Buddhism and Hinduism the home shrine is central, but for Islam, it is the mosque. Typically, the Mosque is constructed like a square box with an arcade that runs around the interior perimeter. At each corner is a tower, one being higher than the others. This is the minaret, from which a Muezzin sings forth the call to prayer for faithful Muslims at the appointed times each day (before watches, this was how the faithful knew the time had come). Today most mosques are outfitted with electronic Muezzin, that is to say that they have a loud speaker in the tower and the *Muezzin* issues the call from down below. It may even be a tape-recorded call to prayer. The tower also can also be used to warn the community of danger. Within the compound, there is a building for prayer, and within the inner courtyard there is a water source. It may be a well, a pool, or a natural spring for using in obligatory cleansing before prayer. If a person sought an audience before a great, high lord in a dusty, dirty Middle Eastern country, the person would not enter all hot and smelly and sweaty with feet covered with dust and the hands filled with grime. The individual would bathe first. Similarly, Muslims do not present themselves before Allah in such a state, but they wash the feet, the hands, and the head as a symbol of bathing, to prepare themselves, to show themselves fit to come into the presence of Allah. After they wash, they enter the building used for prayer where they will either spread out their prayer rug or, in many mosques, there will be prayer rugs already on the ground, where they perform prayer. On the wall nearest to Mecca is a niche, the mihrab, which points in the direction of Mecca. By facing this niche, one is assured of being properly oriented for prayer. Another thing, for which the mosque has been used, politically, is as an armament storehouse. It often continues to be used for this purpose today. The mosque is also a multipurpose community center where classes are taught and the Muslim community gathers.

The Muslim holy day is Friday, when the men, in particular, go to the mosque for prayer, usually the noontime prayer. There are prayers at the Mosque the other days of the week as well, but attendance at the Mosque is optional for those. After the regular ritual of the prayer, they sit right where they are on the

Great Mosque of Cordoba, the medieval Islamic mosque regarded as one of the most accomplished monuments of Moorish architecture in the Spanish city of Cordoba, Andalusia, Spain.

Inside the Cordoba Mosque

prayer rug while one of the religious leaders, standing on an elevated pulpit addresses the community. The address usually focuses on an interpretation drawn from the Quran, or it may be exhortation to live a better Muslim life, or sometimes it may be about a political issue, such as is sometimes reported by western media. Afterward the ceremony is over and the worshipers disperse. Since politics is part of Islam, the address presented could very easily be political. Especially when there is a volatile political situation, it is not unusual after the Friday address for the Muslims, instead of dispersing, to march in some kind of a demonstration. From time to time, in such situations, there are even calls for jihad.

Jihad means "a struggle" and is an idea that goes all the way back to Muhammad himself though he probably meant the inner struggle to be obedient to Allah more than a military action or holy war. Holy war should only be done when it is necessary in order to be and to stay obedient to Allah. One of the decisive factors in jihad is if Islam is threatened. But there is more than one way for such a threat to exist. It may be physical, in which case self-defense is appropriate, including defense of one's territory. But some also include cultures that threaten one's ability to observe Islam. That can call for a holy war against the offending culture as well. This last struggle often exists today within a Muslim society or country. Thus jihad is very interpretative in character. More than simply defending oneself, it can be also defending the right to practice the religion against another culture or another faith. This permits a Muslim to theoretically wage Jihad against anyone anywhere, and against any government or any community or any group of people who are not Muslim if there is a sense of threat. However, to have an official jihad, that is to have a military jihad, a person who has the authority to declare a jihad is needed. Such a person must be a Caliph, or at least a recognized spiritual leader. In Sunni, it would have to be a Caliph. Perhaps an Ayatollah could call a jihad in Shiism.

ISLAM IN AMERICA

- Probably, the second largest religion and the fastest growing religion in America
- About two-thirds are immigrants; one-third are converts, mostly African Americans

- Conversion of African American was encouraged as a separation from white oppression who were mostly Christians
- Christianity was seen as part of the scheme of oppression
- Islam was interpreted as a means to regain self-pride and self-identity
- Conversion to Islam was strongly encouraged in the early twentieth century
- Islam in America is not monolithic
- Muslim movements in the United States:

Noble Drew Ali's Moorish Science Temple of America

- 1913—Noble Drew Ali started a movement, which later became known as the Moorish Science Temple of America
- Ali declared his mission as divinely inspired to "uplift fallen humanity"
- The movement's modest lifestyle—modest dress, gender roles, traditional family structure, and community solidarity—was a model of attraction

Nation of Islam ("Black Muslims")

- Founded by Elijah Muhammad—the messenger of Allah—in the 1920s
- Political focus against white oppression and to empower blacks in America
- Movement undermined by internal conflicts and by allegation of Elijah Muhammad's sexual scandal
- Prominent members and subsequent leaders included Malcolm X (later moved closer to mainstream Islam) and Louis Farrakhan, current leader
- Achievements include combating violence, drug abuse, modest living, responsibleness to one's family, sex education, spiritual discipline and nurturing, and combating social and political injustice

* * *

See the comparative illustration of the criticisms against the treatment of the prophets by the Jewish leaders according to the Quran and the Bible.

83. And when We made a covenant with the children of Israel:
You shall not serve any but Allah and (you shall do) good to
(your) parents, and to the near of kin and to the orphans and
the needy,
and you shall speak to men good words and keep up prayer
and pay the poor-rate. Then you turned
back except a few of you and (now too) you turn aside.
84. And when We made a covenant with you:
You shall not shed your blood and you shall
not turn your people out of your cities;
then you gave a promise while you witnessed.
85. Yet you it is who slay your people and turn a party
from among you out of their homes, backing each
other up against them unlawfully and exceeding the

limits; and if they should come to you,
as captives you would ransom them—while their
very turning out was unlawful for you. Do you
then believe in a part of
the Book and disbelieve in the other? What then is the reward
of such among you as do this but disgrace in the life of
this world, and on the day of resurrection they shall be
sent back to the most grievous chastisement, and Allah
is not at all heedless of what you do.
86. These are they who buy the life of this world for the hereafter,
so their chastisement shall not be lightened nor shall they be helped.
87. And most certainty We gave Musa the Book
and We sent messengers after him one
after another; and We gave Isa, the son
of Marium, clear arguments and
strengthened him with the holy spirit,
What! whenever then a messenger came to
you with that which your souls did not
desire, you were insolent so you called some
liars and some you slew.
88. And they say: Our hearts are covered.
Nay, Allah has cursed them on account of
their unbelief; so little it is that they believe.
89. And when there came to them a Book from
Allah verifying that which they have, and
aforetime they used to pray for victory against
those who disbelieve, but when there
came to them (Prophet) that which they did not
recognize, they disbelieved in him; so Allah's
curse is on the unbelievers.

[35] "It was this Moses whom they rejected when they said, 'Who made you a ruler and a judge?' and whom GOD now sent as both ruler and liberator through the angel who appeared to him in the bush. [36] He led them out, having performed wonders and signs in Egypt, at the Red Sea, and in the wilderness for forty years. [37] This is the Moses who said to the Israelites, 'GOD will raise up a prophet for you from your own peoplea as he raised me up.' [38] He is the one who was in the congregation in the wilderness with the angel who spoke to him at Mount Sinai, and with our ancestors; and he received living oracles to give to us. [39] Our ancestors were unwilling to obey him, instead, they pushed him aside, and in their hearts they turned back to Egypt, [40] saying to Aaron, 'Make gods for us who will lead the way for us; as for this Moses who led us out from the land of Egypt, we do not know what has happened to him.' [41] At that time they made a calf, offered a sacrifice to the idol, and reveled in the works of their hands. [42] But GOD turned away from them and handed them over to worship the host of heaven, as it is written in the book of the prophets:

'Did you offer to me slain
victims and sacrifices

forty years in the
wilderness, O house of
Israel?
43. No; you took along
the tent of Moloch
and the star of
your god Rephan,
the images that you
made to worship;
so I will remove you
beyond Babylon.'

44. "Our ancestors had the tent of testimony in the wilderness, as GOD directed when he spoke to Moses, ordering him to make it according to the pattern he had seen. 45 Our ancestors in turn brought it in with Joshua when they dispossessed the nations that GOD drove out before our ancestors. And it was there until the time of David, 46 who found favor with GOD and asked that he might find a dwelling place for the house of Jacob. 47 But it was Solomon who built a house for him. 48 Yet the Most High does not dwell in houses made with human hands;d as the prophet says, 49 Heaven is my throne, and the earth is my footstool. What kind of house will you build for me, says the LORD, or what is the place of my rest? 50 Did not my hand make all these things?'

51. "You stiff-necked people, uncircumcised in heart and ears, you are forever opposing the Holy Spirit, just as your ancestors used to do.

52. Which of the prophets did your ancestors not persecute? They killed those who foretold the coming of the Righteous One, and now you have become his betrayers and murderers. 53 You are the ones that received the law as ordained by angels, and yet you have not kept it."*

* * *

KEY WORDS

Allah	Muhammad	Ka'aba	Dome of the Rock
Quran	Hadiths/Sunnah	Sharia	Mosque
Hagar	Ishmael	Arabs	Abraham
Caliph	Caliphate	Five Pillars	Sunni and Shiite
Jihad	Sultan	Hijra	Muezzin
Imam	Umma	Sufism	Mihrab
Hijab	Khadji	Fatima	Ali
Nation of Islam	Abu Bakr	Umar	Ahmadyya Movement
Baha'i	Umayyad Dynasty	Mu'awiya	People of the Book

---

*"English Translation of the Holy Quran with Explanatory Notes," edited by Dr. Zahid Aziz and published by Ahmadiyya Anjuman Lahore Publications. Copyright © 2010. Reprinted with permission.

QUESTIONS FOR FURTHER STUDY

1. How are the sources of authority in Islam similar to or different from Christianity and Judaism?

2. Explain the concept of human responsibility in Islam.

3. Discuss the importance of Mecca and the role of Medina in the formative years of Islam.

4. What were the causes of the split of Islam into Sunni and Shia

5. Do you think that the Islamic Umma (community) was idealistic? Why or why not?

6. Discuss Islamic teaching on social justice.

7. Describe the persona of the Prophet Muhammed?

8. Watch the PBS Documentary, "Islam: Empire of Faith" Parts 1 and 2 and answer the following questions:
   a. What is Islam according to this documentary?
   b. What's the significance of the Quran and what are the major beliefs of Islam?
   c. What are Islam's contributions to civilization?
   d. What was the significance of Damascus, Bagdad, and Cordova to Islam and the world community?
   e. What's your evaluation of the content or substance of the documentary?

A Brief Survey of New Religious Movements (NRMs)

INTRODUCTION

Religious observers and practitioners have noted with interest many "new" faces of religions that have appeared in the world of religions and spirituality. Students who study religions and spirituality, world religions, and theological studies show some excitement when it comes to discussing or examining these religions. What are these "new religions?" When and where did they begin? Who founded and are founding them? What do they teach, believe, and do? Why do they exist and how do they relate to conventional or what is described as normative or mainstream religious traditions, as well as the larger society? Ernest Troeltsch made a distinction between natural religions and founded or voluntary religions. Troeltsch's classification of the church, sect, cult, and new age movements is based on the extent of the relationship between the church, the state, the economic order, and the family. How has the church influenced such groups in the social order? How far have they influenced the church? How related are the worldviews of the church and the social order? If the relationship and influence are far apart between a religious community and the social order, he would classify the former either as a sect or cult/new age (which is extremely apart). If the exchange is close but not fused then it is a church type. In-between the cult and church type is the sect. If there is a fusion of the two—religious and social order—then it fits his description of natural religion, whereby natural ties exist between religion and social institutions like the family, polity, economy, warfare, medicine (Livingston 2008). What used to be called cults is now referred to as new age or new religious movements (NRMs).

* * *

On the Difference between Spirituality and Religion by Swenson and Nelson:

> One of the things that we notice is that there are a number of different streams. In some places, they are narrow; in others, they are wide. Just as the streams' courses change, depending on the terrain and amount of water, so too the experience of spirituality changes with a person's context—social, historical, cultural, and religious. And just as each stream sometimes meanders and sometimes rushes down the mountain, so too a person's spiritual experiences may vary throughout his or her lifetime. Despite these differences, all streams share in common the quality of water. These streams of spirituality vary like one person's sense of spirituality differs from someone else's; yet just as the streams are similar, so too the ways that people experience spirituality share similarities in some basic ways.

In this part of our journey, we aim to discover what spirituality is, to determine what makes spirituality distinct from religion, and to consider how spirituality is related to religion. The word "spirituality" shares a root in common with words such as "inspire" and "respirate." These commonalities demonstrate how spirituality describes something that is difficult to see and/or hold and also has the quality of movement.

These commonalities also suggest that spirituality is personal; it can be inside of a person. Furthermore, it can energize and vitalize the person. In these ways, spirituality is like breath or wind. Indeed, the term is derived from this sense of wind or breath, and it came to be associated with the unseen enlivening presence of religious experience. Spirit, then, is what gives a person a sense of spirituality. It is not hard to understand how people began to distinguish spirit from body and the tangible stuff of the material world.

What is the difference between spirit and soul? Both terms, spirit and soul, are used to describe something distinct from the body. Sometimes the terms are used interchangeably. Sometimes, though, people distinguish soul from spirit, believing soul to be something innate and universal; whereas spirit is a special gift that only some people have. To this way of thinking, everyone (and maybe everything) has a soul; by contrast, only some people are "spiritual." Spiritual people are filled with the Divine, and they are so because Divine action manifested itself in their lives to make that happen.

> Many people think of both soul and spirit as something that is immortal, that is, something that does not die. Some of these people also believe that the nature of one's soul is affected by the choices that one makes in life and so determines w\hat happens to the soul after the body dies. Although they think of spirit as immortal, too, they distinguish soul from spirit, considering the spirit to be something that returns to the Divine after death, no matter how a person has lived. So you see that how a person defines spirit and differentiates it from the soul differs depending on a person's beliefs.*

* * *

WHAT ARE NEW RELIGIOUS MOVEMENTS?

The NRMs are new religions that have sprung up across all continents in the last 100 years. They are sometimes referred to as new age movements, alternative religions, marginal religions, nonconventional religions, nontraditional religions, or cults. The term "new age" refers to Aquarian Age, which it is believed to be a soon to come period that will bring peace and enlightenment to the world and unite human beings and God who have been separated not because of sin, but lack of understanding and knowledge of the true nature of God and reality (Brodd et al. 2013, 516). The term has been in use since the 1970s and became more popular in the next two decades (Szerszynski 1992, 8). In this book the terms "new religious movements" and "new age movements" are used to refer to the same phenomena.

In an article, "What is New Religious Movement?" Matt Slick of Christian Apologetic and Research Ministry (CARM), explains the new age movement as "a very complex system with eclectic teachings of salvation, correct thinking," of "correct knowledge," a "feel-goodism," of "universal tolerance," and "moral relativity" (carm.org 2014).

John G. Melton (1999) defines the NRMs as "primary religious groups/movements that operate apart from the dominant religious culture (in our case, the Christian West) in which they are located but seek adherents from their new host culture".

One can understand the identity of the NRMs by examining their general beliefs and features. The beliefs and features include:

---

*From *What Is Religious Studies? A Journey of Inquiry* by Kristin M. Swenson and Esther R. Nelson. Copyright © 2006 by Kristin M. Swenson and Esther R. Nelson. Reprinted by permission of Kendall Hunt Publishing Company.

Interest in contemporary popular culture and lifestyle where there is free movement of people, culture, and ideology, though larger parts of the culture have become more utilitarian or consumerism. Social media provides instant information and exposure to issues in almost any hidden corner of this world. The nature of the twentieth century and this era of the twenty-first century are defined by its being open, highly interactive, and technology-driven.

Strong charismatic leadership: It is said that leadership is everything. When this good notion of leadership is overstretched, worse things happen. This is typical of cults where personality worship (personality cult) could ensue. The founder of the Unification Church, Sun Myung Moon, serves as an example. Sun Myung Moon and his wife have declared themselves the Messiah and, for that matter, messianic parents who determine the one a member of the movement will marry including the day and time of the marriage. People are looking for somebody to follow; someone who can command a resounding and convincing vision and purposefulness, especially at a time of social and cultural transition like the 1950s, 1960s, and 1970s; someone who knows where one is going and what to do to get there. This is especially crucial in a situation of failed leadership as occurred in the Watergate scandal, in the assassination of some influential world leaders like JFK and MLK, Jr., in societies under totalitarian regimes, and in failed states where there seems to be a loss of direction or a feeling of disappointment and where the conventional church seems to have no adequate response.

Individualistic: While many of these NRMs are communal-based, like the Wiccans, the Circle, the Peoples Temple, David Koresh's Branch Davidian, and the Unification Church, there is an undertone emphasis on individualism, such as the teaching on personal improvement that the individual must pursue under the principle of you-can-do-it-yourself. This is more so of the NRMs whose origin is based on Oriental and Western mysticism. The globalized economic, political, and communication culture has eroded what Bronislaw Szerszynski called "particularist and localist understanding of identity" leading to an emphasis on the differences between individual human beings (Szerszynski 1992, 15). As a result, there has been a break in traditional community and neighborliness and their place taken by the global social network where the abstract self seeks their own self-empowerment. The new symbols and vocabulary they have created are their medium of communication and the new community consists of those who understand these symbols and vocabulary. The idea that they cannot redeem or heal the whole society makes them concentrate on the individual, and particularly their own salvation. This is particularly true of the movements that are world-renouncing.

Dysfunctional world: There is a belief that the world is dysfunctional melodrama whereby personal lives and the Western civilization are on a destructive path (Livingston 2008). Most NRMs emerge out of contradiction and tension in modern society between social logics operating in the public and private realms (Szerszynski 1992, 2). It seems like there is "no sweetness here" says the educator and novelist, Ama Ata Aidoo (Aidoo 1970, 56). The world has indeed changed but only for the benefit of a few. For the greater majority nothing has changed. Western civilization with its free market, economic globalization, and all kinds of individual rights (this is not a denial of their efficacy and significance) has left many dreams unfulfilled and society confused. There is a feeling of moral ambiguity, on one the hand, and on the other, moral fundamentalism—a postmodern dilemma, a kind of comedy where the center cannot hold, even if there is a center at all.

Interconnectedness of all life: There is also a belief in the physical and spiritual healing or transformation of the individual. The component of a person—spirit, mind, and body—is interconnected and must stay in harmony through knowledge (consciousness) and spirituality. Hence a belief in "universal vibrational energy" founded on the idea that vibrational changes are associated with consciousness, thus providing a link between matter and mind; the higher one's consciousness the closer one is to cosmic realities. These energies can be harnessed to provide healing to the body and the mind (Livingston 2008). Furthermore, NRMs believe in the interdependence of all living things and have a high regard for modern science—the key to the realization of the tenets of modernity.

Countercultural: The term means against or in opposition to the prevailing dominant culture. The dominant culture of the time, it is believed, also opposes their well-being and is in collision with the aspirations of the younger generation who will not accept things as it is. There is an ideal culture or vision that is worth fighting for, and the dominant culture must be compelled to work toward that. Counterculture of the 1960s was influenced by the Vietnam War, Oriental mysticism, new social spaces created as a result of the emerging social change, political radicalism, and student movements. Countercultural strategy employed to achieve their end was more evolutionary than revolutionary (Szerszynski 1992, 4–5).

THE GROWTH OF NEW RELIGIOUS MOVEMENTS

Sociologists have observed that new age religions have grown to about 14,000 movements within the twentieth and early twenty-first centuries (Brodd 2013, 516). What phenomena have stimulated the growth of this movement? Researchers believe the growth of NRMs has been strongly aided by three phenomena: modernization, globalization, and secularization. Modernization, defined as "the transformation from a traditional, rural, agrarian society to a secular, urban, industrial society," is believed to be the most influential of the three. The era of modernization, which, technically speaking, is fluid, is associated with the period of modern industrialization and enlightenment. Modernization:

- emphasizes the capacity of human effort to bring progress and peace to the world;
- places human beings at the center of the universe—as masters of their own destiny;
- sees higher literacy and advanced knowledge in science and technology as keys to their vision;
- seeks diffusion of political power and erosion of traditional authority; and
- creates a new breed of spiritual "seekers" who do not find comfort or satisfaction in traditional or conventional religions.

Modernization-inspired NRMs became world-affirming type. The certainty of the promise of modernization excited many that were searching for alternative spirituality and a worldview that would not be in conflict with modernity. Modernization created a wide space for such innovation and expansion. The modern world under the control of man will have its own spirituality or religion that is anthropocentric and nontraditional.

The second influence, globalization, has also had significant effect on the growth of NRMs. The *Concise Encyclopedia* defines globalization as the "process by which the experience of everyday life, marked by the diffusion of commodities and ideas, is becoming standardized around the world." Elements of globalization that have influenced the growth of NRMs are inspired cultural interaction, the Internet and social network, mass migration and movement of people, and more importantly the 1893 and 1993 Parliament of World Religions (PWR) held in Chicago that sought to promote the views and "relevance" of the movement. Touching of the effect of globalization on global ethic, the WPR argues

"By a global ethic we do not mean a global ideology or a single unified religion beyond all existing religions, and certainly not the domination of one religion over all others. By a global ethic we mean a fundamental consensus on binding values, irrevocable standards, and personal attitudes. Without such a fundamental consensus on an ethic, sooner or later every community will be threatened by chaos or dictatorship, and individuals will despair" (PWR, "Introduction", 1993).

It further states, "Humankind urgently needs social and ecological reforms, but it needs spiritual renewal just as urgently. As religious or spiritual persons we commit ourselves to this task. . . . Of course religions are credible only when they eliminate those conflicts which spring from the religions themselves, dismantling mutual arrogance, mistrust, prejudice, and even hostile images, and thus demonstrate respect for the traditions, holy places, feasts, and rituals of people who believe differently." Urging the global community toward a culture of tolerance and truth telling, as against lying about others, it further declares, "Finally, for representatives of religion. When they stir up prejudice, hatred, and enmity towards those of different belief, or even incite or legitimize religious wars, they deserve the condemnation of humankind and the loss of their adherents." These statements invariably emboldened the religious communities of different persuasions to accept each other or welcome each other as partners of global ethic for peace, humanness, and justice (PWR, "Introduction", 1993).

The third sphere of influence is secularization defined as a phenomenon that views secular society as the home and promoter of science and looks down upon religious beliefs as subjective and lacking intellectual authority. Historians call this view of religious subordination "Scientific Revolution." New age movements are therefore in bed with scientific postulations of the universe—including social evolution.

The three aforementioned phenomena have also ignited certain factors that have had direct impact on the growth of NRMs. One of the factors is social change. When there is a change in social institutions like the family, traditional norm, and behavior, or some traumatic national catastrophe that shakes society's stability and ethos, people begin to search for new meaning and direction. Individuals who go through personal challenges that alter their lives significantly may seek to find a new way to live. The individual

Five thousand assembled delegates of the historic 1893 Parliament of the World's Religions in Chicago. Courtesy: Parliament of the World's Religions, 2015–2016.

or society may not be able to go back to continue—for there is discontinuity—and therefore may look for an alternative way or create one. Many NRMs were founded or expanded their presence in the 1950s and 1960s (the postwar, postcolonial, sociopolitical, and religiocultural nationalism). A typical example is Jimmy Jones and the Peoples Temple.

Another factor is a revolt against traditions that no longer speak to the aspirations and desires of the time. When religious symbols no longer edify the adherents and religion becomes stagnant, broken, and dry or dead, conscious efforts may be taken to reform them, replace them, or abandon them all together.

THE ORIGIN OF NEW RELIGIOUS MOVEMENT

When and where did it all start? It must be noted that every religion at a point of time in its beginning had been regarded as "new," so the term "new" alone is an insufficient characterization of these phenomena. Hence, the question, what is "new" of the new movements? Buddhism was regarded by some as a renewal and philosophical sect of Hinduism, the same way as Confucianism was to Chinese traditional religion. Christianity was a NRM, a new sect within Judaism for some years until they were completely separated. So what actually would qualify a religion to be classified as a new age religion? The features of NRMs have been examined above. We have also considered some factors that influenced the founding and expansion of NRMs. Social scientists have not come to agreement as to the origin of these movements. New religions emerge whenever factors that change societies and people significantly happen. In the United States, the 1960s, 1970s, and 1980s saw a surge in the emergence or expansion of new religions due to social changes that occurred during that time. It was estimated that about 10 percent of Americans were affiliated with NRMs. (The name, "new age," mentioned before, was first used in the 1970s.) The counterculture of the 1960s (as well as the 1970s and 1980s) brought its new religions when there was a feeling of disappointment as a result of the failure of the counterculture movements to bring the expected social change. The economic downturn in the subsequent decades also saw growth in new religions. Most of the new religions founded in times like that became more world-rejecting, other worldly, or millennialists. Older NRMs emerged from the third quarter of the nineteenth century as a result of social, cultural, religious, economic, and political conditions similar to or the same as that of the second half of the twentieth century.

Concerning their numerical strength, John Melton chides, "That there are no more than about 1,000 New Religions operating in North America means that the estimates of 3 to 5,000 groups that appears frequently in popular literature about "cults" are simply false. There is absolutely no evidence after a generation of study that suggests such a number, and it is difficult to take seriously those who continue to perpetuate such figures." He continues,

> New Religions are also small relative to the host population. In North America the average New Religion still counts its members in the hundreds or thousands rather than the tens of thousands or the hundreds of thousands. To get large figures for membership, one must include the Latter-day Saints [LDS], the Jehovah's Witnesses [JW] and the whole collective of primary and secondary groups that constitute the New Age Movement. The LDS report 5 million members in the U.S., JWs report approximately one million and surveys show New Agers to be between 1 & 2 percent of the population—some 3 to 5 million. Surveys also show over 20 percent of the population as having practiced some form of meditation, and holding beliefs in reincarnation and astrology, though these characteristics do not carry particular information about group

allegiances. Thus, claims that membership in New Religions constitutes 10, 20, or 30 million people are simple baseless exaggerations (Melton 1999).

Melton's study is focused on what he calls "the newer religious groups that have risen since World War II, which will exclude older NRMs and thus reduce the adherents significantly. When older NRMs, like LDS and JWs, are counted as members the estimation of 20 million and above could not be mere exaggeration.

CLASSIFICATION AND EXAMPLES OF THE NEW RELIGIOUS MOVEMENTS

The NRM is a diverse grouping and has been classified according to their regional orientation, spiritual orientation, philosophical orientation, or orientation toward the larger society. There are those who are oriented toward either the Eastern or Western religiocultural traditions or their mysticisms (as neo-Asian or neo-Oriental, neo-Western, or Judeo-Christian) or both. Others lean toward nature and nature religions (such as the neo-paganism). Those that are based on technological innovations, therapy, and medicine (especially alternative medicine) may or may not define themselves as religious entities.

Another widely accepted models of classification are: (1) John G. Melton's model, which classifies the NRMs as 8 religious family groups. They are the *communal* family of religions, the *Latter-Day Saints* family, the *Middle-Eastern* family, the *metaphysical* family, the *psychic-spiritualist* family, the *ancient wisdom* family, the *magical* family, and the *Eastern* family of religions. (2) Roy Wallis's model, which classifies NRMs in relation to their perception of the world as either world-rejecting, world-accommodating (neither reject nor affirm, but adapt), or world-affirming. Examples are the Branch Davidian, Hare Krishna, Brahman Kumaris, Heaven's Gate, the Unification Church, David Bergs's Children of God, and Jimmy Jones and the People's Temple (as world rejecting); Seventh Day Adventists and Jehovah's Witnesses (as world accommodating); and Osho Rajneesh Movement, Werner Earhart, and Transcendental Meditation (as world affirming). (3) Peter Clarke's model, which classifies NRMs according to their personal spiritual transformation that makes them more individualistic, for example, Christian Science, Church of Scientology.

The NRMs are a complex entity making it impossible to define them in a particular way. The NRMs experienced rapid growth from the mid-1960s. Hartford Institute of Religious Research found that there are a number of religious traditions represented in the NRM ranks. These traditions include:

- The Jesus People Movement
  - The Family [Children of God]
  - Jesus People U.S.A.
  - Alamo Foundation Church of Bible Understanding
- Other Christian-related groups
  - Holy Spirit Association for the Unification of World Christianity [Moonies]
  - Crossroads Movement [Boston Church of Christ]
  - The Way International
- Sufism
  - Gurdjieff Foundation
  - Subud
- Hinduism
  - Dawn Horse Communion

- Divine Light Mission [Elan Vital]
- International Society for Krishna Consciousness
- International Meditation Society [Transcendental Meditation]
- Ananda Marga Yoga Society
- The Bhagwan movement of Shree Rajneesh
- Brahma Kumaris
- Buddhism
  - Nichiren Shoshu of America [Soka Gakki]
- Sikhism
  - Healthy, Happy, Holy Organization
- New Age and Human Potential Movement groups
  - Arica
  - The Farm
  - Findhorn The Forum]
  - Insight/MSIA
  - Primal Therapy
  - Psychosynthesis
  - Dianic and Neopagan witchcraft groups
- Ritual magic groups
  - Ordo Templi Orientis
- Satanic churches
  - Church of Satan
  - Temple of Set)
- UFO groups
  - Raelians

Group of men seeing UFOs in the night sky

This study would like to follow the classification based on the new religious groups' orientation toward the traditional /major world religions: Oriental, Christian, Judaic, Islamic, and nature religions.

ORIENTAL OR ASIAN-ORIENTED NEW RELIGIOUS MOVEMENTS

The International Society of Krishna Consciousness (ISKCON): This is a worldwide movement popularly known as "Hare Krishna Movement." This is a religious philosophy derived from the teachings of A. C. Bhaktivedanta Swami Prabhupada (1896–1977), regarded by his followers as "the most prominent contemporary authority on Bhakti-yoga." He tried unsuccessfully to carry out his religious order in India. He migrated to the United States in 1965 to bring "India's message of peace and goodwill" to the Western world. Within a few years in the United States, he gained over a thousand adherents and now has over 300 centers worldwide. The centers are communalistic. The central teaching is that salvation, which is Krishna consciousness, can be attained through the avatar, Hare Krishna, the sole deity of the universe.

The movement attracts exuberant youthful counterculture generation. At initiation, the initiate recites four vows: renouncing meat, drugs, illicit sex, and gambling. He is given a Sanskrit name and promises to chant sixteen times of the Hare Krishna mantra. All positions in the movement are held by men (Swatos 1998).

The Rajneesh Movement: At present called Osho Commune International. This movement was founded by Rajneesh, an Indian professor of philosophy in 1981 in Oregon. He established a community called Rajneeshpuram. Initially, it was a blending of Hindu and Buddhist thought and practice but later included practices of Jewish Hasidim, Islamic Sufism, Marxism, and Freud's psychotherapy. His teachings are eclectic and monistic as disclosed in the following statement:

> My trust is total. I trust the outer, I trust the inner—because outer and inner are both together. They cannot be separated. There is no God without this world; there is no world without God. God is the innermost core of this world. The juice flowing in the trees is God, the blood circulating in your body is God, the consciousness residing in you is God. God and the world are mixed together just like a dancer and his dance; they cannot be separated, they are inseparable. (Brodd 2013, 534)

The movement met opposition as a result of some excesses in their practice. Rajneesh returned to India and died later in 1990. The movement still exists in an informal way.

Transcendental Meditation™: Popularly known as "TM," a copyrighted symbol and Netherland-based, the movement is often named as a sect of Hinduism. It was founded by a student of Guru Dev Singh who it was believed was of "moral stature and compassion." After a spiritual quest, which he began as early as nine years old, Guru Dev emerged as Maharishi (meaning "Great Seer"). By the instruction of his master, he became the teacher of the healing method that is known as *Sat Nam Rasayan*. He named his centers Spiritual Regeneration Movement in 1958; opened similar centers in Los Angeles and London in 1960; then in London in 1961, he opened a center called International Meditation Society. In 1968, the Beatles pop group travelled to learn his meditative practice that caught the world's attention. The goal of Transcendental Meditation is to promote a greater understanding and unity among peoples; world peace, and a strong alliance with evolutionary science. They believe this goal can be achieved if people will practice daily meditation for just twenty minutes, two times every day. The technique gained scientific approval in the 1970s, which some have of late contested (Swatos 1998).

CHRISTIAN-ORIENTED NEW RELIGIOUS MOVEMENTS

The Family International (TFI) or The Children of God (COG) are the most popular of the Jesus Movements (JM) of the 1960s with David Brandt Berg as the prophet and king, who, it is said, goes by many pseudonyms—David Moses, Mo, King David, David Fontaine, Dad, Grandpa. The movement shares the restoration idea of the Moonies. They are premillennial fundamentalists who believe in the 1,000 years' reign of the returned Christ on earth before the final judgment. The group is believed to be antinomian and follow unrestrained sexual teachings that encourage sexual experimentation, nudity, multiple sexual partners, and child sexuality. Their practice, which brought them much litigation, is called "Loving Jesus Revolution." They anticipates imminent end of this age and to spend eternity in Heavenly City (Swatos 1998; Brodd 2013,539-40).

Scientology: The founder is L. Ron Hubbard, who began as a science fiction writer under the name *Dianetics*. In the late 1940s, Hubbard conceived the idea of using science to heal the mind. In 1950 he published a piece in the *Dianetics* that sought to promote lay psychotherapy, which became a bestseller

©360b/Shutterstock.com

Berlin: the Logo at Scientology Headquarters
"Scientology is the study of knowingness.
It increases one's knowingness, but if a man were totally aware of what was going on around him, he would find it relatively simple to handle any outnesses in that."
L. Ron Hubbard

instantly. He later broke from his colleagues in the *Dianetics* movement and established the "Founding Church of Scientology" in 1956. Scientology's key idea is about healing or cleansing the mind of what they called "psychic scars," termed *engrams* by means of scientology, which will enable the person to develop his full potential. Psychic scars come from past damaging traumatic events. A device that is used in some of the processes is called E-Meter. Scientology has had numerous litigations with US and foreign governments. The movement now has opened branches in Russia and other parts of Eastern and Central Europe (Swatos 1998).

Other Christian-oriented groups are Latter-day Saints (Mormons), Christian Science, the Moonies, Branch Davidian, Jim Jones and the Peoples Temple, Heaven's Gate, and many others.

JUDAIC-ORIENTED NEW RELIGIOUS MOVEMENTS

Neo-Hasidic Movement: This movement was inspired by post-Holocaust Judaic thinkers like Martin Buber, Abraham Heschel, Zalman Schachta-Shalomi, and Arthur Green. Hasidim means "piety" or "lovingkindness." Neo-Hasidic movement was a reaction against extreme legalistic Judaism. NeoHasidic is a mystical body that refuses to allow legalism to control their life. And seek to win the young into Jewish spirituality.

A chavurah or havurah is a movement of the NeoHasidic tradition founded in the counterculture era of the 1960s as an egalitarian community to provide a renewed spirituality through prayer and study to counter the "over-institutionalized and unspiritual" society. Architects include Arthur Wakow, Arthur Green, and Michael Lener under the influence of Heschel and Schachta-Salomi. The movement also seeks to attract the secular Jews and the youth.

Modern Kabbalaism (Qabbala). The term means "tradition." Some believe postmodern Kabbalah is a renewed form of the ancient Kabbalah, which was a Jewish mysticism. It is defined as "a set of esoteric (secret) teachings meant to explain the relationship between an unchanging, eternal, and mysterious Ein Sof (no end—infinite) and the mortal and finite universe (God's creation)." This interpretation of Kabbalah teaching is said to be misrepresented. Instead of secret teaching, kabbalah rather teaches the secret. That means Kabbalah's teaching goal is to reveal something hidden, but not to hide something. It is a teaching of wisdom intended for action. Consider this statement, "Inside your body breathes a person—a soul. Inside the body of Jewish practice breathes an inner wisdom—the soul of Judaism." We often call it "Kabbalah," meaning "receiving." Just as Jewish practice is received through an unbroken, ancient tradition from the revelation at Sinai, so is its soul" (Tzvi Freeman 2014).

ISLAMIC-ORIENTED NEW RELIGIOUS MOVEMENTS

New Age Islam: New Age Islam: a post 9-11 movement of Muslims who are concerned with the image of Islam today and seeks to redeem Islam through education and dialogue. It started in April 2008 in New Delhi, India. The movement is guided by the following principles: encourage serious rethinking of all Islamic claims in the light of the twenty-first century; keep the Muslims abreast with the contemporary issues in the Islamic world, stimulate healthy debate among Muslim youth; be mindful of the rich tradition of tolerance, pluralism, and multi-culturalism in the inherited Islamic tradition. An important quotation of Muhammad, which is foundational to the movement is:

> All mankind is from Adam and Eve (Hawwa), an Arab has no superiority over a non-Arab nor a non-Arab has any superiority over an Arab; also a white has no superiority over a black nor a black has any superiority over a white—EXCEPT BY PIETY AND GOOD ACTION. . . . Do not therefore do injustice to yourselves. Remember one day you will meet Allah and answer your deeds. So beware: do not stray from the path of righteousness after I am gone (Sultan Shahin, http://www.newageislam.com 2014).

The movement was founded as a social network to connect all concerned Muslims worldwide to portray a new image of Islam and give a voice to counter the acts of the modern-day jihadists. A concerned member, Rohit Vats, thinks the film "Timbuktu" directed by Abderrahhmane Sissako provides one of the best portrayals of the daunting task facing the movement.

EARTH- OR NATURE-ORIENTED NRMS

The Wicca or Neo-Paganism: Key Text: The Spiral Dance Offer of wine to earth spirits. Modern Wicca emerged around the late nineteenth century and as recent as the 1940s thus becoming one of the newest NRMs. Names associated with its founding in modern times are Charles Leyland, Margaret Murray, and Gerald Gardner. The Wicca is witchcraft and its members are witches. The other name is "the Craft." They believe they celebrate the sacredness of the earth, the beauty of nature, and have more interest in pre-Christian European deities, such as the goddess Artemis of ancient Ephesus and the Celtic god Lugh.

Major festival: Lughnassadh (Lammas—"loaf-mass") named after the Lugh. At their meeting, they break bread in this ritual to strengthen their community or show solidarity. They acknowledge and celebrate seasonal and life cycle rites at a festival called "sabats" (Swatos 1998). Wiccans comprise both males and females, and it is estimated that there are over 100,000 members of which the greater majority are females. Wiccans distinguish themselves from *Satanism*, another new age movement (Swatos 1998). Their ultimate purpose in life is to bring them closer to Nature itself. Nature is Ultimate Reality. They employ magical powers for self-development and also to help others in need.

©tschitscherin/Shutterstock.com

Young palmister reading the future in a hand (the book is 300 years old, no copyright problems)

Witch`s Knot, Wicca, Power of four elements—Earth, Air, Fire, and Water—being the root of all existing matter, an ancient concept.

CONCLUSION

The concerns that created the NRMs must be seen as a part of the larger story of cultural and social change. Also, the NRMs are social phenomena that produce their own symbols and vocabulary that challenge the normative understanding of contemporary society. The NRMs can easily be brushed over and disregarded as oblivion, but the wider society must understand that the NRMs are dealing with real human issues at both the social and personal levels that should not be obscured by sociological technicalities and detachments (Szerszynski 1992, 3). This is vital because the social and cultural changes they react to are as real to them as they are to all others in the larger society. The rituals they employ are signs of their complexities, diverse visions and multi-purpose mission. Szerszynski reports, "The religious and quasi-religious practices they engage in are quite staggering. Wearing crystals, channeling spirits, searching for corn circles and ley lines, regressing to past lives, consulting astrologers and dowsers, going on the ever-burgeoning number of available retreats, practicing shamanic techniques" (Szerszynski 1992, 8). Finally, the reaction of NRMs should not always be misconstrued as a withdrawing from, but a conscious attempt to respond to personal significant changes that the conventional religious institutions have denied.

KEY WORDS

Modernization	Globalization	Secularization	Countercultural
The Wahhabis	Nation of Islam	Millennialist	New Age Movements
David Brandt Berg	Qabalah	Neo-Paganism	Osho Rajneesh
John G. Melton	Roy Wallis	Peter Clarke	Spiritual Regeneration
Engrams	*Dianetics*	*Wicca*	Transcendental Meditation
Lughnassadh	Charismatic leadership		

QUESTIONS FOR FURTHER STUDY

1. What is a new religious movement?

2. Discuss the major characteristics of church-type, sect-type, and cult-type religious groups.

3. Discuss the major characteristics of NRMs.

4. Discuss the types of NRMs. What are the problems associated with these classifications?

5. Explore the historical development, core beliefs, and influence of the following NRMs.

    i.   Latter-day Saints

    ii. Christian Science Church

    iii. The Raelians or UFOs

    iv. Jehovah's Witnesses

    v. The Satanic church

vi. The Church of Scientology

vii. International Society of Krishna Consciousness (*ISKCON*)

References

Aderibigbe, Ibigbplade S. & Carolyn M. Jones Medine, eds. *Contemporary Perspectives on Religions in Africa and the African Diaspora.* New York, NY: Palgrave Macmillan, 2015.

Adler, Joseph A. "Confucianism in China Today," Pearson Living Religions Forum. New York, April 14, 2011.

_____. "Divination as Spiritual Practice in Song Confucianism" Presented to the American Academy of Religion Annual Meeting (Chicago, 2008).

Aidoo, Ama Ata and Ketu H. Katrak. *No Sweetness Here and Other Stories.* Saline, MI: McNaughton & Gunn, Inc., 1970.

The American Heritage College Dictionary, 4th ed., Houghton Mifflin Co: Boston, New York, 2007.

Barker, Eileen, ed., *New Religious Movements: A Perspective for Understanding Society.* New York: Edwin Mellon Press, 1982.

The Bhaktivedanta Book Trust International, Inc., 2002–2013.

Bernard, Rosemarie. "Shinto and Ecology: Practice and Orientations to Nature" "Shinto Religion", *New World Encyclopedia*

Bowker, John. World Religions: The Great Faiths Explored & Explained. DK ADULT, 2006.

Bozarth, G. Richard. "The Meaning of Evolution," *The American Atheist*, Vol. 20, No. 2, February, 1978, p. 30. Atheists acknowledge the theory of evolution strips Christianity of any meaning. Atheist Bozarth sums up their position by writing: "Christianity has fought, still fights and will fight science to the desperate end over evolution, because evolution destroys utterly and finally the very reason Jesus' earthly life was supposedly made necessary. Destroy Adam and Eve and the original sin, and in the rubble you will find the sorry remains of the son of god . . . If Jesus is not the redeemer who died for our sins, and this is what evolution means, then Christianity is nothing."

Brodd, Jeffery, et al., *Invitation to World Religions.* New York: Oxford University Press, 2013. Brown, David H. *Santeria Enthroned: Art, Ritual, and Innovation in an Afro-Cuban Religion.*

Chicago: University of Chicago Press, 2003.

Canizares, Raul. *Cuban Santeria: Walking with the Night.* Rochester, VT: Destiny Books, 1993, 1999.

Carpenter, Dennis D. "Practitioners of Paganism and Wiccan Spirituality in Contemporary Society: A Review of the Literature." James R. Lewis, ed., Magical Religion and Modern Witchcraft.

Albany: State University of New York Press, 1996.

Certeau, Michel de. *The Practice of the Everyday.* Berkeley, CA: University of California Press, 1984. Clark, Mary Ann. "Santeria" in Zellner, William W., ed. *Sects, Cults, and Spiritual Communities:*

A Sociological Analysis. Westport, CT: Praeger, 1998.

De La Torre, Miguel A. *Santeria: The Beliefs and Rituals of a Growing Religion in America.* Grand Rapids, MI: Eerdmans, 2004.

Dopamu, Abiola Theresa. "A Socio-Religious Evaluation of Predestination, Destiny and Faith among the Africans," Published in *Proceedings of the Proceedings of the 9th International Academic Conference*, May 2014, pages 343-357.

Durkheim, Emile. Elementary Forms of Religious Life. Free Press; Reprint edition. June 1, 1995.

Eliade, Mircea. *The Sacred and the Profane: The Nature of Religion.* Translated by Willard R. Trask. New York: Harper and Row, 1961.

Ellwood, Robert S. Alternative Altars: Unconventional and Eastern Spirituality in America. Chicago: University of Chicago Press, 1979.

Encyclopedia Britannica, "Total population. UN medium variant figures for mid-2010, as given in World Population Prospects: The 2008 Revision."

The Encyclopedia of Religion (New York: Macmillan Publishing Company, 1987) Vol. 4, p. 25.

Esposito, John L., Darrell J. Fasching, and Todd Lewis, *World Religions Today*, 4th ed., (New York: OUP, 2012).

Fisher, Mary Pat. *Living Religions.* 8th ed. Upper Saddle River, NJ: Pearson, 2011.

Freeman, Tzvi. What is Kabbalah: The Soul of Judaism. Chabad-Lubavitch Media Center. 2014. Chabad.org. Accessed October 18, 2014.

Geertz, Clifford. "Religion as a Cultural System," in *Anthropological Approaches to the Study of Religion,* edited by Michael Banton. London: Tavistock, 1971, pp. 1–21.

Geertz, Cliffor. "Religion as a Cultural System" (1966; reprinted in The Interpretation of Cultures). New York, NY: Basic Books, 1973.

Herskovits, Melville J. "African gods and Catholic saints in the New World Negro belief," in *The New World Negro: Selected papers in Afroamerican Studies*, ed. Francis S. Herskovits, (Bloom- ington: Indiana University Press, 1937, 1966), 321–29.

Kristin, Swenson and Nelson Esther, *What is Religious Studies? A Journey of Inquiry. 1st ed.,* Dubuque, IA: Kendall Hunt Publishing Co., 2006

Lefever, Harry G. "When the Saints Go Ride in: Santeria in Cuba and the United States," in *Journal for the Scientific Study of Religion, vol. 35, no. 3* (September 1996), 318–330.

Levy, Lawrence J. "A Study of Divination within Santeria, an Afro-Cuban Religion, as a Psycho- therapeutic System," unpublished Research Paper Submitted In Partial Satisfaction of the Requirements for the degree of Doctor of Psychology (Nova Southeastern University, Center for Psychological Studies, 2000).

Livingston, James C. *Anatomy of the Sacred: An Introduction to Religion.* 6th ed. Upper Saddle River, NJ: Pearson Prentice Hall, 2008.

Melton, J. Gordon "The Rise of the Study of New Religions." A paper presented at CESNUR 99, Bryn Athyn, Pennsylvania - Preliminary version, 1999.

Miller, Williams, ed. "Old Man's Advice To Youth: Never Lose A Holy Curiosity," *Life Magazine* (May 2, 1955), 64.

Mosquera, Geraldo. "Africa in the Art of Latin America," *Art Journal* 5:4 (Winter 1992), 30–38. Murphy, Joseph M. "Santeria" in *Encyclopedia of Religion, vol.13,* ed. Mircea Eliade. New York: McMillan, 1987.

Olmos, Margarite Fernandez and Elizabeth Paravisini-Gebert. *Creole Religion of the Caribbean: An Introduction from Vodou and Santeria to Obeah and Espiritismo.* New York: New York University Press, 2003.

Otto, Rudolf. *The Idea of the Holy: An Inquiry into the Non-Rational Factor in the Idea of the Divine and Its Relation to the Rational.* 2nd ed. Trans. John W. Harvey. London: OUP, 1950.

"The Rise of the Study of New Religions," A paper presented by J. Gordon Melton at *CESNUR 99,* Bryn Athyn, Pennsylvania - Preliminary version © J. Gordon Melton, 1999

Rutz, Vicki L. and Virginia Sanchez Korrol, eds. *Latina in the United States: A Historical Encyclopedia, vol. 1.* Bloomington, IN: Indiana University Press, 2006.

Sandoval, Mercedes C. "Santeria as a Mental Health Care System: An Historical Overview." Social Science & Medicine. Part B: Medical Anthropology. Vol. 13, No. 2 (April 1979), 137–151.

Scribner's, 1999. Cited in Jeffrey Brodd, et al. *Invitation to World Religions.* New York: Oxford University Press, 2013.

Sharpe, Eric J. "Study of Religion: Methodological Issues." In The Encyclopedia of Religion vol. 14 [editor in chief, Mircea Eliade] New York: Macmillan, 1987.

Shermer, Michael. "What Is Pseudoscience?: Distinguishing between science and pseudoscience is problematic," *Scientific American,* September 1, 2011.

"Shinto Religion", New World Encyclopedia. 2003.

Smart, Ninian. *Worldviews: Crosscultural Explanations of Human Belief.* 3rd ed. New York:

Spuler, Michelle and Michelle Barker. *Developments in Australian Buddhism: Facets of the Diamond.* Vol. 22 of Routledge Curzon critical studies in Buddhism. Psychology press, 2003.

Szerszynski, Bronislaw. "Religious Movements and the New Age: Their Relevance to the Environ mental Movement in the 1990s." A Report Presented to Centre for the Study of Environmental Change, Lancaster University, 1992.

Tate, Peter. *Flights of Fancy: Birds in Myth, Legend and Superstition.* New York, NY: Delacorte Press in Covid Corner, 2008.

Vicky and Virginia, 207

Internet

Berling, Judith A. "Confucianism." Asia Society: www.asiasociety.org. Accessed April 19, 2016.

Babb, Lawrence. "Jainism." New Dictionary of the History of Ideas. 2005. Retrieved August 04, 2016 from Encyclopedia.com: http://www.encyclopedia.com/doc/1G2-3424300395.html

BBC, "Religions: Candomblé" http://www.bbc.co.uk/religion/religions/candomble/beliefs/ beliefs.shtml (24 May 2011). Accessed October 13, 2014.

Bishop Gilbert Burnet, *History of his Own Times* (vol. I, bk. I, sec. 96). Everyman Paperbacks, 1992.

Cited in www.WorldofQuotes.com. Accessed September 24, 2014.

Bowker, John. "Kami no michi." *The Concise Oxford Dictionary of World Religions.* 1997. Encyclopedia.com. http://www.encyclopedia.com. Accessed April 23, 2016.

Buddhist Peace Fellowship. www.buddhistpeacefellowship.org 2012. Accessed March 15, 2015.

Cuban Information Archives, Document 0337: Afro-Caribbean Religions. March 1995. This is a yearly report by the Miami-Dade Police Department. http://cuban-exile.com/doc_326-350/ doc033.html, Accessed July 19, 2011.

Deshphande, M. S. "Light of India or Message of Mahatmaji" at http://www.mkgandhi.org/ religionmk.htm. Accessed September 24, 2014.

Durkheim, "The Sacred and Profane" http://routledgesoc.com/category/profile-tags/sacred-and-profane. Accessed March 16, 2016

Fine Art America. "Santeria Mythology Greeting Cards," http://fineartamerica.com/art/all/santeria/ greeting+cards. Accessed August 2, 2011.

Fox, Robin Lane. *Pagans and Christians,* 492, cited in "Marcion, the Canon, the Law, and the Historical Jesus" by Chris Price (October 2002) at www.christianorigins.com/marcion.html

Harper, Douglas. Online Etymology Dictionary (2012-2014). Www.etymoonline.com. Accessed December 2, 2014.

Halsall, Paul (Jan. 1996), "Edict of Milan" (from Lactantius, De Mort. Pers., ch. 48. opera, ed. 0. F. Fritzsche, II, p 288 sq. (Bibl Patr. Ecc. Lat. XI). The text translated in University of Pennsylvania. Dept. of History: Translations and Reprints from the Original Sources of European history, (Philadelphia, University of Pennsylvania Press [1897?-1907?]), Vol 4:, 1, pp. 28-30. This text is part of the Internet Medieval Source Book, at http://legacy.fordham.edu/halsall/source/edict-milan.asp

Hara, Masakazu. "Shinto." Encyclopedia of Science and Religion. 2003. Accessed August 3, 2016 from Encyclopedia.com: http://www.encyclopedia.com/doc/1G2-3404200466.html

Idaho State Historical Society. Idaho State Archives at www.history.idaho.gov. Accessed April 20, 2016.

Intelligent Design, "Explaining the Science of Intelligent Design," www.intelligentdesign.org, April 15, 2016

"The Concept of Kami." http://www.socsci.uci.edu/~rgarfias/aris/courses/japan/kami. Accessed August 3, 2016

"Kairos" Wikipedia. Accessed August 1, 2016

Koconis, Benjamin. "Santeria Lives on in the District," a report on a Santerian workshop held in Washington DC on June 26, 2010. http://www.washingtoninformer.com/faith. Accessed March 8, 2011.

Lazaros, Ros. "Spreading the Gospel of Afro-Cuban Music: Pop music: Santerian priest, LA."

LA Times (December 17, 1993). http://articles.latimes.com/1993-12-17/entertainment/ca-2899_1_cuban-music. Accessed July 19, 2011.

Lau, D. C. *Confucius: The Analects.* Harmondsworth, Penguin Books, 1979. From *Lun Yu - The Analects of Confucius,* trans. James Legge (*The Chinese Classics,* 1861), D. C. Lau, and R. P. S. Couvreur at http://wengu.tartarie.com/wg/wengu.php?l=Lunyu&no=6. Accessed April 25, 2016.

Marx, Karl. "Critique of Hegel's Philosophy of Right," pp. 261-313 at https://www.goodreads.com/work/quotes/313609-critique-of-hegel-s-philosophy-of-right. Accessed August 1, 2016

Mertz, Rafi and Ron Bugaj. "Timeline of Human Spirituality." Compiled January 7, 2005: www.ifdawn.comesa/timeline.html. Accessed August 4, 2016.

Miller, Uzoma O. "Santeria's Convergence of Music, Dance and Spirituality: Historical Note (Sep- tember 23, 2002), 1–3.http://historicaltextarchive.com/sections.php?action=read&artid=441. Accessed March 8, 2011.

Miller, William James. "Sacrament". The American Church Dictionary and Cyclopedia. http://www.studylight.org/dictionaries/acd/view.cgi?n=589. 1901. Accessed July 31, 2016

"Native American Religion" in *Encyclopedia of Death and Dying:* www.deathreference.com. Accessed April 20, 2016.

New World Encyclopedia Contributors. "Shinto." New World Encyclopedia, September 14, 2015. http://www.newworldencyclopedia.org/p/index.php?title=Shinto&oldid=990679. Accessed August 3, 2016,

Parliament of the World's Religions, "Introduction" in *Toward Global Ethic*, Chicago, September 4, 1993; https://parliamentofreligions.org/sites/default/files/TowardsAGlobalEthic.pdf. Accessed April 15, 2016.

Quartz Hill School of Theology, "What Is Theology?" at www.theology.edu/theology.htm. Accessed 4/15/2016.

Ramberg, Bjørn and Gjesdal, Kristin, "Hermeneutics", The Stanford Encyclopedia of Philosophy (Winter 2014 Edition), Edward N. Zalta (ed.): http://plato.stanford.edu/archives/win2014/entries/hermeneutics/. Accessed December 20, 2014.

Richardson, James T. "Transcendental Meditation" in *Encyclopedia of Religion and Society*. Edited by William H. Swatos, Jr., Hartford Institute of Religious Research at www.hirr@hartsem. edu. Accessed October 15, 2014.

Romberg, Raquel. "Revisiting Creolization" from the School of Arts and Sciences Conference Archives, University of Pennsylvania. http://www.sas.upenn.edu/folklore/center/Confer- enceArchive/voiceover/creolization.html. Accessed July 19, 2011.

Santeria Botanica site: http://www.viejolazaro.com/en/?gclid=CP6a48PftKoCFYeD5QodUQS49Q. Accessed August 3, 2011.

Shahin, Sultan. New Age Islam: Mapping an Agenda for the Twenty-First Century at www.newageislam.com, Accessed December 2, 2014.

"Shinto." *Encyclopedia of Social Sciencs.* 2008. Accessed August 3, 2016 from Encyclopedia.com: http://www.encyclopedia.com/doc/1G2-3045302438.html.

"Shinto Faith Statement" in *Faith in Conservation* by Martin Palmer with Victoria Finlay, published by the World Bank in 2003: http://www.arcworld.org/faiths.asp?pageID=74. Accessed August 3, 2016.

Slick, Matt. "What is New Religious Movements." Christian Apologetic and Research Ministry at www.carm.org. Accessed October 14, 2014.

Slideshare.com, "Confucius" @ http://www.slideshare.net/Myobii/confucius-presentation. Accessed April 25, 2016.

Smith, Cathy. "Santeria: The Way of the Saints," http://historicaltextarchive.com/sections. php?action=read&artid=441. Accessed August 2, 2011.

"Son (music)." *Wikipedia.org.* http://en.wikipedia.org/wiki/Wikipedia:FAQ/Copyright. http://historicaltextarchive.com/sections.php?action=read&artid=441. Accessed July 19, 2011.

Swatos, William, Jr. ed. "ISKCON". In Encyclopedia of Religion and Society, 1998: http://hirr.hartsem.edu/ency/index.html. Accessed October 15, 2014.

Taliaferro, Charles, "Philosophy of Religion", *The Stanford Encyclopedia of Philosophy* (Winter 2014 Edition), Edward N. Zalta (ed.): http://plato.stanford.edu/archives/win2014/entries/philosophy-religion/. Accessed December 20, 2014.

Vats, Rohit. "Timbuktu: Biting, Haunting Critique of Sharia" published on November 29, 2014 at http://www.newageislam.com. Accessed December 2, 2014.

Vocabulary.com. "Primal" at www.vocabulary.com/dictionary/primal. Accessed April 19, 2016.

Wertz, Richard R. Chinese History: Confucianism, www.ibiblio.org/chinesehistory, Accessed April 23, 2016.

Why Islam Project. "Cairo, Egypt." www.whyislam.org. Accessed April 15, 2016.

Zimmer, H. R. Philosophies of India, Campbell, J., ed. Princeton University Press, 1969 from http://books.google.com/books?id=bRQ5fpTmwoAC. Accessed October 19, 2014.